'Scratch'

A Salcombe Boy

ABOUT THE AUTHOR

BILLY 'SCRATCH' HITCHEN has lived a life that could never be repeated.

One of the country's first NHS babies to be born in the early hours of July 5th 1948, he took full advantage of the freedom offered to a young boy growing up in post war Britain.

Aged just fourteen, in 1963, he played hooky from school after the Easter holiday and ran away to sea. Illiterate and innumerate, by the age of nineteen, he had sailed around the world five times and mastered the 3Rs along the way. When he eventually came home to Salcombe in South Devon in 1973, he had used up many of his nine lives. Undaunted, he started a new career in the fishing industry, one of the most dangerous occupations in the world. After a rapid rise to skipper, he went on to fish for the next three decades in every sea area from Dover to Rockall.

Surviving storms and groundings, collisions and near fatal accidents, finally, he ' swallowed the anchor' and came ashore more than forty years after running away to sea. He then started two businesses which he has run successfully for the last twelve years, one a live shellfish export business to the Far East and a boatyard sailing business. Both are still running today.

Scratch has now written his autobiography, a unique and vivid record of recent maritime history – an inspiring tale of one man's courage and determination.

'Scratch'

A Salcombe Boy

*The story of one man's courage and
commitment to the call of the sea*

BILLY 'SCRATCH' HITCHEN

Most of the photographs in this book were taken by myself with a small Instamatic camera that I always carried on my travels. The few professional images are listed below.

By kind permission, the following pictures have been used in this publication.
SY Norian - Beken of Cowes
Salcombe - Lorna Yabsley - cover picture
McDermott Inc - various pictures from their in-house magazine, Jaramac 1971
Carl 'Willoughby' Savage - photographs from his personal archives
Salcombe Harbour map - Nick Walker Printing Ltd

Matador
9 Priory Business Park,
Wistow Road, Kibworth Beauchamp,
Leicestershire. LE8 0RX
Tel: 0116 279 2299
Email: books@troubador.co.uk
Web: www.troubador.co.uk/matador
Twitter: @matadorbooks

ISBN 978 1789014 075

Printed and bound by CPI Group (UK) Ltd, Croydon, CR0 4YY
British Library Cataloguing in Publication Data.
A catalogue record for this book is available from the British Library.

Matador is an imprint of Troubador Publishing Ltd

For our grandchildren:
Will, Frankie, James and Harry

Contents

Acknowledgements

I would like to thank and acknowledge the people who have generously given their time and skills during the production of this book: Nick Walker for expertly producing a huge number of black and white photos from their original source and for going the extra mile with his professional help and advice on all printing concerns; Richard Hunt for giving his on-going PC support and for his professional ability in printing the trial run - The Final Years of Freedom; Heather Buchanan, for her practical knowledge, her enthusiasm and encouragement; Jenny Brown, who picked up the pieces and did sterling work on typing large portions of the manuscript at a critical stage and who has so kindly promoted my efforts; Tony Boullemier, for his sound guidance and advice; Susie Lewis and Rachel Wilcox, for their brilliantly clever pen sketches; Sylvia McKenna, my sister, for typing, proof reading and editing the raw material and for her belief in me. Finally, to the many shipmates along the way, for their indomitable spirit in a world that is the heart of my story and which made me the man I am.

When I began writing my story, I was not aware of the difficulty I would encounter in knowing what to remember and how much to forget. I have studiously endeavoured to be accurate in my details and to avoid giving offence to anyone. Achieving this has been my toughest challenge.

Billy Scratch Hitchen

PROLOGUE

Slithering up through the fore hatch, I crept silently back aft and lowered myself carefully into *Saucy Sue*. I slipped the rope and was off. It was a row of about 100 yards across to *Norian*.

Tying *Saucy Sue* up to *Norian*'s buoy, I pinned a small note to the centre thwart: 'Gone to sea on *Norian*. Be okay, Billy.'

Midnight was soon upon me. It was Good Friday, 1963. I was 14 years old.

My excitement was immense. The smell of steam, hot oil and coal fire was almost too much to bear.

'Let go forw'd.'

'All gone forw'd.'

Ding a ling. Ding a ling ding.

The telegraph rang Slow Ahead.

The engine hissed and suddenly, clank clonk, the flywheels turned and in beautiful unison, the shaft turned and the huge propeller turned. We were under way and as we slipped down Salcombe Harbour the starboard oil lamp spread a green glow across the water.

Little did I know then that I had started a journey which, in the next forty five years, would take me through tempest, typhoon, hurricane, calms, fogs, snows and close to shipwreck. I would rise from cabin boy to skipper. I would steer the last of the great Cunarders into New York Harbour and berth safely alongside in Manhattan to then return her, for the last time, to Southampton. I would go round the world five times before the age of nineteen covering many thousands of miles across the four corners of the earth. It was to be a long, long journey. I would meet many people, good and bad, who would all influence me in some way or another. I would teach myself to read and write and to do arithmetic. I had not been a good scholar during my nine years at school. School was a fog, but at last I had come out of the fog. I was to learn about the thing that I wanted to learn about – the sea.

Norian slipped out of Salcombe Harbour and into the English Channel.

I still did not know where we were going. Just by the funnel, the Engine Room door suddenly opened. A very dirty looking character appeared. Swearing and cursing loudly, he leant on the rail and rolled a cigarette. Doug Richards was Chief Engineer of the *Norian*, a thoroughbred Steam Engineer and a Cornishman. He was also Chief Engineer of the *St.Meryn*, a large Falmouth Harbour Tug. He was showing *Norian's* owner, Lloyd's Underwriter, Simon Sitwell, the skills required of a Steam Engineer.

'And who are you?' he asked.

'Billy Hitchen,' I replied. 'Just signed on as cabin boy.'

With these words my childhood ended.

INTRODUCTION

1948-1963

Whether or not I was the first National Health baby to be born is debatable, but I entered this world in the early hours of July 5th 1948 and I didn't cost a penny. Being the youngest of four children, I had an elder brother and two elder sisters.

We lived in the small village of Streatley beside the River Thames, where my mother was headmistress of the little school. My sister, Sylvia, was much older. She was born just before the outbreak of war and was by now at school in Abingdon near Oxford. My dad was in the Grenadier Guards and had served throughout the war with them. Sadly, this had taken its toll on his health and by the time of my first birthday, he had become seriously ill with TB.

My father spent nearly two years in Peppard Sanatorium, set in wooded countryside near Henley on Thames. Surgeons removed seven ribs from his left side in order to collapse most of the lung and three ribs from his right side for the same purpose. He was given a new drug, Streptomycin, the first anti-biotic ever used in the treatment of Tuberculosis. Few patients were considered strong enough to face up to this pioneering surgery but he surprised even his surgeons by surviving a series of dreadful operations.

By 1951 my dad was at last discharged from Peppard but was advised to move away from the foggy, damp atmosphere of the Thames Valley, find fresher air and a milder climate. Hence our move to the small South Devon village of East Portlemouth on the Salcombe Estuary, where my mother became the last headmistress of the tiny Church of England village school.

It was solely due to my father's illness that I did not grow up in the heart of England and become, maybe, a builder or a farmer. I would never have gone to sea and I would never have lived my remarkable life.

*

It was snowing when we left Streatley, the first day of January 1952. On February 6th, only a few weeks later, Queen Elizabeth II came to the Throne.

We set off, all our belongings packed into our small Hillman car and its trailer, my dad driving west across Salisbury Plain. It was dark by the time we reached the narrow lanes of Devon

My memories of Streatley are nil. I was two when we left, but this is really when my life began. East Portlemouth was to become a boyhood dream. It gave me an unforgettable childhood: carefree days endlessly spent with wild, boyish adventure, roaming from dawn 'till dusk in complete freedom. A small steep path led down from our house to the estuary with its beautiful wooded coves and white sandy beaches. Talk about 'Swallows and Amazons'! It was a paradise of fishing, sailing, rowing and swimming. What more could a young boy want?

*

The first big shock of my young life was school. I hadn't allowed for going to school at all and I remember clearly my first day at East Portlemouth village school – sudden confinement and a bit of discipline. This was not going to work. I played truant from a very young age and this behaviour did not rest well with the headmistress, my mother. After about six months, she had had enough. A phone call to Mrs Hawkins in Salcombe and I was expelled from East Portlemouth School to continue my education across the water with Mrs Lapthorn at the Salcombe Infant School.

My attendance in Salcombe was a little better mainly because my sister Sylvia, about to start her teacher training in London, was a 'helper' at the Infant School and made sure I crossed the ferry each day. Life ticked by like this until I was seven. Mother still refused to have me back at East Portlemouth and so, on leaving Salcombe Infants, I enrolled at Salcombe Boys' School

First day at school, East Portlemouth, 1953. This was not going to go well.
Back row (l to r): Fishy Trout, myself, Eddy Wood, Doug Gordon.
Front row (l to r): Carol Gordon, Dawn Penny, Eileen Powlesland, Mary Tucker.

with Chimp Childs at the helm. Discipline was harsh. The cane was out most days and not just for me, I hasten to add.

I was soon given the nickname of Scratch. I would say 90% of us had nicknames. That was the Salcombe way. I was also called the Bearlander . This was the name given to anyone from East Portlemouth. It was well known that bears still ran free in the woods of East Portlemouth!

Schooling on the other side of the Estuary gave rise to a rather strange situation – split loyalties between my school friends and my buddies at home in East Portlemouth. Only about two hundred yards of water separated us, but rivalry between the Salcombe-ites and the Bearlanders was always there. School days were spent in one place, evenings, weekends and holidays in another, but I knew where my true loyalties lay – East Portlemouth.

The view from my bedroom window, East Portlemouth, 1955.
Lion in the foreground with Ocky Stone leading and Ben Weymouth at the rear with one of the farm dogs.

*

I suppose I was about eight years old when I acquired my first boat. Well, it wasn't really a boat, it was a telegraph pole. We were swimming off Ditch End beach one day when it came floating down the creek from South Pool. There were five of us village boys in the gang: Fishy Trout, Doug Gordon, Ears Steed, his brother, Rob, Eddy Wood and me. We swam out, pulled the pole in and pushed it across to the beach. There was much excitement. Who would be the captain? What would we call it? We finally named it *The Black Shadow* after a pirate ship Fishy had heard about. We moored it up on Ditch End beach with a bit of old rope and a big stone for a stern anchor. Yes, we were very proud of our ship. The next day we made paddles out of some branches, heaved her off the beach and set course for Salcombe but we finished up on Snapes Point with more splinters in our backsides than a porcupine has quills and filthy from impregnated creosote. Eventually, we did manage to cross the Harbour but only after learning a bit more about tidal flow.

The Black Shadow disappeared one night and that was the end of that. I think Bob Martin, the Harbour Master, towed it away. Ears said we hadn't moored it up well enough. Who knows? But what fun we had out of that old telegraph pole.

*

Of course, not all the adventures in my early childhood were centred around the sea. The village farm was also a great focus of fun and amusement and a huge learning curve all thrown into one.

In the 1950s the Village Farm, as it was known, was operating pretty much as it had been for the last century or so. There was very little automation and it didn't acquire its first motor tractor until 1958. I remember the arrival of a David Brown Field master – what excitement! All of us kids got a ride on the back of it that day. The fella chosen to drive it was a nice, happy go lucky chap called Bob Rendle, who I don't think had ever driven a vehicle in his life and had to learn pretty quickly about such modern things as a clutch. Bob's nickname was Buggering Bob, so quite a few 'buggers' could be heard in those first few days with the new tractor. But he began to master it without killing himself.

Looking back, the arrival of the tractor heralded the passing of a magical way of life in East Portlemouth. Up until then, the only source of power on the farm came from the two beautiful Shire horses, Lion and Duke. These two powerful animals were the backbone of pretty well all the farming operations: harrowing, ploughing, harvesting, the carting of milk, corn, feed, hay. Everything revolved round Lion and Duke. One farm worker, who was called the horseman, came from the old East Portsmouth family of Stones. Arthur, married to Mary, was known as Ockey. Ockey Stone was not a big man in stature. He was a quiet, gentle countryman, who only once in his entire life ventured out of East Portlemouth into the great wide world beyond. In 1914 he and two other boys from Salcombe, Sid Luscombe and Bill Spry, ran away to Plymouth to do their bit for King and country. Lying about their age, they joined the Royal Navy and all three soon found themselves in the biggest naval battle since Trafalgar – the Battle of Jutland! Needless to say, they all survived and lived to a good old age. Ocky, now an old man, told me a lovely story years later when I met him in a pub. Prior to the Battle of Jutland, the battle fleet was moored in Scapa Flow. Ockey, Bill and Sid, because they came from Salcombe and could handle small boats, were sent around the fleet to replenish rum supplies. Well, of course, at only fifteen years of age, the rum got the better of them and they were found unconscious, drifting aimlessly through the Scapa Flow battle fleet. All three went into the Battle of Jutland with hangovers from hell and 'on jankers'.

*

Back on the farm, though, Ockey was brilliant. Often, when ploughing or harrowing with Lion and Duke, he would let a few of us sit up on those strong, broad backs, our weight probably feeling like nothing more than a few sparrows to them. Lion was a little more frisky while Duke was pretty quiet, so it was boys on Lion and girls on Duke.

The hay barns were our playground in the winter months and we spent days building camps with the hay bales, creating tunnels and dens and hideouts. That it didn't all collapse and suffocate us was a miracle.

All the village milk and cream came from the farm which had to be collected daily in small alloy containers. With wartime food rationing still in force, nearly all our needs were supplied by the farm. In about 1957, a dairy was set up in Kingsbridge and that was where all our village farm milk ended up every day. Ernie and Mary Green, who lived at the farm, started a milk delivery operation and our milk began to arrive on the doorstep in bottles. It seemed daft to have our milk go all the way to Kingsbridge and then come back the next day in bottles.

The village shop and bakery was the only place for miles where we were able to buy groceries and provisions. It was situated near the village green, tucked into a row of little white cottages on the steep hill that carried on up to the church. The shop cum bakery was owned by the Thornton brothers and sisters, seven of them, if I remember correctly. They all had a role to play in the running of their shop, all except for one brother, Cyril. Cyril had an old horse called Bob and he spent his days walking Bob up and down the lanes in all weathers, very seldom riding him, an old sack pulled across his shoulders. You never saw Cyril without Bob and you never saw Bob without Cyril. We used to get an occasional ride on Bob, often on Millbay beach We would pretend to be the Lone Ranger, but we could never coax him into any fast action. He would only ever walk, so our childhood fantasies never amounted to much with old Bob.

To my knowledge, the Thornton brothers and sisters never married. They all seemed to live happily together, looking after their shop and bakery. Phil was the brother who delivered the bread to the houses, weighed down by an enormous bread basket on his arm. He got around the village in an old bread delivery van which was always breaking down and Phil would often be seen hunched over, winding up the starting handle.

Come the Spring and another great pastime began; seagull egging.

Today there is a huge problem in coastal towns with the seagull population and this is because children no longer go seagull egging. We would gather hundreds of eggs from the cliffs and those that weren't used by our mothers in the kitchen, were used in egg fights and the seagull numbers were kept low. All the girls in the village kept well clear of our gang during the seagull egging season. The last thing they wanted was to be hit in the back of the neck with a seagull egg. If you were not seagull egging, happy hours were spent in the many gullies in the rocks between Sunny Cove and Gara Rock, fishing for Wrasse or Cunner, or, if you cast out far enough, the occasional Bass. This was a rare prize to take home to your Mum.

*

Although I never really knew it at the time, a division ran through the village between church and chapel. Of course, we all went to the same village school, except me, but I could never understand why, come Sunday, we went to either the Church of England church of St. Winwalloe or the Weslyan Chapel. Both places were practically next door to each other and every Sunday both were full of worshippers, myself included. But one great event every year was the Chapel Harvest Tea. After standing still for the good old Wesleyan Grace to be said, we dived into plates of sandwiches, mountains of cakes and buns, scones thick with strawberry jam and lashed with clotted cream, all washed down with orange squash. We didn't come up for breath but did manage to stuff some leftovers up our jumpers on the way out.

In the Spring of 1956, the rector of East Portsmouth, the Reverend Major, decided to start what was known as the East Portsmouth 1st Sea Scout Troop. All of us local kids of around my age immediately joined and I can remember being given a blue jumper with Sea Scouts across the chest and a round sailors hat with Sea Scouts around the brim and a sort of scarf to be worn around the neck. I felt very proud and smart in this uniform which sowed the seeds, in those early days, for what was to be a lifetime at sea.

The biggest highlight in the Sea Scouts was a very early introduction to sailing. A local boat builder, Hugh Cater, gave up one evening a week to take us sailing. We only reached backwards and forwards across South Pool creek from the Rectory foreshore in a Salcombe Yawl, Y20, which was kindly lent by Mr Wright who lived in the village.

With Sea Scouts over, the best bit was when Mrs Major, the Reverend's wife, produced a tea with sweet tasting cakes and buns, a real treat for us kids when such luxuries after the war were still few and far between.

*

One winter, heaven knows what year it was, Doug Gordon was given an old pram dinghy. It was in pretty poor condition and its sea going days well over. It snowed quite hard that winter and just after Christmas the plan was to pull the old pram up to the very top of Portlemouth hill, climb aboard and toboggan all the way down. The run down should have been the best part of a mile if we had managed to steer. As the village was completely cut off, passing cars would not be a problem and being a boat, we thought it would travel pretty straight.

But we had a bit to learn.

We climbed into the pram dinghy right up near the church, on a very steep part of the hill. We shook and rolled; nothing. Fishy and I were sitting in the stern so we jumped out and pushed and shoved. Suddenly, she started to move. We just managed to roll ourselves back into the old boat when away she went. The hedgerows acted as guides and kept us on track. We were picking up speed and by the time we got down to the village, we were really motoring and shouting with delight, but our run was doomed. Just outside the farm we hit a large concrete gate post.

The game was up. The pram dinghy exploded and the five of us were thrown in all directions. We sustained cuts and bruises but I had also hit my head on something pretty hard and was knocked senseless.

The first thing I remember was Ears saying, 'I think Billy's dead.'

I was lying face down in the snow. A nail from the planking had caught the top of my head, leaving a longish gash, causing it to look worse than it really was, the snow becoming a startling red all around me. There was not much left of the old boat so I abandoned the scene and staggered home. Mum and Dad were out, but Sylvia patched up my head and all was well. God, we had some fun in East Portlemouth in those early '50s.

*

In the summer of 1956, my dad was starting to get his strength back. He was at last able to go back to work and took a job as a civvy driver at RAF Prawle. On Saturdays or holidays I would go to work with him on the back of his old 16 H 500 Norton. The deal was, if I rode to work with him, I then had to walk back the three miles home. I thought this was pretty good. One day, he let me sit on the tank and operate the clutch and throttle. That was a real treat and my love of motorbikes was born.

It was in that summer that Dad bought our first boat. It was a 14ft clinker built launch with a one and a half HP Stuart Turner engine. Heavens knows why, but we went all the way over to Paignton Harbour to pick it up. Looking back, I would have thought that there were plenty of boats in Salcombe Harbour. Anyway, we borrowed an old trailer and went off to meet a man called Louis Gale who had built her. She was called *Kittiwake* and we proudly launched her into the Salcombe Estuary from the foreshore at Yalton. She was painted white, had a red bottom and was varnished inside. *Kittiwake* brought us unlimited pleasure. Most Saturdays

My Dad. He had his left lung removed in 1951 aged 40.
But lived to 82 firing on one piston as he always used to say.

we would sail up to Kingsbridge for the weekly shop. It was quicker than driving through the lanes. It took me no time at all to handle her on my own, getting familiar with her temperamental Stuart Turner engine and my interest in engines began.

At about this time, Mum and Dad started taking in Bed and Breakfast guests during the summer months. I was sometimes asked to take these visitors for a cruise around the Estuary in *Kittiwake*, and although only nine years old, this was well within my capabilities. My instinct for boats and the water was beginning to show promise.

The following summer, Mum and Dad splashed out again and bought a small houseboat that came up for sale in the Bag area of Salcombe Harbour. She was called the *Exmoor Lass* and was 30ft long, clinker built. She cost £300 which was a lot of money in the 1950s. She was not in good condition, looking back, and I think my dad was probably stitched up. His knowledge of boats was not good. So by the summer of '58, we left our little house in East Portlemouth to live aboard *Exmoor Lass* and the house was let out to holiday makers. It must have been fairly good business because we were still at it in1963 when I left home.

I can't remember where she came from, but we had also acquired a pram dinghy called *Saucy Sue*. She was only a small 8ft pram, similar to the one we had taken tobogganing. But at least *Saucy Sue* was seaworthy.

*

The late 50s slipped by. The long summers were magical and the Salcombe Estuary was my playground, its wooded creeks and inlets constantly filled with new adventures. My best mate at this time was Ears – real name, Rick Steed. We were inseparable. I was a couple of years older than Ears, so I was always the leader. Mill Bay valley was a great hunting ground for us and we would spend days up there searching for war equipment that American GIs had left behind after their departure for D-Day. One of our best finds was a clip of live 303 bullets. We managed to fire them across the valley by securing them to a gate post and clouting them with a hammer. We never knew where they landed, but they made a huge bang, echoing all through the valley.

Things were not going too well on the academic front, though. In the Spring of '59 I was in my last year at Salcombe Boys School. Chimp Childs, as we called him, had retired, thank God – no more cane. A new much younger headmaster had arrived, Sid Gibson. He was a nice friendly chap and treated me well. But school was just hell for me. I did take some interest in geography. Sid made it come to life. He had a huge globe and would take us all around the world, describing countries and continents which stirred my imagination and got me thinking of faraway places.

Mrs Preston was my class teacher for the first two years at the boys' school. She was a kind lady and tried her best to help me. Maths was my really weak link. It was just a fog. Two and two made five as far as I was concerned. In the spring of 1959, I was in my last year at Salcombe Boys'.

One day, Sid said to me, 'Better have the day off tomorrow, Billy. There is not much point in you coming in.' Music to my ears. But the reason was that the rest of the class was going to sit an exam called the 11 plus. So I had the day off school and with another couple of boys, also not up to the challenge, went fishing.

The strong rivalry between the Salcombe-ites and the Bearlanders remained but I always managed to keep a foot in both camps. That summer I left Salcombe Boys' School and was enrolled at Kingsbridge Secondary Modern. Almost another four years of sheer torture was about to begin, but because I was no longer attending school in Salcombe, the move, at least, made me a true Bearlander.

*

Now in the first year at Kingsbridge I was, of course, placed in the lowest stream – no surprise there. Our main subjects

Not up to taking the 11+ so went fishing.

Salcombe Boys' School Sports Day, 1957. Already starting to show interest in sport.
(l to r): Peter Crocker and myself.

were metalwork, woodwork and gardening. They didn't even let us do geography, which was a disappointment. But, I began to excel at sport and started getting recognition for an achievement of my own doing, something I had never before experienced. During my four years at Kingsbridge, I captained all our main sports – athletics, cricket and rugby. I was selected to play for Devon County Schools as wing forward, or flanker, as they call it today. That day was the true highlight of my school days. I had a lot of help from a teacher called Charlie Dagger. He really pushed me to get into the County side. Charlie taught metalwork, but spent all lesson chatting to me about rugby. He drove me to matches all over Devon in his little old Austin A40 car. Charlie Dagger was Welsh and rugby was in his blood. Going to sea put an end to my rugby career, but sport certainly helped me through those years at Kingsbridge Secondary Modern School.

*

In the winter of 1960, I joined the Air Training Corps – the ATC. We were 1876 Squadron. I had a Royal Air Force uniform to wear and felt very smart and proud. I think it was the marching and discipline that were good for me, but best of all there were no exams, so it suited me fine. We would be off marching across Dartmoor or visiting RAF camps. One day we went to RAF Mountbatten in Plymouth and were taken out in an Air Sea Rescue launch. In the summer of 1961 we all went on a coach to RAF Marham in Norfolk for a week's camp. What an experience! It certainly put paid to any thoughts about trying to join the RAF.

After a couple of days at RAF Marham it was time for us to take our first flight. We went up, one at a time, in a Chipmunk Trainer. My name was called. I strapped on my parachute and

Devon Schoolboys 1st XV 1962-3.
Two Kingsbridge boys: back row: second left, myself, far right Roger Pope.

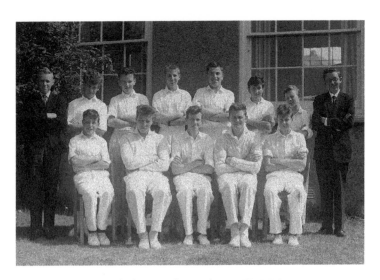

Kingsbridge Secondary Modern 1st XI 1962-3.
Back row (l to r): Michael Pearn, Toothy Tucker, unknown, Mike Lynn, Kenny Brown,
Chris Rogers.
Front row (l to r): Bailey Lewis, myself, John Buckland, Chris Warren, Mike Babbage.

Kingsbridge Secondary Modern Athletics Team 1962-63.
Back row (l to r): unknown, unknown, unknown, Mike Andrews, Toothy Tucker,
unknown, unknown, unknown.
Front row (l to r): Marlene Baker, Chris Warren, Mary Prouse, myself, unknown,
Michael Pearn
Sitting: unknown Janet Teasdale.

crossed the runway to the waiting aircraft. I felt like a real Battle of Britain pilot off on a sortie. I climbed into the back seat behind the pilot, strapped myself in and put on the leather flying helmet with earphones and mouthpiece.

'You ready, Hitchen?' asked the pilot.

'Yes, sir,' I replied.

'Have you ever flown before?'

'Yes, sir'.

One of the older cadets had told me to say ' yes' or I would not get to do any aerobatics, so I lied. I had never been anywhere near a plane in my life.

The old pilot knew the truth. 'I'll have you, you little sod,' he must have thought.

We took off and reached for the sky. After about ten minutes, the pilot came across on the radio.

'Hold tight!' was all he said.

I don't remember much about the next ten minutes except I couldn't ask him to stop because the flying helmet was suddenly full of breakfast. I didn't know if we were upside down, rolling the barrel, looping the loop or what. I was in some mess and so was my end of the cockpit and I prayed for it to end. We landed pretty quickly, thank God, and taxied to a halt. The engine died and I knew for certain that I was never going to join the RAF.

'Get this lot cleaned up then,' said the pilot. 'You've got an hour.'

Cleaning the inside of a Chipmunk Trainer is not an easy task when it has just been used as a food mixer. I did manage to clean it up after an hour or so, but I never went flying again with 1876 Squadron. The camp was really good fun, though. I also got to fire a Bren Gun but ended up with a nose bleed because I couldn't hold it tight enough to control the recoil.

*

Back home and war was still raging between the Salcombe-ites and the Bearlanders. It wasn't too serious – boys stuff, the odd scrap, chucking stones and sticks, catapult fights and rammings on the water. Poor old *Kittiwake* and *Saucy Sue* were beginning to look a bit battle weary, but my gang, Fishy, Ears, Doug, Bob and Eddy somehow managed to patch them up, so my dad never knew. Perhaps he did but turned a blind eye and had a chuckle.

It was around the fifth of November 1961 when I hatched a cunning plan. We would arrange a battle on Whitestrand Car Park and teach the Salcombe-ites a final lesson. Battle plans were thrashed out with the Salcombe lot during the dinner break at school and they agreed to meet for war at 6.30pm that very evening.

For anyone not familiar with Whitestrand Car Park, it is surrounded on three sides by pubs and buildings. The fourth side is on the water front. It was spring tides and high water was at approximately 6.30pm. That was part of the plan. We would tie milk bottles along the starboard side of *Kittiwake* and load them up with shilling rockets that were supposed to be used on firework night. We would also be armed with empty baked bean cans, each one stuffed with a Penny Cannon and these would be lobbed ashore after the rockets had been fired. Surely, the Salcombe-ites would run for their lives and never recover from an attack like this.

That night, as soon as it was dark, we all met to prepare *Kittiwake* for battle – great excitement. About that time we gained a new gang member, Yuri. Children had recently been evacuated from Hungary during troubles with Russia and one or two had surprisingly come to East Portlemouth. The eldest was 12 years old and he joined the gang. We could not pronounce his name so just called him Yuri after Yuri Gagarin, the first man in space. He was very pleased with his new name and being called after an astronaut. He didn't seem to mind that it was Russian.

His English was almost nil, but we had hours of fun teaching him how to swear, which was hilarious at school, or so we thought.

At last we were ready to set sail. There was one small set back that we had not prepared for – a stiff easterly breeze blowing down the Harbour. This not only made it rough for the crossing, but also made for pretty choppy water off White Strand, our firing zone. However, onward we sailed into battle. We didn't load the milk bottles until we had crossed the Harbour – had to keep our powder dry. As close as I could to 6.30pm, I brought old *Kittiwake* in for the broadside. I could make out enemy silhouettes on the quayside.

'Fire!' I gave the command.

The roll in the choppy sea caused the first two rockets to fire straight down into the water. *Kittiwake* then rolled to port and the other four rockets did the business. One went flying into the toilet block, facing the sea in those days, ricocheting round the inside of the building like a mad rat until it had run its course. Another went clean over the roof of the Victoria Inn and disappeared out of sight. The last two rockets scurried across the Car Park at ground level. The Salcombe-ites ran for their lives. I recognised Ching, Goo Goo, Eggy, Pansy Potter, Bimbo and Barney in flashes of light made by the rockets. We made another pass and then launched our salvo of grenades, the baked bean cans. I don't think we had the range with them and several just fell into the sea, but there were quite a few good bangs.

We disappeared into the night and back across the choppy Estuary to East Portlemouth, congratulating each other on the success of our attack.

Next day, on the school bus, everyone was talking about it. Once in the school playground, we awaited the arrival of the Salcombe bus . The reaction from the Salcombe-ites was a bit withdrawn. They thought our attack was amazing and wanted to join our two gangs together. After that we did get a bit more friendly. We were all slowly growing up. Girls were starting to appear in our lives and things were about to change, for ever.

Looking back on that November evening in 1961, we were lucky to have got away with it. The Salcombe boys were lucky not to have been hit by the rockets and we were lucky to have survived in *Kittiwake* with her temperamental old petrol engine. She could have exploded into flames at any time. But we did get away with it and 'boys is boys!'

I didn't quite get away with it, though. The next day, when I arrived home from school, my dad grabbed me by the scruff of the neck.

'What were you doing in *Kittiwake* last night?'

'Nothing,' came the classic reply.

He marched me down the small, steep path to where *Kittiwake* was moored.

'What's that then?'

Down *Kittiwake*'s starboard side were six black burn marks from where we had launched the rockets.

'I suppose the seagulls did that.' he said.

Well, I got a good hiding, but he never knew the full story. The final years of freedom they surely were.

*

The following summer the house was let out again so it was back to *Exmoor Lass* in the Bag. I had taught myself to sail a bit in *Saucy Sue*, but she didn't have a centre box and so I could only run or reach with the wind. On Saturday afternoons I would be down on Small's Cove, the little beach opposite the Yacht Club. This was where all the dinghy sailing took place and if you were lucky enough you would get a chance to crew. I did a few races in a National 12 with Terry Stone who lived in the village and also in a Yawl with John Stone, one of Terry's nephews. Terry was also Alec Stone's uncle. Alec was a world class helmsman, a brilliant boat builder and a sailing legend. My sister, Sylvia, crewed a couple of seasons with Alec. No one could look at them in the Harbour, winning every trophy going and also competing nationally. Alec went on to helm single handed in a Solo in which he won the Nationals eight times and the World Championship in 1971. And he lived at Good Shelter, just down the road. Wow!

Meanwhile, when not out hoping to pick up a bit of crewing, I would often row *Saucy Sue* round the Harbour looking at the beautiful yachts that came in and sometimes chatting to the crews. Harbour Master Bob Martin had retired by now and our new Harbour Master was Laurie Prynn, a Cornishman from Looe. He had been in Salcombe many years and often I would ride with him in his launch, *Our Boys,* picking up Harbour dues. Laurie Prynn was good to me and taught me a lot about boat handling and seamanship.

By September 1962 we moved back to the house for the winter. The winter of '62 – '63 was very cold. We had heavy snow after New Year and that winter the Beatles broke into the world of music with 'Love, Love me Do'. By February they had appeared on telly for the first time on 'Thank Your Lucky Stars'. We didn't have a telly, so I went next door to watch them.

*

By the end of March 1963, the snow had melted and one fine day, into the harbour steamed a very interesting looking ship. She anchored off the Ferry Inn. I was soon in *Saucy Sue* rowing out to take a closer look . As soon as I got up to leeward of her I could smell the unmistakable smell of coal fire, hot oil and steam. She was about 80ft long, painted blue with white superstructure and a large yellow funnel from which escaped the whiffs of steam and smoke. She was called *Norian*, registered at Irvine in Scotland. I thought she was magnificent. She had an aura of power about her, combined with elegance and style and the biggest ensign I had ever seen, flying from her beautiful counter stern. Laurie Prynn told me she was on passage from Scotland to London and had pulled into Salcombe for repairs after coming through heavy seas in the Irish Sea and around Land's End. She would be in Salcombe for a few weeks and was going to be on a mooring in the Bag not far from *Exmoor Lass*. 'How wonderful,' I thought.

Sure enough, Laurie put her on a fore and aft mooring, just above *Exmoor Lass*, the following day.

Easter was approaching fast. The weather had improved. The house was ready to let out for the coming holiday season and embarkation day was upon us once again – another summer aboard *Exmoor Lass*.

Not for me though! A new chapter in my young life was about to begin.

I rowed over to the *SY Norian* late one afternoon. I had noticed stores and provisions being loaded aboard for some time. She was obviously preparing for a voyage.

I pulled alongside the hanging gangway.

Simon Sitwell was a tall gangly man, a good six foot in height with blonde hair and blue eyes. He was wearing a dirty white shirt, red neckerchief and jeans. I never imagined for a moment that he was the owner. I was later told he was a relative of the famous Sitwell literary family.

'What do you want, son?' he said, in a friendly enough voice.

'I'm looking to go to sea, sir,' I said. 'I've just left school and my cards are not ready yet.'

Someone had told me you have to have 'cards' to get a job.

'Can you peel spuds and shovel coal?' he asked.

'Yes sir,' I replied immediately.

'Can you wash up and clean toilets?'

'Yes, sir.'

'Will you be seasick?'

'No, sir.'

'We sail tomorrow at midnight. Be on board by 11pm. You've got the job.'

'Thank you, sir. My name is Billy Hitchen. How long is the voyage?'

'Three to four months,' was his reply. And with that he disappeared down below, back to his beloved engine room.

Rowing away from the *Norian* I had to pinch myself to make sure it was true. I had thirty six hours before sailing time. Would I ask Mum and Dad if I could go and risk losing the opportunity of a lifetime, or should I just run away to sea? I chose the latter. If she was sailing at midnight, I could sneak out of the foc'sle hatch of *Exmoor Lass*. Most evenings Mum and Dad listened to the classical music from Semprini on the wireless before switching out the lights at about 9.30pm. I would sit it out until then.

I gathered my thoughts. Sailing day was a nervous day. The next twenty four hours would be a tense time if I was going to go through with my plan.

SY Norian in the Bag, Salcombe, loading provisions and getting up steam, Easter 1963

I packed a small duffle bag with all my worldly belongings, a sheath knife and my wellies. I hid the bag under the seat on *Saucy Sue*. I went to my bunk in the focs'le quite early that night and lay there listening to Semprini Serenade. Mum and Dad were creatures of habit but at last the programme finished and I heard, 'Goodnight dear,' from Mum. The lights went out. Before long sounds of gentle snoring broke the silence. It was time to go.

Slithering up through the fore hatch, I crept silently back aft and lowered myself carefully into *Saucy Sue*. I slipped the rope and was off. It was a row of about 100 yards across to *Norian*.

Tying *Saucy Sue* up to *Norian*'s buoy, I pinned a small note to the centre thwart,

'Gone to sea on *Norian*. Be okay, Billy.'

Midnight was soon upon me. It was Good Friday, 1963. I was 14 years old.

My excitement was immense. The smell of steam, hot oil and coal fire was almost too much to bear.

'Let go forw'd.'

'All gone forw'd' .

Ding a ling – ding a ling ding.

Steam Yacht Norian at Cowes Regatta, 1963 - resplendent with her buff funnel and her big ensign. Cabin boy, Billy, on the foredeck.

The telegraph rang Slow Ahead.

The engine hissed and suddenly, clank clonk, the flywheels turned and in beautiful unison, the shaft turned and the huge propeller turned. We were under way and as we slipped down Salcombe Harbour the starboard oil lamp spread a green glow across the water.

Little did I know then that I had started a journey which in the next forty five years would take me through tempest, typhoon, hurricane, calms, fogs, snows and close to shipwreck. I would rise from cabin boy to skipper. I would steer the last of the great Cunarders into New York Harbour and berth safely alongside in Manhattan to then return her, for the last time, to Southampton. I would go round the world five times before the age of nineteen, covering many thousands of miles across the four corners of the earth. It was to be a long, long journey. I would meet many people, good and bad, who would all influence me in some way or another. I would teach myself to read and write and to do arithmetic. I had not been a good scholar during my nine years at school. School was a fog, but at last I had come out of the fog. I was about to learn the things that I wanted to learn about – the sea.

Norian slipped out of Salcombe Harbour and into the English Channel. I still did not know where we were going. Just by the funnel, the Engine Room door suddenly opened. A very dirty looking character appeared. Swearing and cursing loudly, he leant on the rail and rolled a cigarette. Doug Richards was Chief Engineer of the *Norian*, a thoroughbred Steam Engineer and a Cornishman. He was also Chief Engineer of the *St.Meryn* a large Falmouth Harbour Tug. He had met Simon sometime in the past and was showing him the skills required of a Steam Engineer.

'And who are you?' he asked.

'Billy Hitchen,' I replied. 'Just signed on as cabin boy.'

And with these words, I left my childhood behind.

PART ONE

SEA SHIPS AND
SEAMANSHIP

One

SY NORIAN

'Get the bloody kettle on then,' he said. 'Don't just stand there.'

I produced two big mugs of tea and giving one to Doug, immediately made a good friend. He passed me his tobacco tin.

'Want a roll?'

'Okay. Thanks.'

I tried to roll my first cigarette, but was unsuccessful.

'Give it here.'

Doug deftly rolled it for me. And so I sat on the engine fiddly and enjoyed my first hand rolled Old Holborn cigarette with Doug Richards, Chief Engineer.

'Where are we sailing to?' I asked Doug.

'Where are we bound, you mean.'

I had learnt my first nautical term

'French coast, as far as I know. St. Malo or Dinard I heard.'

My heart lifted. There was no chance of them getting me back to school if I was on the French coast.

It took me a few days to settle into the routine and knowing what jobs were expected of me. Mostly, as Simon had said, it was peeling spuds and washing up in the galley, cleaning brass and paintwork on deck and shovelling coal in the engine room. The worst job was trimming the coal in the bunkers. Because of my size and being the youngest, I had to crawl into the bunkers and rake the coal back to the engine room hatches. It was best to go in wearing only a pair of shorts, come out as black as the ace of spades and then wash off under a hot pipe in the engine room before appearing back on deck. The engine room and stoke hole of a coal burner is a pretty mucky place, but the engine, always gleaming and flashing in the dull light, effortlessly, it seemed, produced the power to drive shaft and propeller. The engine room was one of my favourite places.

On deck I learnt to splice rope and wire, how to steer by the compass and how to box the compass by all its quarter points. I learnt how to take bearings and understand the meaning of different lights, how to distinguish lighthouses and buoys by their flashing sequences. I was back at school but at last, learning. I was no longer in the fog.

*

When we were in St. Malo, I explained to Simon, or Mr Sitwell, as I always addressed him, that I had only left a note for my parents to say that I had gone to sea. To my amazement, he didn't seem too concerned but said he would phone Laurie Prynn at the Harbour Office in Salcombe to say all was well. That was the last I heard about anything until I got back to the UK twelve weeks later. Our voyage continued all through the summer of '63. We ventured down into the Bay of Biscay, calling at many French ports. Years later it occurred to me that I never had a Passport. But, once again, this was yet another magical thing of those days. No one ever asked me for a

Passport and I never offered one. To be honest, I never knew I had to have one.

The weeks passed and by late July we had arrived back in Poole, Dorset. I was well settled in to shipboard life and never even considered going home. Simon Sitwell had to go back to London on business for two weeks, so we picked up a mooring off the Royal Motor Yacht Club at Sandbanks.

'Now then, Billy,' he said. 'Everyone is going home for a week or so. I'm leaving you in charge of *Norian*. You know how everything works. You're the Captain.'

*

I felt so important I could have burst, but I didn't. Simon came on deck wearing a suit. I couldn't believe it was him, bowler hat and all. Simon was born into the wrong dynasty. He was part of the famous Dame Edith Sitwell family. They were expected to wear suits and work in the city. Simon in his real life was an Underwriter at Lloyd's Shipping, but in his make believe life he was a steam engineer, much more at home covered in coal dust and oil. In another life he would have been a chief engineer in the Merchant Navy, but his fate was sealed at birth. He had to be a city gent and only act the part of chief engineer. He bought the *Norian* because she was a coal burner. He could have had any yacht he wanted, sit back on the stern with cigar and a large gin and tonic, but that was not Simon. I had great respect for Simon Sitwell. He was a man I looked up to and, of course, he gave me my first job at sea. For that, I would be forever grateful.

For the next two weeks I was alone on the *Norian*. It was the first time I had looked after myself on my own and I loved it. Mostly I went ashore in the evening and bought fish and chips. I did try to cook a bit but without much success. After a fortnight

I received a telegram from Simon via the RMYC. He would be back the next day. Prepare for sea – music to my ears.

Simon and Doug returned with a fellow called Len Morton. Len was also a city gent but an experienced seaman. He was a nice man and he taught me a lot over the next few weeks. With them was another fellow by the name of Charlie Lamplugh. Charlie was to skipper the *Norian*, ex Merchant Navy who also knew his stuff. Simon said we were going to Cowes Week and presented me with a set of white overalls and a white peaked cap.

'Better look the part, Billy.'

I felt very smart and important in my whites.

Cowes week August 1963: the weather was good. *Norian* looked at her best with her huge ensign and yellow funnel. One day I went off in our small tender boat by myself and pulled alongside the Royal Yacht *Britannia*. Hand over hand, I inched myself along the full length of her hull from stem to stern. Her top sides shone like a mirror. No one said anything. Security wasn't too tight in those days.

One day Simon and Doug came back on board with a guest and I was introduced to Uffa Fox. He asked me a lot about Salcombe and said he knew it. Uffa Fox, sailing icon of his era, world famous boatbuilder and designer, shook my hand and said he wished me the best of luck with my career at sea.

*

As always happens in life, all good things come to an end. Simon announced that after Cowes Week he would take *Norian* back to London where she would lay up for winter. Sadly, I would have to be paid off, as he put it. I thought that sounded very nautical.

By the beginning of September we entered the Thames, always called the London River by seafarers. We steamed past the Royal Docks, East India Docks and Surrey Commercial, finally swinging into St. Katherine's Dock. The *Norian* lay alongside. Her boilers were shut down and she became a dead ship. My first voyage was over. I would never again be called a 'first tripper'.

I spent a few more days on board mostly cleaning the engine room. Doug and Len took me ashore a couple of times. We visited the Tower of London and the Merchant Navy War Memorial on Tower Hill. I had a ride in a London taxi and went into two pubs with Doug and Len, drank Guinness, only one bottle, but I felt very grown up. After all, I was fifteen now.

My wages on *Norian* were £2/10s a week all found. Simon did not settle on this figure until I had passed a two week trial period, but when I passed he back dated my wages and when I paid off *Norian* I had accumulated £36. I was rich.

'Now then Billy,' Simon said, 'on a more serious note, what about your future?'

The rest of the crew unanimously decided that I should join the Merchant Navy. Doug was sure it was the only way forward for me, as long as I was happy to put my hand in my pocket and buy my own tobacco. He said he was fed up with giving me roll ups.

Simon handed me an envelope which simply said 'To Whom It May Concern'. 'Take this to the Merchant Navy Office in Plymouth when you get home. If they don't let you join up it will be their loss.'

I said my good-byes to Charlie, Len and Ken Puttick. I forgot to mention Ken earlier. He was also on the crew and I think came from south east London. Simon shook me firmly by the hand and wished me good luck. Doug and I caught a bus to Paddington Station. Doug was going home to Falmouth and I to East Portlemouth. I never saw Simon or any of the London crew again, but they were all responsible for launching me into my chosen career. Doug and I travelled back to the West Country together. I left the train at Totnes Station after saying a final good-bye to Doug, not knowing then that our paths would cross one more time many years later.

Two

MR PROFIT

Life back at East Portlemouth seemed very dull. My Mum and Dad were fascinated listening to all my adventures. I am sure they were relieved. That morning when they read my note to say I had gone to sea, in their hearts they knew I would be okay. I was ready to fly the nest, as my mother told me, years later.

'Well, what are you going to do now, Billy? Join the Merchant Navy?'

'Oh yes!' I said. 'Mr Sitwell said I could join. All I have to do is take this envelope to the Shipping Federation in Plymouth.'

I honestly imagined I would be on my way to Australia by the end of the week. As often happens, things did not work out as hoped.

I crossed the ferry to Salcombe and bought my bus ticket to Plymouth with a change at Kingsbridge. By mid morning I was in Plymouth looking for the Shipping Federation. After getting a few directions I entered a tall building at St. Andrew's Cross, climbed up the stairs to the fifth floor and there it was, marked on the door, British Shipping Federation, Plymouth Pool. This was it. My future lay beyond that door. I knocked and entered. It was apparent to me that the six months on *Norian* had given me a certain confidence, which over the coming years was only to increase. The *Norian* and the men I had met on her had taught me more skills than I had realised. I certainly looked and acted above my years.

Mr Profit sat behind a big, old oak desk, an elderly bespectacled chap and a man I was to get to know well over the next few years.

'How can I help you, son?', were his opening words.

'Oh well,' I thought, 'here goes'. I was now in possession of my first Passport so I told him my real age.

'I've come to join the Merchant Navy.'

With that I handed him the envelope from Simon, still unopened. He opened it up and quietly started to read.

'Very good', he said finally. 'This is a very good reference. Take care of it. You can join the Merchant Navy, but not yet.'

My heart sank.

'You are too young. You will have to go to Training School.'

'But,' I argued, 'Mr Sitwell said I could go straight in.'

'I don't care what Mr Sitwell said, you have to go to school for about six months.'

The word school sent a cold shiver down my spine. There was no way in hell I would ever go back to anything that even resembled a school.

Mr Profit was very understanding but said to go to sea you had to be sixteen years of age or have twelve months sea experience on trawlers, tugs, yachts etc. under your belt.

With no intention of going back to school, I chose the latter.

'I'll see you when I'm sixteen then, Mr Profit.'

'I'll look forward to it, son.' He stood up and shook my hand. 'Get some sea time in and come back.'

A very dejected Billy Hitchen left the Shipping Office that

day. It didn't look like I would be in Australia for Christmas. I walked down to the Barbican and wandered round the docks. Two colliers were unloading coal from the north east of England. It seemed so unfair that I couldn't join them. I could do the job with my eyes closed. Finally I caught the bus back to Salcombe. There was only one thing for it, get some sea time in before next summer, 5 July 1964, my sixteenth birthday.

Back in Salcombe the first chap I bumped into was Laurie Prynn, the Harbourmaster.

'Hello, Billy. Paid off the *Norian* then?'

I told him the whole story of the voyage and finally about the Merchant Navy and the sea time problem.

'Well,' he said, 'Richard Cove is looking for crew on his fishing boat the *Newbrook*. Go and see him. I'm sure you'll get a job. He's always looking for crew.'

Three

NEWBROOK

It was not going to take long to find out why Covey was always short of crew!

I soon found the *Newbrook, SE 33,* tied up alongside Coves boatyard at the end of Island Street. I jumped down and landed on her deck. Richard was in the wheelhouse talking to another fishing vessel on the radio. He ended his conversation with a short whistle and then, 'Cheers and gone.' I was sitting on the large gunwhale of the *Newbrook* when he came out of the wheelhouse.

'Aye, aye! What do you want?' were his opening words, 'And stand up. No-one sits down on the *Newbrook.*'

'I know you,' he said, ' you're a Bearlander, Hitchen.'

I could see this was going to be a bit different from the *Norian.*

'Yes, Billy Hitchen and I am looking for a job fishing.'

Richard Cove was a big man, over six foot and a good 18-19 stone, hands like shovels, drank like a fish, worked like a dog and expected the same of his crew.

Richard Cove, 'Covey', a legend in his lifetime, aboard *Newbrook*.

'Come over here,' he said. 'Pick that up.' I looked down at what was known as the end pot, an extra heavy pot at the end of each string of pots to act as an anchor. Inside the pot was chain and concrete. I attempted a lift. It was impossible.

'Stand back,' he said and he rolled the pot onto its edge, put it against his knees and leant back. The pot left the deck.

'Now, have another go.'

I did exactly as he had shown me. The pot left the deck, but only by a few inches.

'We've got fifteen of those and three hundred and sixty a bit lighter,' Richard grunted. 'Be here at 3.30am tomorrow morning. We'll be at sea for twelve hours so bring some grub. And don't be late, we won't wait for you.'

And that was that, no big formalities, I was signed on the *Newbrook* .

We left Salcombe harbour at about 3.45am the following morning. We rowed the net boat out to the *Newbrook* which was kept on a deep water mooring. The big Gardner engine burst into life.

'Chuck her off then, Boysie,' Richard yelled up to the forcastle head. Leopard and Russell were the other two crew members. They knew me, so no need for introductions.

'Going to be a bastard day,' said Leopard. 'Coming in a gale later.'

The three of us started to cut up bait behind the wheelhouse. Going down the harbour I could hear the wind whistling in the rigging. I was a little apprehensive. The *Newbrook* started to pitch and roll. The decks were soon well awash. Christ!

'Hold on,' shouted Russell.

The *Newbrook* went under water and surfaced again like a U Boat.

'All still there?' shouted Richard. 'Another one coming. Hold on under water.'

Down again we went and again resurfaced. Everything on deck was awash. We tried to hold on to the boxes of bait and the tea chests.

'Look out! Another one coming,' yelled Covey.

This one was even bigger than the other two. It shook the Newbrook from stem to stern. Richard said later that we must have hit the sand to make her shake so much. I never really knew what we hit but it was bloody hard. We had crossed Salcombe Bar in a Force 6 south easterly with a half ebb tide on and in pitch darkness. No wonder *SE 33* was always short of crew!

I don't remember an awful lot about that first day. I couldn't believe the conditions we worked in. We were up to our knees in water, clinging to the gunwhales and foredeck, but somehow managing to haul and shoot 360 large crab pots. By the end of the day we had almost 2 tons of crabs on deck.

We came back into Salcombe harbour at around 4pm. It was just getting dark and the ebb tide was full on again. But now we had a south westerly gale up our ass. Richard said to leave most of the crab behind the wheelhouse to keep the weight back aft.

'There will be some big creamers on the Bar, so hold tight boys.'

He wasn't far wrong. The *Newbrook* must have surfed back in over the Bar at about 15 knots. Once again, water was almost at gunwhale height At last we found calmer water just off the Castle and finally rounded up to the mooring nearly fouteen hours after letting go. I didn't know what time of the day it was or what day it was. I was shattered.

It took us another good hour to get the catch ashore, after which Richard grunted, 'Okay, 3.30 in the morning. Don't be late.' and with that, disappeared into his house to drink a bottle of gin.

I rowed back across the harbour in faithful old *Saucy Sue* and staggered up the steep path to our house. Putting the alarm clock on for 2.30 am, I went straight to bed. I slept for eight solid hours and just about got up in time to get some grub ready for my next day on *Newbrook*. As I rowed across the harbour again that morning I seemed to know that today would be no better than yesterday. I was right. Day two was just about the same as day one, apart from the fact that I knew a little more about what was going on.

The thing that terrified me more than anything else was shooting away the gear. My job was to stand in front of the wheelhouse facing forward and pass the pots to Leopard who was on the starboard gunwhale dropping them over the side. Covey, as usual, did everything at full speed, including shooting away. Almost half a mile of inch and a half rope would snake its way past your feet at speed. Many good men have been caught up in the gear and been pulled overboard during this operation. I lost one myself years later when I was skipper of *Burutu* . The worst direction of all was shooting away straight into the sea.

The *Newbrook* would never lift to any sea so most of the time you were working under water.

Through it all, Covey was a very good seaman but was as wild as the wind. I can remember one occasion when he was up on the foc'sle hauling in gear in a full gale without oilskins and soaked to the skin, still yelling orders around the deck, remaining wet throughout the day, fortified only by a good swig of gin. One day, before going to sea, he cut off a finger with a bandsaw while cutting up bait skivers. He still went to sea and when he came home that evening he took his finger up to the doctor to see if anything could be done. Covey was certainly a one off. They don't breed 'em like that any more. He never made old bones. I don't think he made it past sixty. His body was clapped right out but he was a legend in his own lifetime.

I survived on the deck of the *Newbrook* for almost a month. I was beginning to think that perhaps Training School would have been the better option. I had made my bed and now I had to lie in it. But fate was about to step in and take control of my destiny.

On the *Newbrook* we were hauling away in typical nasty weather when one of the pots came up badly and spun up around the backline. It was my job to lift the pots as they broke the surface. I was trying to untwist this pot when my right hand was pulled into the gunwhale roller. When it was released my right index finger was almost severed and badly crushed and my finger nail was missing. Covey had a quick look at it and then told me to 'bugger off back aft and sort it out'. I could no longer take part in any more of the day's fishing so I wrapped my hand up in a saltwater rag and spent the rest of the day hanging on to the mizzen mast. Finally, when all the gear was finished, we turned for home. Covey called me into the wheelhouse. Crew were never allowed in there. This was sacred ground.

'Let's have a look then,' he grunted. 'Huh! Thought it would be worse than that. Better get up and see Dr. Hammond when we get in.'

My days on *Newbrook* were over. Dr. Hammond put my finger in a splint and told me I would get a new finger nail in time. I went down to see Covey next evening when he came in from sea. I told him I had to finish. I couldn't go on. It was too much for me at just 15. Physically I was not up to it. It was a man's job. Covey was a bit disappointed.

'Pity,' he said. 'You had the makings of a good hand.'

He gave me nearly £40 for my month's work, more than I had earned on *Norian* all the previous summer. If you worked on *Newbrook* you were the best paid fisherman in town but it was said in Salcombe that the back of the *Newbrook's* wheelhouse was not big enough on which to write the names of all the men who had worked on her.

Four

ISLAND CRUISING CLUB

Throughout life I discovered you don't get anything for nothing and now I had a busted hand to prove it. Anyway, I had to get another berth if I was to get my sea time in before next summer. Once again it was Laurie Prynn to the rescue. Laurie was doing his rounds when he spied me on Ditch End pier. He coasted alongside in his launch *Our Boys*.

'Aye, aye! What's happened to you?' He saw my bandaged hand.

'Caught it in the roller,' I said.

'I heard someone was hurt on the *Newbrook*. That Covey is a maniac.'

He gave me a lift over to Salcombe. Rowing for me was out of the question for a few days.

'Well,' said Laurie,' we'll have to get you another berth. How about trying the I.C.C., the Island Cruising Club? I'll put a good word in for you with Ted Pearce. You'll be all right but don't go in to see him with your hand all bandaged up. Looks like you've been in a scrap.'

A few days later I walked into the I.C.C. with an unbandaged hand. Ted Pearce was a very tall man. In fact it was Major Pearce. He was ex-military but he never stood on ceremony and everyone knew him as Ted.

'Yes, Billy, we can offer you a job but because we are a club the wages are very poor. You would be getting £1/10s a week, all found though. I believe you would learn a lot with us and I heard you want to join the Merchant Navy. We will give you a good understanding of basic seamanship.'

Ted was right and at the Club they could not believe my knowledge and capability for one so young. What Len, Doug and Co had taught me on the *Norian* was about to come into its own. I could splice wire and rope and my boat handling skills were A1. I knew about navigation and lights and buoyage. I knew the compass back to front and had a basic knowledge of diesel engines. Within one month I was on £2 a week.

The I.C.C. at that time had a cadet section for youngsters between 12 and 17 years of age. These kids were from inland and had not grown up in boats as I had and so naturally I was light years ahead of them in every skill possible to do with boats and the sea. For me it was quite a turn around having left school barely nine months back, unable to read or write or do even simple arithmetic. The following Easter I was to skipper the Club launch, *Shamrock*, for a while. It carried twenty passengers.

'No one is to know how old Billy is,' Ted instructed his staff. 'We'll get shot if his age is public knowledge.'

I spent the winter of '63-'64 working in the engineers shop under the clever guidance of Eric Jedynak. Eric was a good man and a very good engineer. He came to Britain during the Second World War. He was a pilot in the Polish Air Force. Like many of his generation he was very modest about his wartime flying but I did see photographs of him in Spitfires and Hurricanes, which spoke for themselves. We got on well that winter and

Top: 2nd Mate aboard *Provident,* aged 15. A time in sails and steam, summer 1964.

Bottom: Eighteen months after running away to sea, now 2nd Mate aboard *Provident.* With my proud Mum, East Portlemouth, autumn 1964.

he promised to take me as Second Mate the following summer when he would skipper the *Provident*, a 70ft sailing trawler built in 1924, for the sailing season.

Eric was true to his word and just after Easter 1964 I sailed as Second Mate of the *Provident* with Royston Raymond as First Mate. What an honour! I was given my own watch with four hands under me. I didn't find it any problem at all, I revelled in it. No one on board knew my age except Eric and Royston. It was better that way.

Our voyages were all to the Channel Islands and the French coast, usually lasting a week or ten days. Eric had to take a trip away for some reason, so two ex-merchant seamen, Roy Claire and Stan Crow replaced him and I sailed as Second Mate under them. They were excellent seamen, both ABs on cargo ships. Stan had been torpedoed during the war and was now Head Rigger at the Club. Men like these became my friends, my teachers and my 'university lecturers' in all that mattered – the sea, ships and seamanship.

The summer of '64 slowly started to slide by. My time was divided between sailing on Provident, launch driving and engineering. My sixteenth birthday came and went. I thought long and hard about going to see Mr Profit again but something told me to stay put. I was learning a hell of a lot about the sea and other interests had started to appear in my life – women and drink.

Five

JEFF SCOTT, SCOTTY

I had my first love affair that summer with a young lady called Caroline. She was a lot older than me, around twenty, but as I looked older than my years it didn't seem to matter. It was my first sweet taste of love and we spent most of the summer together. I took her to the Galley Restaurant one night for dinner. We had a bottle of wine and I felt very grown up. At 16 I could go into any of the pubs in Salcombe and be served, even though I was underage. Nobody gave it a second thought, as long as you had money in your pocket and you didn't get legless. It was one night that summer and the King's Arms was heaving. I was drinking with Stan Crow when he introduced me to a shortish fella, Jeff Scott. Jeff was a stocky man with wavy hair and piercing blue eyes He wore a speckled jersey, a peaked cap and blue serge trousers and I was never to see him in much else for the next 30 years. He was not a local Salcombe man, ex Merchant Navy and came from Brightlingsea in Essex. He served his time as a boy and then as Mate on Thames Sailing Barges. He had arrived in Salcombe by sea and married a local

Salcombe girl, Lil Edgecombe. He made Salcombe his home. Over the coming 15 years I was to sail thousands of miles with Jeff. I can say, without a shadow of a doubt, I learnt more about the sea and seamanship from Jeff than from any other person I sailed with.

Jeff never really told you anything. You watched what he did and copied accordingly when the time came. In all the miles we sailed together I hardly ever saw him look at a chart. It was all in his head like a homing pigeon. He was a remarkable man, but to him it was just natural and what you did, nothing special.

Jeff had started a small business called Scott's Yacht and Ship Delivery Service and this is precisely what he did all over Europe and as far south as Africa. After a couple more bottles of Guinness the King's Arms began to sway. Jeff suddenly asked if I could run up to Southampton with him to pick up a houseboat for the Quick brothers. I had two days off work from the I.C.C., so 'What time are we off?' I asked. 'As soon as the pubs kick out. We'll catch the flood off the Start, and carry it all the way to past the Bill, tuck in under Studland and carry a slack up to the Needles, anchor up for a couple of hours and then up the Solent with the guts of it up our ass.' That was Jeff's navigation sorted out and it happened just like he said it would. This man would teach me a lot.

We had the use of a 65ft ex Scottish Trawler called *Linnet*. She was powered by a 6 L 3 Gardner engine and her towing capabilities were good. She belonged to a friend called Roy Middleton with whom Jeff did many delivery jobs, but Roy was not on hand for this one. Hence I got the job. We duly arrived at the top end of the Hamble River where it is crossed by the main road to Portsmouth. 'There she is, Scratch, over there.' I was known as Scratch from way back when I went to Salcombe Infant School. It was my nickname. Jeff only ever knew me as Scratch. And that's the way it stayed. Your nickname was only with you at home, so on all my travels I was known as Billy or Limey.

'She's hard aground, Mate,' said Jeff. 'Can't wait around for her to float. We'll miss the sodding tide. I'll put you ashore on that pier. Go across the mud and put a line on her so we can pull her off.'

And that was how it was. Within 10 minutes I had secured a good chain and wire to her and was back on board the *Linnet*. Jeff gave the old Gardner engine the *Bells of Shannon* as he called it, a good jerk and a twang, and the flat bottomed houseboat came skimming across the mud and made a very impressive launch into the Hamble River. A good cheer went up from a nearby boatyard, whether to acknowledge our launching technique or whether to see the back of the old houseboat I never knew. A bit of both maybe.

Two hours saw us down off Yarmouth on the Isle of Wight.

'We'll chuck the pick out for a couple of hours and wait for the tide to come round,' said Jeff.

As soon as the anchor held we were ashore and off to the pub.

'She'll be all right there, soggy bottom,' said Jeff. He just seemed to know everything you needed to know but made nothing of it. That was his charm.

We entered the pub which I think was called the Bluebell. It was heaving as pubs always seemed to in those days. Jeff was quite well known in the pub and I reckon he stopped there often to wait for the tide.

'Where bound, Scotty?' someone yelled.

'Back down Channel to Salcombe with a tow. Be home by dinner time tomorrow.'

Once again we set sail at kicking out time. The tide had 'come round' as Jeff called it and we caught the young ebb out through the Needles. Soon we were slushing down the English Channel at a good 10 knots.

'Hold her in after the Bill, Scratch', Jeff said. 'I'm going to get my head down'.

He trusted me completely to keep a good watch and as the *Linnet* had an autopilot, I spent most of the night sitting on deck watching the tow. Most of the traffic was coasters. There were not many yachts about back then. I pulled her into the north west after rounding Portland Bill and saw the loom of Berry Head at Brixham. Jeff had said to put Berry Head on the port shoulder after the Bill and then to call him an hour later. It was first light when I called Jeff. He came up and took over.

'Well done, Mate.' he said. 'We'll hold her well into the north across Lyme Bay and miss the flood. We'll be home for last orders at dinner time, you watch.'

I went below, crashed down on a bunk and remember nothing more until we crossed Salcombe Bar. We knocked *Linnet* out of gear and brought the tow alongside. Within fifteen minutes we were in the King's Arms. Last orders were just being called.

'Told you we'd make last orders, Scratch', Jeff smiled.

I had never before seen navigation like that. Jeff had not consulted a book or a chart the entire trip. It was navigation I was keen to learn.

Six

BACK TO MR PROFIT

Jeff gave me £15 for the trip. He said I was a good hand and would take me again anytime. I was to hold him to his word many times in the coming years, but in the meantime the long hot summer of '64 was slipping by fast. I seemed to be doing more launch driving and less sailing on *Provident* with Roy and Eric. By the autumn of that year, I decided it was time to pay Mr Profit another visit. I was over sixteen and had the sea time in. I was ready to join the Merchant Navy.

Jeff gave me a lift to Plymouth one fine morning and back into the Shipping Federation I went. MrProfit remembered me immediately.

'You've grown a bit,' he said.

I was just over six foot tall and weighed about 13 stone and a half. I suppose he didn't get many kids of fifteen knocking on his door and demanding to join up.

'Right, pay attention!' he said. 'You have to have a medical examination and also pass the Lantern Test.'

'What's the Lantern Test?' I enquired.

'To see if you're bloody colour blind.'

I'd never thought about that.

'What if I am?'

'You'll have to be a steward!'

'Christ Almighty,' I blurted out. 'I don't want to be a bloody steward!'

'Pass the Lantern Test then,' he said.

He gave me two slips of paper. 'Here,' he said. 'Go to the Mercantile Marine Office on the Barbican and give them these. And go to Woolworths and get two photo shots of your face.'

I left his office a little concerned. I was a bit worried about this Lantern Test. The Medical shouldn't be a problem.

Plymouth Mercantile Marine Office was a gloomy old building on the Barbican, the oldest part of Plymouth, not a stone's throw from the Pilgrim Steps where more than three hundred years ago the Pilgrim Fathers had set sail on their voyage to America. I entered and handed my slips of paper to a gruff old man who told me to take a seat and I would be called. Ten minutes later I was led into a blackened room and told to sit down.

'What can you see?' a voice said.

'Nothing,' I replied.

Silence. About a minute passed.

'What can you see now?' asked the voice again.

'Red light,' I said.

'What now?'

'Two red lights.'

'What now?'

'Two more red lights.'

'And now?'

'Two green and one white.'

'Now?'

'Red and green.'

'Okay, you've passed.'

The lights came on and I felt great relief. This was the first and only exam I had ever taken in my short life and I had passed. I wasn't going to be a steward. I felt very good.

I sailed through the medical. My only concern was that at the age of nine I had fallen out of a tree and had broken my left arm and shoulder. Perhaps they would detect a weakness. I never told them and they never asked, so that was all right. Next stop Woolworths for the mug shots.

Armed with my photos and exam passes I returned to Mr Profit.

'No Catering Department for you then,' he chuckled.

'No, sir.'

'One last thing. You will have to join the NUS, the National Union of Seamen.'

Quick, back down to the Barbican and into the NUS office. I was now a Union member. I had no choice. This was 1964. By the time I got back to Mr Profit he had made up my Discharge Book and a red ID Book.

'There you are, Junior Ordinary Seaman Hitchen. You're in the British Merchant Navy.'

I felt very important indeed. Mr Sitwell would be proud, I thought.

'Now then, a ship,' he said. My heart jumped, but, alas, just like the previous year, I would not to be in Australia for Christmas.

'Because you have not been to Training School, you will have to go on Home Trade ships for the first six months.'

That meant ships that ply their trade between Brest and the Elbe and all around the UK. I didn't mind too much. At least I was in and I was going to join my first ship. I was to find out later that this was just a scam by the Federation to get crew on to clapped out old coasters plying their trade up and down the

Irish Sea in winter, carrying coal from Ayr in Scotland to Yelland Power Station in North Devon. This was the meanest route anyone could be on. Still, you live and learn, as Ron Sweetland soon said to me.

Ron was one of the first ABs I met. He was on the run because he had a girlfriend in Ayr and he spent the night with her every five or six days or so, if he was lucky. Ron was a great one for sayings: 'Fanny will draw them further than dynamite will blow them.'

'Right,' said Mr Profit. 'the *Halcience* is in Yelland and she needs a JOS, Junior Ordinary Seaman. She is sailing at 11pm tonight, so you had better get your skates on. Here is a railway warrant. Change at Exeter for Barnstable and then get the Number 10 bus to Appledore. It stops at Yelland Power Station and you can walk from there. Report to the First Mate.' And that was that.

PART TWO

HOME TRADE, UNION CASTLE AND SCOTTY

One

MV HALCIENCE

I had to get home quickly and then to Totnes Station, all last minute but when you've got to go, you've got to go. I finally arrived at Yelland Power Station at 9.30pm that evening. On leaving the bus the conductor pointed out the entrance to the Power Station. It was blowing a gale, pitch black and chucking it down. The pier at Yelland out to the coal berth must have been about a mile long. By the time I found the ship at the coaling berth I was like a drowned rat. I climbed down a ladder with my bag of belongings and on to the deck of the *Halcience*. She was all battened down and ready for sea, but what a wreck she was. I can't remember her age, but she must have been built before the First World War. She was a typical three island coaster, accommodation aft and midships, two hatches aft and one for'wd of the bridge. A voice yelled down from the bridge through the driving rain,' You the Ordinary Seaman?' 'Yes, sir.' 'Get up here then.'

I ascended the ladder and finally entered the bridge.

'Name?' he said.

'Hitchen, sir.'

'I'm not sir. I'm the Mate. Call me Chief.'

'Yes, sir, – sorry, Chief,' I corrected myself.

'Come and sign here; Home Trade Articles,' he said.

I had no idea what he was talking about but I had just signed on my first Merchant Ship. Home Trade Articles were a little different from deep sea Articles. Home Trade Articles meant you could pay off with 48hrs notice. Deep sea were for two years unless you came home to a UK port.

We sailed that night from Yelland spot on 11pm. The river out past Appledore is quite tidal, so there was no room for error. The old *Halcience* poked her nose out into the Bristol Channel and Christ Almighty, it was just like being back on the *Newbrook*. She was light ship and heading back to Scotland in a full north westerly gale. I honestly thought she was going to shake herself to bits, but no, she held together. She had seen it all before. Every other wave the prop came clear of the water and cavitated until it shook the whole of the stern section. How the funnel stayed on I shall never know, but it did. Forty hours later we arrived at Ayr on the west coast of Scotland to load coal for – guess where? Yelland! It was still blowing a gale, but the rain had turned to snow.

The *Halcience* was owned by The London Rochester Trading Company. All their ships ended in '*ence*'. I was later to serve on the *Kindrence* and the *Cressence*, needless to say between the west coast of Scotland and Yelland on the coal run.

And so I settled into life on the old *Halcience* up and down the Irish Sea in all weathers. Crews came and went. Even Ron Sweetland paid off one day in Yelland to go and marry his sweetheart. Then one day a fellow called Bert Clements arrived to sign on. Bert was a nice man, hell of a piss head, smoked like a train, but had a heart of gold. He must have been in his late fifties, had been in the Merchant Navy throughout the war and was

MV Halcience loading coal in Ayr, Scotland. She was my first ship in the Merchant Navy. The old 'rust bucket' as Bert Clements called her.

now in the twilight of his seagoing career. There was nowhere in the world he hadn't been and I listened to his stories of deep sea voyages in amazement. He had been on tankers, liners, tugs, cargo ships, ferries. You name it, Bert had been there and done it. Bert knew Mr Profit well. I told him what Mr Profit had told me about Home Trade for six months.

'Load of crap,' said Bert. 'If you want to go deep sea pay off this old rust bucket and get yourself down to Southampton. The Union Castle fruit ships will be sailing to the Cape this time of the year. Bugger Mr Profit. Get yourself on one of those and get some sunshine on your back.'

The next time in Yelland I took Bert at his word, paid off the *Halcience* and headed for Southampton, deep sea and sunshine. Arriving at Southampton by train I had to make my way to the docks area. Bert had told me that the Shipping Federation Pool was in Canute Road just along from the big Cunard Building and Union Castle House. Already excitement was growing. Sunshine, palm trees, blue seas and golden sands began to appear as these huge Shipping Offices stoked the fires of my imagination. Yelland Power Station and the Irish Sea already felt like another lifetime, left behind.

Bert had told me to go to the Pool, look at the board and pick a ship, one looking for Ordinary Seaman. It would give the name of the ship, where bound and crew she was looking for. Well, I must have picked a good day, there were ships going all over the world.

'This is more like it,' I thought. 'This is why I joined the Merchant Navy.'

Two

SHIPPING FEDERATION: SOUTHAMPTON POOL

Paraguay Star: two ABs; four stewards; one deck boy – South
America

Suivic: four ABs; two greasers; one donkey man; one deck boy –
Australia, New Zealand, Round the World

British Glory; two ABs; one deck *boy; one steward* – Persian Gulf

Edinburgh Castle: six ABs; two DHUs; two waiters; four greasers;
four donkey men; two cooks; one baker – South African
Mail Run

Golfito: one AB; one donkey man; two stewards – Central
America, Caribbean

Richmond Castle: one AB; one EDH; two Ordinary Seaman; one
deck boy; three greasers – South African Fruit Run

'Aye, aye, that's me!'

The Pool was a buzz of sailors all getting ships, talking,
shoving, pushing, joking, shouting, smoking and even drinking.
I approached the small barred window. There were a couple

of guys in front of me. I overheard that they were joining a BP Tanker at Fawley. I was relieved they weren't Ordinary Seamen about to join the *Richmond Castle*.

'Next,' shouted the clerk behind the bars, a wizened little man wearing small spectacles on a long beaked nose. I had been listening to what the other seamen had said at the window and simply said the same. 'Ordinary Seaman, *Richmond Castle*,' I said with all the confidence I could muster and handed my discharge book through the bars. He opened the book. There were a few seconds silence.

'Your first trip deep sea?' he said. My heart sank.

'Yes,' I replied. 'I've been on the coast for a while.'

He looked up and gave a smile. 'Yes, and I see that you got a very good report as well.'

He gave me a slip of paper, *Richmond Castle* Berth 6 Cargo Dock. 'Get down there quick. I'm sure she sails tonight.'

I almost ran down to the ship for fear the clerk would call me back, but no, I was off to South Africa. 'Good old Bert!' I thought . 'I owe him a pint if I ever see him again.'

The *Richmond Castle* looked huge as I approached her. She was around 7,000 tons and the old *Halcience* was a 400 tonner. Her fine cut bow looked enormous towering over the dock. She was painted in distinctive Union Castle lilac, the colour of Cape sunsets. Her accommodation, masts and derricks were white and just behind No.3 hold, her enormous funnel was painted red and black. I had never been so close to a ship this size before. I thought she was massive, but in time I was to sail in much bigger vessels.

I climbed the gangway and onto the main deck by hatch No 4, went into the accommodation and into the Sailors' Mess. Blow me down! There was a face I knew! Tony Wiltshire was a local Kingsbridge boy. I could just remember him being a fourth year at Kingsbridge Secondary Modern when I was an eleven

MV Richmond Castle in Port Elizabeth, South Africa, February 1965 on my first deep sea voyage. 'I looked up at her huge bow and beautiful lilac topsides.'

year old first year. I didn't really know him. First years didn't mix much with fourth years. He had joined the Merchant Navy five years earlier and was now a seasoned hand.

'Hello, Shag,' he said in a friendly voice. (Tony called everyone Shag.) 'I know you, don't I?'

'Billy Hitchen, East Portlemouth.'

'That's right,' he said and gave me a good handshake. 'Tony Wiltshire, Kingsbridge. Come on Shag, we've got to sign on in the Mate's cabin.'

Tony immediately took me under his wing. We were the best of mates for the whole trip. I felt he took pleasure in guiding me and showing me the ropes as it were. There were many tricks to learn about life in the Merchant Navy.

I stood alongside Tony in the small queue to sign on. Tony, at the last minute, pushed me in front of him. It was my turn to sign on. I was a Junior Ordinary Seaman. That was my official rank. The Mate never looked up from his desk.

'Junior Ordinary Seaman Hitchen,' he said.

I was just about to say, 'Yes, Chief.' when Tony's voice came from behind and said 'Senior Ordinary Seaman.'

'Senior Ordinary Seaman.'

'Yes, Chief,' I said.

I was signed on as Senior Ordinary Seaman, the quickest promotion I had ever had or ever would have thanks to Tony, a difference to my wages of £10 a month. When we left the Mate's cabin Tony proudly informed me that my newly acquired rank also entitled me to beer and cigarettes, known as slops. Good old Tony. He was a younger version of Bert, knew all the tricks. We shared a cabin together that trip. That way, he said, we would get on the same watch. He was dead right.

'Come on, Shag. A last pint before we sail.' Tony was down the gangway and hailing a taxi. I just followed. Two hours before shore leave ended.

Gatti's Bar was near Bargate in the centre of Southampton, a famous bar known by seamen the world over. In we went. It was like the Wild West and I loved it. Tony introduced me to a South African called Neville. He came from Port Elizabeth and was also signed on the *Richmond Castle*. He was on his way home as long as he could pull himself away from blonde Sandy, his Southampton girlfriend. After a couple of hours in Gatti's Bar it was time to get back to the ship. Sandy was in tears. Neville promised to return on the next available ship. 'Believe that, you'll believe anything,' said Tony. That didn't help.

Ten minutes later we were all aboard. We dropped the derricks, battened down the hatches and made ready for sea. Two tugs arrived and gently pulled the *Richmond Castle* away from the quayside. Ropes were let go and our bow was pulled around to point down Southampton Water and onward down the Solent.

Ding a ling, ding a ling! The telegraphs rang down to the

engine room – Slow Ahead. The huge propeller turned and we were on our way.

'Don't stow the ropes,' the Mate ordered. 'We are only crossing to Antwerp. We still have part cargo to discharge before we head for South Africa.'

We passed through the eastern entrance of the Solent, past the Nab Tower and set course for the Straits of Dover and then on up into the North Sea to Antwerp. There was a good easterly gale blowing down the English Channel, but the *Richmond Castle* just brushed the waves aside. It was nothing to her. I remember being on the starboard wing lookout thinking how the old *Halcience* would handle this weather. I was pleased to be on the *Richmond Castle*. We were making about 15 knots into this gale, which was just about the fastest I had ever been on water. Our watch finished at midnight. We were to do the 8-12 watch outward bound. I crawled into my bunk that night feeling pretty good about things.

Three

ANTWERP AND MARLENE DIETRICH

We entered the Schelde River at first light next morning with a pilot aboard. We gently navigated up the river to Antwerp. It took about four hours to reach Antwerp and because it was our watch on deck, 8-12, I was expected take my turn at the wheel. I didn't find it daunting at all. It was the first time I had been on the wheel under the direction of a pilot. Here I was, just 16 years old, steering a 7,000 ton cargo ship up the Schelde River.

'Starboard 10 degrees.'

'Starboard 10 degees,' I replied.

'Midships.'

'Midships,' again I replied.

'Port 15 degrees.'

'Port 15 degrees.'

Now that I was a Senior Ordinary Seaman my responsibilities had somewhat grown. To have control of this huge cargo ship made me feel like an AB, all thanks to Tony's quick promotion plan at signing on, just to get more beer and cigarettes.

We docked in Antwerp just after mid-day. The *Richmond Castle* slowly eased alongside. Before long we had stripped off the hatch boards and were discharging the remaining cargo. We would be in Antwerp for twenty four hours before sailing for Cape Town. Antwerp was buzzing with ships from all over the world, discharging and loading cargo. Late that afternoon I walked around the docks reading the names and ports of registration of a few of these ships. I knew that one day I would visit all those faraway places.

On my return to the ship I was greeted with, 'Come on, Shag! Where the hell have you been? We're off ashore, Danny's Bar and you'll love it.' A quick wash behind the ears, comb through the hair, a clean T shirt and I was ready. It was just getting dark when Tony, Neville and I raced through the dimly lit cobbled streets of Antwerp's dockland. Tonight was to be an eye opener for this naïve young boy from a small village in South Devon.

'Here we are,' Tony announced at last and we walked into a dimly lit cellar type bar. It seemed quite busy, waitresses working the tables and not bad looking either. We found a table not far from a small stage where an elegant tall blonde lady was singing a very seductive kind of song. I asked Tony if she was Marlene Dietrich.

'Who?' he said.

'My Mum is a fan of hers. Wait till I tell her I've seen her live!'

Tony gave Neville a wry smile.

Looking round the bar I soon recognised a couple of familiar faces, the Second Mate and the Second Engineer, plus a few others from the ship. An hour or two passed. The Belgian beer was flowing and the night was beginning to swing, but somehow everything did not seem to be as it should. One of the waitresses got into a fight with our Second Engineer and they were not pulling punches. It finally dawned on me! Even Marlene turned out to be a man. All settled down again and peace was restored in Danny's Bar but the Second Engineer had a black eye all the way to Las Palmas.

We sailed outward bound for Cape Town at about midday the following day. I shall never forget sailing down the Schelde River late that afternoon, sitting on the stern of the *Richmond Castle* watching the lights of Antwerp and Belgium disappearing into the distance. With a can of strong lager in one hand and a Capstan Full Strength in the other, 'This is the life,' I thought.

Four

THE FAIREST CAPE

The ship soon settled into seagoing mode. Tony, Neville and I were 8-12 watch outward bound, 12-4 on the African coast and 4-8 homeward bound, but that was a long way off. Four days out of Antwerp we called at the Canary Island of Las Palmas for bunkers. Las Palmas was the main bunkering port for all Union Castle ships bound for the Cape. We had a quick run ashore at Las Palmas because we could not get straight on to the bunkering berth. Once again Tony knew exactly where to go. I bought a bottle of Bacardi to go with the beer on the long haul down to the Cape.

It took two weeks to get to Cape Town. Crossing the line on the equator was a bit of a laugh and I managed to get away with it fairly lightly, but the Deck Boy had a hard time. Once again, my promotion paid dividends. I couldn't believe how hot it got in the tropics. Most nights I slept outside on the hatches under the stars of the southern hemisphere, locating the Southern Cross, its compass like formation pointing due south to the pole. It was very dark on the after end of No.4

45

and No.5 hatches. Most of the crew slept up there and I would quite often trip over someone in the night. Passing close to Dakar and Monrovia I could smell Africa, spicey and pungent. Finally we closed the South African coast off Walvis Bay. The hinterland was becoming mountainous as we approached the Cape. We passed the *Edinburgh Castle* homeward bound. The two ships came quite close and our whistles blew in salute. I felt very proud that a huge ship like the *Edinburgh Castle* would acknowledge us. The Second Mate told me that it was company policy to acknowledge where possible.

It was dark when we pulled into Table Bay. We rounded up off Cape Town and rumour quickly spread, as rumours do, that we were to anchor for five days to wait for a loading berth. And so we dropped anchor about a mile off Cape Town.

Dawn broke next day and I saw a sight that would stay with me all my life – Table Mountain, with cloud slowly spilling down from across the flattened top. It was an incredible sight, and there was Cape Town tucked up underneath the mountain. Over the next five years my travels would take me to many of the most beautiful sights in the world: Sugar Loaf Mountain, Sydney Harbour, Tahiti, the Manhattan skyline, the Bay of Islands, but none would live up to my first sight of Table Mountain – 'the fairest Cape in all the world,' wrote Sir Francis Drake.

The rumours were correct and we stayed at anchor for the next four days. They were the longest days of my life. I don't know how rumours start in a ship, but they do. I think they come down from the Captain's steward to the galley. The galley always seemed like the most reliable source of information. On the fourth day, however, the rumours came to fruition. The Bosun ordered the pilot ladder to be lowered and we were on our way.

'Del Monica's tonight,' said Tony. 'Get ready for Cape brandy.'

The anchor slowly but surely graunched up through the hawser pipe.

Ding a ling, ding a ling the telegraphs rang and the *Richmond Castle* pointed her bow towards Cape Town. Tony, Neville and I were always on the forecastle for docking along with the Bosun and First Mate. As we slowly entered the harbour the bow tug assumed position underneath our bow.

'Lower away,' said the Mate.

We lowered the hawser down to this beautiful tug which looked more like a yacht than a tug. It was immaculate. The varnished bridge glistened in the sunlight, the brass work shone. After the hawser cable was connected I heard the telegraph on the tug ring. We were standing about 60 to 70 feet directly above her and I could see right down through the engine room hatch. I watched as her giant engines burst into life, flashing and gleaming. I was reminded of that first night on the *Norian*. Cape Town tugs were all coal fired, triple expansion engines, just the same as the old *Norian* – a vanishing age, the age of steam and sail, disappearing before my eyes. In years to come, I would be among the last of a very few who could say that they had served their time in both sail and steam.

The *Richmond Castle* was gently nudged alongside by the beautiful Cape Town Harbour tugs. We tied up about three berths behind the mail boat berth. The bow of the *Transvaal Castle*, later to become the *SA Vaal*, towered above us. As soon as we had secured alongside, the gangway was swung out and lowered to the quay. And then a strange sort of thing happened. Black dock workers swarmed onto the deck like flies and started setting up camps with tarpaulins, lighting small fires to boil water and make tea. It felt very strange to me, almost an intrusion into our little world that had been our home for the last month. However, things soon appeared to become organised chaos and it all seemed to work. Many of the dockies, as we called them, disappeared down the holds and apples, oranges and grapefruit were soon coming aboard. Tony said we would be on the coast loading for about three weeks. He wasn't far out. Before we were fully loaded we called at Port Elizabeth and East London before returning to Cape Town to top up.

Five

TEACH YOURSELF SUMS

Tony, Neville and another AB called Tarzan took me ashore for my first night out in South Africa and it sure wasn't a let down. We had a couple of beers in a pretty rough bar just outside the dock gates. Then our fearless leader, Tony, announced it was time to hit Del Monica's. It was a real sailors' bar cum club. We went up a small flight of stairs and I could hear piano music and the noise as we approached, entering through two batwing doors. Well, we could have been back in Gatti's Bar in Southampton. Against the wall, by the bar, was some old queen playing the piano. She could play any tune you wanted and she didn't stop playing all night even when she was having a drink or a smoke. We found a table and sat down.

'Bottle of brandy and four glasses,' Tony ordered. I think the name of the brandy was Limousin. Ice and coke was also put on the table. Tony poured the drinks and the fun began. All sorts was going on in Del Monica's. There didn't seem to be any house rules – card games, singing, dancing and in the first hour I witnessed two punch ups with more to follow. As I was to learn over the next five years, the world was a very small place to the average deep sea Merchant Seaman. The ships were really just a means of transport from bar to bar all around the world: Del Monica's, Cape Town; Monty's Hotel, Sydney; Ma Gleeson's, Auckland; Joe Beef's, Montreal; Navigators, Durban; English Bar, Christchurch, New Zealand. The list goes on and on and I would visit all of them in the coming years. They will all be gone now, of course, bulldozed down to turn the old docklands into sought after apartments. Little do the people living there now know of the wild parties held there 50 years before and once again another age was disappearing before my eyes.

After a few more brandies we left and went on to a nightclub or two. I honestly do not remember getting back to the ship, but next morning I woke up in the right bunk but Tony and Neville were still missing. They showed up within the hour bragging about their conquests, ending the night at the top end of Adderley Street. There were three girls, they said, but I had passed out so they put me in a taxi back to the ship.

'A little less brandy for you tonight, Billy,' said Tony.

And so my first week in Cape Town passed by. We went ashore every night as soon as we had finished loading cargo.

It was now slowly becoming apparent to me just how much of a disadvantage my complete lack of maths was starting to have on my life. Up until the time I left school, maths was a complete blank. I could just about read and write, but Maths was a fog. I suppose the teachers had tried their best, but it was no use. The funny thing was, I could say my eight times table with no problem. It was just like a poem, but I hadn't a clue what it meant. I had an understanding of British currency, but having to deal now with foreign exchange, I was back to square one, trying to convert different currencies into Sterling. Other simple things like playing cards and darts I had to shy away from. Being thick was not something you would openly admit to in 1965.

One afternoon I was walking through one of the poorer districts of Cape Town, which I am sure was a black area. Apartheid was in full swing in South Africa in those days and I probably shouldn't have been there at all. But I was. I came across a very small bookshop, just a corrugated iron shack really. My guardian angel, who looked after me many times in the coming years, had guided me there. Not as though I had ever read a book in all my life, I was drawn inside. I looked around for a short time and then I saw it, a dog eared old book called, Teach Yourself Sums. I picked it up and glanced inside. Everything was in very big simple print. I imagined it was aimed at people in the black townships who had never been to school. I fell into that category, or so I thought. That day was a turning point for me. The book worked wonders. I never became the world's greatest mathematician, but after a couple of months, quietly on my own, I had mastered basic maths. I kept the book for many years to come, not that I could learn any more from it but because it was like a friend. Whoever wrote it was a genius. It must have helped thousands of people in my situation. I like to think so, anyway.

Tony was right about our time on the South African coast. It took about three weeks to completely fill the holds of the *Richmond Castle* after four or five days in Port Elizabeth and East London. It was early in the fruit season and I think the fruit was only coming down to the coast in dribs and drabs. We carried no other cargo but fruit. Finally, with three or four more days back in Cape Town to top up, we were fully loaded. The old *Richmond Castle* was well down to her load line and felt very steady in the water. We were ready to head for home.

Six

DOUBLE HEADER

When we sailed from Cape Town the weather was poor, driving rain and a strong wind. This was a bit of a shock as it had been beautiful all the time we were on the coast, but heading north we soon got into better weather. Our orders were for Europe. We would be told ports of discharge on entering the English Channel. And so we started the long, slow monotonous slog up from the Cape.

The *Richmond Castle* was not what was known as a good feeder, meaning the food was not very good. I think the Chief Cook had shares in Union Castle with company interests always at heart. It felt we were on a near starvation diet in the Mess, so I was always hungry. One night, we were up near the equator, Tarzan and I pinched some hard boiled eggs and bread from the galley. We went back aft behind No.4 hatch and scoffed the lot. Next morning, when the Second Cook and Baker discovered the loss, there was hell to pay. Tarzan said just keep quiet, so we did. In the end the Chief Steward blamed the Cook for leaving the galley door unlocked. We never got our hands on any more eggs but she was always a hungry ship.

We didn't stop at Las Palmas homeward bound for bunkers but pressed on for the English Channel where we finally received orders for Gothenburg, Sweden. This was a bit of a downer for most of the crew as they envisaged being home in Southampton the following day. I didn't mind at all. Gothenburg was to be my next foreign port of call. Tony, being the old maritime lawyer he was, pointed out that if we were to discharge all our cargo at Gothenburg, we could be ordered straight back to the Cape. Our Articles read we could only pay off in a UK port within the Home Trade limits. Gothenburg was well outside Home Trade limits. This risk was always taken when signing on a cargo ship. You could be on that ship for two years as long as she stayed away from Home Trade limits.

Three days after receiving orders we docked in Gothenburg and started to discharge immediately. Every few hours a new rumour would spread around the ship as to the amount of cargo we were to unload. Towards the end of the fourth day it was not looking good. There was very little cargo left in the ship and Tony was to be proved right yet again. By the end of the fifth day in Gothenburg everyone on board was resigned to what was known as a 'double header'. The Bosun was to inform the crew officially that we would not be returning to the UK this trip, we were to batten her down and that night we would sail for the Cape of Good Hope.

It was not good news at all for the married men from the Captain down. The worst part for them was sailing back down the English Channel with the lights of England twinkling away on our starboard side, but outward bound again we were – the Cape for orders. I was never caught out again in this sort of situation. Personally, I wouldn't have cared if the Bosun had told us we were bound for New Zealand. For me it was all a great adventure.

And so, in the Spring of '65, the old *Richmond Castle* plodded

MV Richmond Castle in the tropics. A view across her boat deck where Tarzan and I acquired the hard hard boiled eggs to supplement our meagre rations.

her way south to the equator and then onward to South Africa. Our time on the coast was similar to our previous voyage, apart from calling at Durban for a few days. Loading was quicker as the fruit season was now well under way. Calling again at Port Elizabeth for five days I caught up with a girl called Sandra I had met the previous trip. She was a very tall blonde of Dutch descent, I imagined, very attractive, but serious promises were out of the question. I still had a lot of living to do. I never saw Sandra again after that trip, but we did write a few letters to each other. Perhaps she couldn't read mine and that was why she stopped writing. I shall never know

At last, we were fully loaded in Cape Town when good news spread around the ship like wildfire. We were homeward bound for Southampton to discharge full cargo in the UK. Everyone aboard was smiling with this news and the homeward trip went well. We had good weather all the way to Las Palmas, where we stopped for bunkers, and then onwards north about five days to Southampton. I recognised the Start light as we came up the Channel and the Portland Bill. None of the others seemed to know anything about navigation, so what I knew, I kept to myself; better that way. But the Second Mate was interested to know about my previous seagoing career. He was a nice fella, came from the New Forest and was intrigued to hear about Scotty's navigational skills. He agreed that navigating around the coast required much more skill than navigating to South Africa. I only remember his name as David, but I was to sail with him again as First Mate on the *Rustenburg Castle*. That was not a double header, just a quick run down to the Cape and back.

Finally we passed through the Needles, up the Solent and into Southampton water. Tarzan came up with a classic observation as we pulled alongside.

'When you think about it,' he said in his strong Portsmouth accent, 'all we've really done is a trip round the Isle of Wight.'

'What are you talking about?' said the Mate

'Well, Chief,' said Tarzan, 'we went out through the Nab and came in through the Needles. That's just going round the Isle of Wight except that we went to South Africa twice on the way.'

A remark like that stays with you all your life. Good old Tarzan.

We finally pulled alongside at 8am. Sandy was on the quay waving with a few other girlfriends and wives.

Ding a ling, ding a ling, the telegraphs rang down – Finished with Engines – and our voyage was over.

'All right tonight, Nev!' said Tony.

Neville was down in the well deck blowing kisses to Sandy.

'Gatti's Bar for lunch time,' said Tony.

He was spot on. All hands were in high spirits We paid off later that morning and sure enough, first stop was Gatti's Bar. I walked down the gangway and along the dock and had a last look at the old *Richmond Castle*. She didn't look quite as spick and span as when I first joined her. There were streaks of rust now running across her beautiful lilac topsides and weed was beginning to grow around her waterline. She had steamed nearly 30,000 miles on her two trips to the Cape and had brought home tens of thousands of cases of apples and oranges. Within eight or ten days she would do it all over again.

Tony soon had a taxi organised and we all went to Gatti's. It was as if we had never left.

Seven

RETURN TO BASE

And so my first deep sea voyage came to an end. I had a very good report in my Discharge Book, about £30 in my pocket and a railway warrant to get home. What more could I want? I am not sure where I slept that night. The celebrations for the end of our voyage lasted well into the night. The last time I saw Tarzan some woman was bundling him into a taxi. It is strange in a way, but so true, the saying, 'ships that pass in the night'. After paying off from a ship you rarely saw any of the crew again. It was sad really because over the past six or so months you had become best buddies. I did catch the train back to Devon the next day with Tony. When we got back to Kingsbridge we had a couple of drinks together but after that I never saw him again. It was good to have met him though. He helped and guided me a lot on that first trip, especially with my promotion.

Back in Salcombe things had not changed very much. I went across to East Portlemouth to see Mum and Dad. They were interested to know all about my voyage to South Africa but I somehow I did not want to stay at home any more. I had left home when I was fourteen and a half and it was hard to go back now. I was much happier looking for new adventures. I did not have to look far. That night I ran into Stan Crow, guess where – the King's Arms.

'Where have you been? Haven't seen you for ages.'

I told him about my first deep sea trip.

'I did a double header once on the *Brocklebanks*. We were away for 16 months.'

Made my double header look a bit tame.

'Scotty is looking for you,' he said. 'He's heard you were home. He's off to the east coast tonight to pick up a Swan 60 to take to the Med. Better get your ass round there quick.'

Scotty's house was only a stone's throw away from the King's Arms. I was there within minutes.

'Christ, am I glad to see you, mate. Got your kit? Lil's just doing up some grub then we're away. Burnham on Crouch to the Med. Okay?'

How could I refuse.

'John's coming with us. Just the three of us.'

John was Jeff's son, a couple of years younger than me. He was tall and slim and had a big shock of curly auburn hair. He was a gentle sort of guy, very softly spoken but even at just fifteen years of age, showed great skill in seamanship. Over the next three and a half years we were to become the best of mates. We were on a ship together in the summer of '68 when John was murdered in Rotterdam. The Harbour Police asked me to identify his body that had been in the water for two weeks. It took a long time for me to get over that.

The three of us left Salcombe that night at about midnight for Burnham on Crouch, Essex. Jeff had a lot of connections there, Burnham and Brightlingsea, his home town. We drove up in Jeff's old Mini. Jeff let John and I drive during the night although we were both well under the legal driving age, no driving licence and no insurance. I don't know how we had learnt to drive, but boys just could back in the sixties. Jeff sat alongside and said that if the cops stop us we must dive in the back and he would swivel into the driving seat. We never had to put it into practice and that morning we arrived in Burnham.

Eight
_____

TO THE MED WITH SCOTTY

The Swan 60 was a beautiful yacht, only a couple of years old. The owner didn't look too impressed with John and me with our leather jackets and winkle pickers. But Jeff assured him we were up to the job. The owner's wife nipped ashore and returned with two pairs of posh yachting shoes that would protect the deck from our winkle pickers. I am sure this put the owner at ease. He was more worried about his decks than getting his boat to the Med. Jeff finally shook hands with the owner and said he would see him in Barcelona in two weeks time. How did he know he would be in Barcelona in two weeks? Only Jeff knew that. That was his magic.

If a Swan was not called a Swan, it would have been called a Greyhound. It was one of the fastest yachts I have ever sailed, apart from *Velsheda,* a J Class, years later. We did have fair wind it's true, but we didn't drop under 10 knots for the first five days. We ran across the Thames and rounded up at the South Foreland

Jeff Scott with me on *Corunna of Burnham*, in the Bay of Biscay, en route from London to Port d'Andratx, Majorca, summer 1968.

for a northerly reach right down the English Channel. As we approached Ushant the wind let more into the North West and this gave us another broad reach across the Bay of Biscay.

'Just keep her on the Rhumb line across here.' said Jeff, 'parallel with the southbound ships. They will all fetch up at Finisterre tomorrow. We'll pull inside them. They will all pass 10 – 15 miles off and we want to be inside that.'

There were charts aboard, but Jeff hadn't touched them. I'm sure he could see over the horizon. The sixth day out saw us well down the Portuguese coast but, alas, the wind was beginning to fade and come on the nose. We bore her away a bit and started the engine. She still held 6 – 8 knots with full sail on. By nightfall it was dead calm and so we took all her sail off.

'We'll stop at Gibraltar tomorrow night,' said Jeff. 'A run ashore to the Old Bull and Bush will do us good, anyway. We are on good time and we are nearly out of fags and beer.'

Early the following evening saw us alongside in Gibraltar. We were well on schedule to be in Barcelona within the two weeks. A good run ashore that night was just what the doctor ordered. We didn't leave Gib until the following afternoon. Scotty, the old devil, had been up to the Yacht Club and picked up a 55ft Fleur-de-Lis motor yacht to take back to Southampton, which was good news all round; a free ride home and get paid for it.

The last leg up the Spanish coast to Barcelona was a doddle, lightish onshore winds and the knocker on. She still made 8 knots. Needless to say we got there a day before the owner's arrival. He was so chuffed that he took the three of us up to the Yacht Club for a slap up meal. He even seemed to approve of the winkle pickers and was more interested in telling his mates what a record breaking voyage his fine yacht had just made.

Nine

HM CUSTOMS AND EXCISE AND BLACK JAKE

Next day we caught a train down to La Linea and crossed the border into Gibraltar. The Fleur–de-Lis was a fine gentleman's motor yacht. She had twin Gardner diesels but the best she could make was about seven and a half knots knots. She was quite badly weeded up and I guess that didn't help. We left Gibraltar for the UK well loaded up with fags and booze. Jeff wryly indicated that we would not be going directly to Southampton but would stop at Salcombe to unload our cargo.

The *Lady of Rudding* was a fine ship but I have never been on anything that rolled as much. Several times I wished to hell we were back on the Swan. During the voyage home the diesel engines faltered often. It was just shitty fuel; change the filters; bleed them through and off again. Not a pleasant job when rolling your gunwhales under, but all good experience. John and I were learning so much from Jeff but we didn't know it at the time.

Twelve days out of Gib we picked up the loom of Eddystone light.

'Just right,' said Jeff. 'We didn't want to go in in daylight with this lot on board.'

In the last hours of darkness we crept up Salcombe harbour and rounded alongside Jeff's launch on its mooring off Snapes Point. We quickly and quietly unloaded the contraband into his small launch. John stayed aboard the *Lady of Rudding* in case Black Jake, the Customs Officer, should arrive but we knew there was little chance of that. Black Jake liked his bunk too much. Within an hour we were back aboard, boxes of cigarettes and drink safely stashed away in Jeff's store in the park. We hoisted the yellow Quarantine Flag and then we all three turned in and slept like babies.

Sure enough, at about 9.30 am, knock, knock on the hatch door.

'You there, Scotty?' Jake called.

'Aye aye, Jake. Come aboard.'

The usual formalities followed.

'Anything to declare, boys?'

'Yep, two hundred fags and a bottle of whisky.'

'Just sign here then.'

And that was that. We were ashore and in the King's Arms by 11 am.

My Christ, wasn't there a party at Jeff's house that night! There was gin, rum and whisky galore and everyone was given two hundred cigarettes. Jeff was a very generous man and I don't think he was happy until it had all gone. I'm sure I can even remember Black Jake himself, quietly sitting in a corner, sipping a brandy. I went to many such parties at Jeff's house. Everyone knew when Scotty had had a good trip. And this had been a good one – one down to the Med and one back.

We took the *Lady of Rudding* to Southampton a couple of days later and then it was up to Burnham to pick up the Mini – driving lessons again on the way home. The final years of freedom and they had to end.

Ten

MOTOR BIKES AND
MV KINDRENCE

I honestly don't know when I learned to drive. As I said before, it was just what boys did. In the summer of '64 I had bought my first motorcycle, at least, my first legal one. When I was thirteen a fella called Hugh Cater gave me a 250cc Panther. I don't know why he gave it to me, but he did. I certainly didn't have any money. I used to drive it round the village at night with a mate of mine called Fishy Trout. We had quite a spill on it one night – hit Chivelstone Cross signpost and went to school next day feeling very sore. As an old farmer's wife, in her broad Devon, told me years later, 'Boys is boys and maids is glad of it.'

I acquired a Provisional License in the summer of '65 and went to take my test on my 500cc Norton. You were only supposed to have a 250cc as a learner driver, but the examiner didn't seem interested in how big the bike was and passed me with no problem. So the L Plates soon went into the bin. I still have the same Norton today, fifty years on and still ride it to

MV Cressence punches her way down the Irish Sea loaded
with coal for Yelland power station.

John on the right and myself with another crew member in the Pig and Whistle on
board *RMS Oriana*, early 1966.

Pig and Whistle *RMS Edinburgh Castle*, John far left, myself second left.
She was a happy ship.

Vintage Shows and Rallies. It's quite unusual to have owned the
same vehicle for over fifty years.

It was becoming apparent to me that I did not actually learn
much about seamanship in the Merchant Navy – womanizing
and drinking, yes. My time with Jeff was when I was in the
learning groove. The really good thing about the Merchant Navy
was that you could come and go as you pleased. There was no
fixed leave. As soon as you had paid off a ship, it was entirely up
to you when you got another one. For most Merchant Seamen
it was when the money ran out, unlike the Officers and Cadets
who were indentured to a specific company. You could sign on
with any shipping company going to any part of the world which
took your fancy. This situation particularly suited me. Whenever
Jeff was busy I was at home, mostly in the summer and when
winter came I was off to sunnier places.

Jeff's son, John, was also keen to join the Merchant Navy and in the summer of '66 he turned sixteen and joined up the same way as I had, through Mr Profit. Of course, he was given the usual story – you will have to go on the coast for six months. So we both joined the *MV Kindrence* at Yelland and did a few runs up to Scotland and back on the coal run. Not for long, though – Jeff got in touch to say he needed crew. He had four coal fired harbour tugs in Swansea to go to the breaker's yard at Siloth on the Solway Firth. We signed off the *Kindrance* on our return to Yelland and were soon back in Salcombe.

Eleven

TUG DELIVERY DRAMA

There were no flies on Jeff when it came to saving a few quid. He had a small motor yacht, about 30ft, a Silver I seem to think. It was to be delivered to Cardiff that same week, so all the crew for the tug delivery piled aboard this small motor yacht to travel from Salcombe to Cardiff. He saved a mint on train fares and got paid for it. You see what I mean about learning from Jeff. There were seven of us altogether: Roy Middleton, owner of *Linnet*, Chief Engineer; Henry Bowden–Leigh; a piss artist, Ernie Edgecombe; Jeff's brother-in-law, Mick Hallam, just a bit older than John; and me–and of course, our fearless skipper, Jeff.

Jeff's plan was as follows: pick the best two tugs, that is, the pair in the most seaworthy condition and do it in two trips, steam one and tow the other. This steam one and tow the other was a trick we were to use again the following summer with two minesweepers to Italy. The tugs had been laid up for a year, but, undaunted, Roy got the coal fires going and soon, with that lovely old smell of fire, steam and hot oil, I was back on the *Norian*. I seem to remember it was about 24 hours before we had enough pressure to turn the old engines, but turn they did. The familiar clank, clonk and a hiss of steam and they were away. A few of the old tug crew had organised a farewell party to see the tugs off. Any excuse, we didn't need any encouraging, so a proper Swansea dockside party was held, plenty of wine, women and song until the wee small hours. There were a few sore heads next morning.

And so, on a beautiful summer's day, our little flotilla steamed out of Swansea and set course for the Hats and Barrels to the south west tip of Wales. The weather was fantastic, clear blue skies and the sea was a mirror. But Scotty had a plan.

Both tugs were dripping with beautiful brass fittings – wheels, navigation lights, telegraphs, signs and more. Jeff's plan was to slip into Fishguard, box a load of this stuff up and send it home to sell at a later date. So after entering St. Georges Channel, we rounded Strumble Head and into Cardigan Bay. We brought the two tugs alongside each other and all hands proceeded to strip the old tugs of their brasswork. After an hour or so, the after deck of the tug we were using to tow had a good pile of marine memorabilia being boxed up ready for shipment back to Salcombe.

'We'll anchor one tug outside Fishguard, pop in with the other and get this lot on the train back to Totnes.' said Jeff with great authority, as though he did this every day of the week. 'Brother Bill will come and pick it up from Totnes with his lorry.'

Bill Edgecombe was another of Jeff's brothers-in-law. The Edgecombe family was pretty big in Salcombe.

Good plan, but for Jeff another drama was about to unfold. To handle a triple expansion steam engine an engineer has to get used to the engine. It has no gearbox. To put into reverse you have to completely change the rotation of the engine and that is very tricky unless you are used to the engine. Roy had only changed rotation once with this engine, a fact that Jeff had forgotten.

And so Jeff attempted to bring this 150 ton tug alongside the pier at Fishguard in the correct manner – shoulder towards the quay, opposite helm on and a good kick astern would swing her alongside. Should have been no problem at all until he rung down for half astern and got half ahead. The powerful tug took no prisoners and hit the quay with good force. Suddenly, all hell let loose with a tremendous hissing of steam and smoke. The funnel completely sheared off at deck level and came crashing down like a tree almost wiping out the starboard wing of the bridge.

'Christ Almighty,' and a few other choice words, our captain yelled, as the funnel disappeared over the starboard side of the tug. It turned out that the base of the funnel was rusted right through and the stays were also rotted out. Had we been in any weather, it would have been lost overboard long before. Escaping steam was coming from the steam pipe up to the ship's whistle which bent right over and shut itself off. Coal smoke now billowed up from the gaping hole in the boat deck.

Well, to cut a long story short, we got our boxes onto the train as soon as we could, slipped out of Fishguard, picked up the other tug at anchor and high tailed it out of Cardigan Bay. Afterwards Roy claimed he was sure the engine was going astern. As the funnel fell on the starboard wing it knocked the telegraph to full ahead. By this time he was completely confused so he put the engine into neutral. Thank God! Otherwise we would have gone right through the quay.

Fortunately for us we had a light headwind for the rest of the trip up to the scrapyard at Siloth. This kept most of the smoke out of the bridge, but the afterdeck was a no-go area. When we finally pulled into the scrapyard, the fact that we had no funnel took gaze off the fact that we also had no navigation lights. We all caught the train back to Swasea and delivered the other two tugs without incident. It was still flat calm and this time the funnels stayed in place. John and I hitch-hiked all the way back to Salcombe, about 400 miles. It took us a couple of days but we saved our train fare which we could then add to our wages. Jeff had only a couple of small deliveries on his books for the rest of the year.

Twelve

JUDGE MCGOOGAN

A small job came up through Jeff. A fella called Norman, who owned a small Dunkirk Little Ship called the *Sun Star*, had asked Jeff if he would help him take the yacht up to Southampton. Jeff said, 'No, I'll take it up to Southampton, but I don't do helping.' Jeff would only go to sea as skipper, and so he should. So I agreed to help Norman up to Southampton with the *Sun Star* for £30 and a fare home. Done deal. A good mate of mine called Wills, who I had come through school with, would come along also and so we set sail for the short run up to Southampton. It should have taken 24 hours at the most, but Norman had other ideas. On the first day we sailed to Brixham, about 18 miles around the coast. This wasn't much good. At this rate it would take around a week to reach Southampton. It would have been better for Norman to have gone on the bus and let me and Wills whizz up to Southampton. After two days we finally stopped in Poole. This wasn't going at all to plan. We should have been back home by now. That night in Poole, Norman asked Wills and me if we would go ashore and get some fish and chips for supper.

Norman gave Wills and me just enough money to buy some fish and chips, so off we set. On our return to the dock there was no sign of Norman or the *Sun Star*! He had done a runner, knowing it was only a few miles across the bay to Southampton.

'What now?' I said to Wills.

'Christ knows,' he said.

It was no good trying to hitch-hike. It was now around ten o'clock and dark.

So I pinched a car. A small Triumph Herald was parked in a pub carpark with the keys still in. In we jumped. I started up and we were homeward bound. I didn't know it then, as we drove off, but I was about to learn one of the biggest and harshest lessons of my young life. Looking back on it all these years later, that night changed the course of my life forever, and for the better. Thinking back, it was a crackers thing to do. I don't think we had enough petrol to get us more than 50 miles. I managed to find my way out of Poole, God only knows how, I hadn't a clue where I was going, but at last we were on the right road from Poole to Bridport. We thought we were pretty slick but, within 20 minutes or so, the blue light appeared in the rear view mirror.

'Put your foot down Scratch,' yelled Wills.

I did, but we were no match for the powerful Zephyr 6 police car and the highly trained drivers. We were doomed. The police car didn't try to overtake us, but really just followed us across the Dorset Heights. Finally they stopped us at a level crossing in Bridport. I remember thinking I would make a run for it, but no chance. It was a fair cop, as they say. We spent that night in the cells at Bridport Police Station.

It was not a nice feeling to be locked up. I certainly didn't fancy too much of that. Justice moved fast the following day. We appeared before Judge McGoogan at Poole Magistrates Court. Judge McGoogan reminded me of the little clerk in the Shipping Pool at Southampton, a small wizened up little fella with gold rimmed glasses. Our case was read out to him and it all happened so quickly; 'Twelve weeks in a detention centre. Off you go.'

Wills and I were dumbfounded. Christ, that was swift justice. Well, our feet didn't touch the ground for the next six weeks. The regime was modelled on the first six weeks of National Service, everything at the double, even having a shower and eating, but time passed very quickly. I behaved myself and got out two weeks early. It was a big wake up call for me. I thought Judge McGoogan was a proper old sod. I am sure he was not and if he was alive today, I would shake his hand and thank him. I never got into trouble again – a short sharp lesson.

PART THREE

DEEP SEA, THE *QUEEN MARY* AND JOHN

One

RMS ORIANA AND RMS QUEEN MARY

So by Christmas, John and I travelled up to Southampton to get a berth deep sea. We stayed away for about five months.

Our first trip was around the world on the beautiful P&O liner the *Oriana*. Known as the Queen of the Pacific, she was a very fine ship and very fast, about 50,000 tons. This was my first trip on a liner but the chances of learning anything to do with the sea were nil. In fact, we both soon found the daily work routine boring and repetitive; washing down paintwork, holey stoning the decks, polishing brass. I never went near the bridge the whole trip. But the social life was way hay!

The main hub of entertainment when at sea was the crew bar, fondly known as The Pig and Whistle. We were on day work, so every night at sea was spent in The Pig and Whistle and every night was party night. Beer was cheap and when The Pig finally closed there would be parties going on in every other cabin.

It was the fastest trip I ever did around the world, about three months overall. We had good runs ashore in Samoa and Fiji. In San Francisco, where we were loading cases of Levi Jeans, we, of course, managed to acquire a case to share among the deck crew. I took my lifeboat ticket in Vancouver on that trip. What a scream that was, with a whole crew of queens from the Catering Department. All in all, it was a very memorable trip. We must have done about twenty ports. Over the next few years I sailed on quite a number of liners The really good thing about them was that you knew exactly how long you were going to be away. The biggest problem was you never paid off with much money, it was all a big party. In all, I sailed on sixteen ships during my time in the Merchant Navy. Royal Mail Line, Cunard, Shaw Saville, Union Castle and Blue Star were my main deep sea companies. London Rochester, Everards, RFA, Comben and Longstaff sailed Home Trade. In the end, I preferred Home Trade. It was more hands on and at least allowed me to get involved with some of the seamanship.

Good bye *Queen Mary* – a long 'paying off' pennant clearly visible from her aftermast.

RMS Queen Mary, October 1967, leaving Southampton for the last time, bound for Long Beach California.

John and I paid off the *Oriana* in early February1967. We called Jeff to see if any good deliveries were coming up, but it was pretty quiet so we hung around Southampton for a few days. Finally, John's uncle, Gerry Scott, who was a skipper with Everards, probably the biggest coasting company of its day on Home Trade, asked John if he wanted to join him as crew on board his ship the *Clarity* for a few months until the summer. John agreed to sail with him. I reckon he knew he would learn a lot from his uncle. I am sure he was right. I sailed myself a number of times with Gerry when he occasionally skippered the *Linnet*. He was a very cautious skipper, unlike Jeff. He did everything by the book, always plotting his position on charts, but a lot of his navigation came naturally. He was very highly thought of by Everards and had been with them for many years. As a boy, like Jeff, he had served his time on spritsail barges on the London River and its approaches. This apprenticeship really did turn out some very good seamen, but also very modest seamen.

And so, John and I parted company for a few months saying we would meet again in the summer for the delivery season with Jeff.

I wandered along to the Southampton Pool in Canute Road. On the blackboard it read *Queen Mary*, Abs and EDHs wanted. EDH, Efficient Deck Hand, was my rank at that time, but with that rank you could also sail as AB. So I stuck my nose through the grill and said, 'EDH, *Queen Mary*.'

'Take this report to the Bosun,' usual procedure.

And so I joined the *Queen Mary*, holder of the Blue Riband throughout the fifties, until she lost it to the American liner *United States* and probably the best loved and the most famous liner of all times, except, of course, the *Titanic*, who had a brief but infamous career compared to the *Queen Mary*'s thirty years on the high seas.

The *Queen Mary* was a city in herself. At the time I honestly did not appreciate the honour I had unknowingly bestowed upon myself. This was a final peep into the decadence and glamour of Edwardian transatlantic travel that the luxury liners of the early twentieth century represented. Those who experienced this and who are still around today must now be few and far between. I feel privileged to have been one of them. In all, I did around six trans Atlantic crossings in her. During the second crossing one of the quartermasters became ill and he paid off in New York. The Chief Quartermaster came down to the mess and asked if anybody wanted the job. Of course, I immediately volunteered and in the flick of a lamb's tail I was promoted to quartermaster on the *RMS Queen Mary*. The wages were not much different, only a few quid a week, but the food was a lot better in the quartermasters' mess. I wore blue serge bell bottoms and a blue jersey with Cunard across the chest and a white peaked cap with Queen Mary on it. The quartermasters' watches were all spent on the bridge. One of us was on the helm at all times. Every day, at midday, we sounded her enormous fog horns so that the passengers could adjust their watches east bound or west bound accordingly. The clocks changed every day. It was a huge thrill to press the big brass buttons on the wing of the bridge for four seconds, look aft and see the steam escape from the massive whistles on the front of each funnel, followed by the deep bloodcurdling sound of the fog horn. It would be impossible to recreate that sound on a modern fog horn.

I must have helmed the *Queen Mary* into both Southampton and New York several times during my time with her. If it was your watch and you were at the helm, you brought her in. The ocean terminals at Manhattan were simply wooden piers sticking out into the Hudson River. I seem to remember that docking at Manhattan was much trickier than in Cherbourg or Southampton, where the berths lay alongside the quay. There were always many more tugs in attendance in New York, Moran's Tugs with a big M on the funnel.

When I am in my car today, moving along at 45mph, I look out at the passing hedgerows. That was the speed the *Queen Mary* travelled when she held the Blue Riband, twice the speed of today's modern liner. Have a look yourself next time and think of the *Queen Mary*, all 83,000 tons of her.

I paid off the *Queen Mary* and phoned HQ in Salcombe. 'Still not much doing', from Jeff. 'Give it another few weeks.'

Two

RMS FRANCONIA AND *RMS ANDES*

I had not seen Canada and fancied a look up the St Lawrence Seaway. So I signed on another Cunarder, the *Franconia*, a much smaller ship, around 30,000 tons. It was a quick trip to Canada and back, up the St Lawrence to Quebec and Montreal, but Christ it was cold! I think the *Franconia* was almost at the end of her career, at least with Cunard. They often sold them on to some Greek or Panamanian owners who would squeeze a further ten years or so out of them before they finally went for scrap.

It was to be yet another trip across the North Atlantic in winter. Well, it was spring really but the weather was still pretty atrocious. I remember being on watch in the crow's nest for a couple of hours at a time. The crow's nest was situated half way up the foremast. The foremast of the *Franconia* was a huge steel tube with a diameter of roughly 3 ft. To get up to the crow's nest was not easy, especially if you were 6 ft tall and broad in the chest. Entry was through a small door at deck level. To get through this door meant lying down on the deck and pulling yourself through. Once inside you had to slither into an upright position and begin a climb of a good 100 ft up to the crow's nest. The crow's nest itself was not much bigger than the tubular mast, so it was a very cosy operation squeezing past the lookout you were relieving. This feat accomplished, you then faced two hours in pitch darkness on lookout. I don't remember ever seeing anything. I think we were supposed to be looking out for icebergs, but I certainly never saw one.

Communication back to the bridge was by wind up telephone and a bell. The only time I remember calling the bridge was to ask if they could get the small heater to work. They said they would look into it, but without much success.

When the ship dived down into a bigger wave than usual, the whole mast shook like some dreadful fairground ride. The crow's nest was certainly not a pleasant place to be, but at times, during a daylight watch, the view in heavy weather was magnificent.

I did three North Atlantic crossings on the *Franconia*, six to eight weeks in all. Once again, The Pig was the main attraction each night and so, finding myself back in Southampton by early May, I phoned Jeff.

'Nothing going yet,' I was told, 'only small yacht deliveries around the coast, but get home for June. We've got a big dredger to go to Bruge in Belgium for scrap, but I'm going to try and salvage a cargo ship on the way.'

'I'll be there,' I told him. It sounded like a good one to me.

A couple of days later I signed on the *RMS Andes*, a classic old liner that belonged to the Royal Mail Line. Built in 1939, she survived the Second World War as a troop ship and was given back to the Royal Mail Line in1947. She was a classic old lady of the sea, retaining the glamour and style that belonged to a passing age. I can't say the same about the crew accommodation, which was definitely 'upstairs, downstairs'. The deck and engine room crowd, as we were known, were eight or ten to a cabin and that wasn't much fun in the hot weather, but I am honoured that I had the privilege of sailing on one of these fabulous old ships, of an age that was rapidly disappearing.

I did a Mediterranean and Adriatic trip on the *Andes*, and that was enough, given the cabin accommodation. Once again, it was a continual party from leaving Southampton to our return three weeks later. The crew bar, The Pig, was situated at almost waterline level and it was incredible to watch the sea rushing past the portholes. It gave an idea of the speed at which we were travelling.

Three

ANNIE LEWIS

Back in Southampton, with both feet on terra firma once more, it was time to head for home and see what all this dredger and salvage business was all about. John was already home, having paid off the *Clarity* a week earlier. There was a good buzz going at Jeff's house when I arrived. Roy was there, our Chief Engineer, and there was great excitement about the salvage job. We were all going to be rich. The plan was as follows: we had to deliver the old harbour dredger from Aberdeen in Scotland, to Bruges in Belgium for scrap. Jeff had done a few jobs for the Beker Brothers Yard in Bruges, and so they knew him well and that he was the kind of man to take a gamble en route. We were to go to Cuxhaven at the mouth of the Elbe River which runs up to Hamburg. In Cuxhaven we were to pick up details of a stranded cargo ship called the *Emmanuel M*, about 7,000 tons, which had been driven ashore onto notorious sand banks west of the entrance to the Elbe. Beker Bros had bought the wreck and all they had to do was to get it to their yard at Bruges. This was where Scott's Yacht and Delivery Service came into play. The sand banks were dangerously shifty and that is why the *Emanuel M* was trapped. The sand built up around her on the one tide and on the next, she was almost free.

'Piece of piss,' said Jeff. 'We'll soon get her off with a dredger.'

However, nature is a powerful lady. Man often thinks he is above her, but she will always win in the end.

Beker Bros offered Jeff the use of the dredger at no cost and half the scrap value of the ship if we could deliver her to Bruges. A hundred or so thousand pounds was a considerable amount in 1967, and so you can see how we were all going to be rich. The ship itself was quite seaworthy. We just had to get her to float. We needed the expertise of Isambard Kingdom Brunel, but we were a hundred years too late.

The *Annie W Lewis* was a typical harbour dredger of her day. They spent their whole life in harbours around the UK. She would have been built well before the Second World War and had kept Aberdeen harbour dredged all that time. Once again, we were back in the age of steam. She was powered by a good sized triple expansion steam engine, and that was just for propulsion. Being a bucket dredger, there were several more steam engines

Myself by starboard propeller of *Annie Lewis* on
Cuxhaven Sandbanks, summer 1967.

Annie Lewis hard aground, Cuxhaven
Sandbanks, summer 1967.

in her engine room to drive her dredging equipment. The good
thing as far as the crew was concerned was that she was oil fired
– no shovelling coal.

In late June, 1967, the *Annie Lewis* sailed from Aberdeen
harbour for the last time, bound for the scrapyard, but quite an
adventure lay ahead. She was not what you would call a proper
seagoing ship, all right for coastal hops, but thank God, the North
Sea was calm that June and we duly arrived in Cuxhaven about
thirty six hours later. She only made around 4 knots at best. She
would never have been a contender for the Blue Riband.

At Cuxhaven, Scotty was given local charts of the sandbanks
by Jan, a Dutchman built like a giant, who was to accompany us
to the site of the wreck. The following afternoon we arrived on
location at the *Emmanuel M*. She was a typical medium sized
cargo ship of that era, German built in the mid fifties, very
similar to what was to be my last ship in the Merchant Navy, the
Canberra Star of the Blue Star Line, also built in Bremen in the
mid fifties.

The *Emmanuel M* was light, that is to say she carried no
cargo on board when she went aground on the sand dunes. A
navigational error had put her up there. Jan, the huge Dutchman,

MV Emmanuel M stranded, Cuxhaven,
1967.

MV Emmanuel M on Cuxhaven Sands,
summer 1967. She never sailed again.

gleefully told us that no ship had ever been salvaged from these sands. They move every tide, forming new lakes and channels.

'You think you come off, and then next tide, all different,' were his words. 'After two veeks, you give up and go Cuxhaven for good drinking and voman.'

Jan was just about dead right. For two weeks we dredged channels, put hawsers aboard, pulled her, pushed her, dredged more channels to allow the sea into her small lagoon, all in vain. Our £100,000 was slowly sinking into the sand with the ship we had come to save. We got the *Annie Lewis* stuck for about five days and thought we were going to lose her as well. Beker Brothers would not thank us if they had both ships stuck in the sand.

The weather was beautiful, calm, hot and sunny, and so we rigged up a huge death slide on a wire hawser from the forecastle head of the ship, down to the stern of the *Annie Lewis*.

This gave us hours of entertainment during the five days we were trapped, but, alas, after two weeks, the tide was cutting away again and Jeff had to admit defeat.

Sure enough, when we got back to Cuxhaven, there was big Jan.

'Ah, now we go Hamburg, vomen and drinking.'

What else could we do? We shut down the boilers of the old *Annie Lewis*, put on clean jeans and tee shirts and with a sub in our pockets, ashore we did go.

'Ve go Vinckle Strasse,' instructed Jan. 'I take you on train.'

And so it was that we all jumped aboard a train to Hamburg with Jan leading the way. Jan made quite a sight on the train, must have been 7 foot tall, blonde hair, wearing blue shirt, enormous baggy trousers and biggest clogs I have ever seen, like a pair of rowing boats. Well, it took us the next forty eight hours to do all we had to do in Hamburg. It was mental. I don't really recall what Strasse we were in. It didn't really matter. I can see why John, Paul, George and Ringo had had such a good time there only a few years before.

All good things must come to an end and slowly, in dribs and drabs, and as our money began to run out, we managed to crawl our way back to the *Annie Lewis*. Ernie Edgecombe was the last one back and had to come aboard to ask Jeff for some money to pay the taxi. What a run ashore that had been. No one ever knew what happened to Jan, we never saw him again, but Beker Bros assured us he was all right when we saw them in Bruges.

And so we fired up the boilers of the old *Annie Lewis* for the last time. This was to be her final voyage, but she had one more trick up her sleeve. We slowly plodded down the German and Dutch coast to finally arrive off the entrance to the Bruges Canal. Gently, Jeff nudged the old ship into the first lock from the sea. Now, as I have explained, everything on the *Annie Lewis* was powered by steam, even the heavy steering was steam assisted by a set of small steam pistons behind the steering wheel. This mechanism was now badly worn by age which meant that when you went hard over to port or starboard, the wheel would shudder and vibrate. The wheel was attached to what is known as the Boss by an enormous nut. Unbeknown to our fearless skipper, the nut had become quite loose with all the shaking and vibration. As we entered the lock, which was crowded with holidaymakers, Jeff was in his correct position on the wing of the bridge to bring her alongside, but in order to line her up, he decided a quick nudge ahead was required with a hard to starboard on the helm. So back into the bridge he disappeared. I heard the telegraph ring and Roy down below responded well with a quick nudge ahead on the engine. Jeff then gave the wheel a full spin to hard a-starboard and returned to the wing of the bridge, only to be followed by the ship's wheel rolling out onto the wing of the bridge behind him. A very red faced skipper ran back to the bridge, dragging the wheel behind him to be returned to the boss, to the cheers and amusement of the crowds on the quay. Jeff, to his credit, returned to the wing, removed his cap and gave the audience a huge bow. You never knew what was coming next on Scott's Yacht and Delivery Service.

The *Annie Lewis* gently eased out of the lock and into the Bruges Canal which was dead straight for a mile or so, leading up to Bruges itself, where you could see the historic old medieval town in the distance. We lashed the wheel to the boss in order to steer her these last couple of miles. I think that the enormous nut that had held it on had been lost overboard in the excitement at the lock.

Jeff rang down for full ahead and called down the voice pipe to Roy to give her the *Bells of Shannon* up this last stretch. And so the *Annie Lewis* went to her graveyard in a blaze of glory, with Roy giving her everything she'd got. She probably made 5-6 knots and I thought she was going to shake herself to pieces, but she held together and we rounded up at Beker's scrapyard. Jeff gave a prolonged blast on her old steam whistle and then rang down – finished with engines. All was silent and the *Annie Lewis* had completed her final voyage. The cutting torches would be the next thing she would experience.

It was always emotional taking a ship to the scrapyard, like taking a faithful old horse to be shot. Strangely enough, if she were still around today, she would be a tourist attraction as a ship of historical interest.

Four

MOTORCYCLE DIARIES IN CORNWALL

We paid off the *Annie Lewis* and came home. The homeward trip was pretty uneventful. Funds were low after the few days in Hamburg. John and I split up with the rest of the crew in Dover. We always tried to hitch hike home in order to save the train fare and then pocket it. We tossed a coin and one of us would sit in front of the other an hour at a time, because the chances of getting a lift were always much better if you were on your own. Sometimes the one that left first got home last, don't ask me how. On that occasion it took me about twenty four hours to get home. I slept for a few hours at night in a hay barn on the Salisbury Plain and spent the next two days scratching my ass because of fleas, but it was cheaper than a hotel. Back in Salcombe, I soon met up with John and we both decided that a holiday was just what the doctor ordered.

We scrounged together a few quid washing up in a hotel. And so, with an old tent and a couple of sleeping bags borrowed from a yacht that Jeff was looking after lashed to my Norton, off we set for a five day tour of Cornwall. Life was so free and easy with no big plan of where we were heading, we just followed our noses. I think we made Mevagissey the first night, and then on to Falmouth, one night in St. Ives, Padstow and then back up the A38, over the moors and back home. The Norton never missed a beat, although it did stop charging so we couldn't travel at night, but it was summer and there was plenty of daylight.

Years later, in about 2008, I went to see The Motorcycle Diaries, a film about the Argentinian born revolutionary Che Guevara who finished up his days with Fidel Castro in Cuba. He left Buenos Aires with his best mate and they travelled across South America on a motor cycle exactly the same as mine, a Norton 500 Es.2. Seeing the film all those years later reminded me so much of that summer of '67 when John and I set off.

Back in Salcombe, things hadn't changed that much, but we got a pretty vocal reception from Jeff.

'Christ Almighty, where the hell have you two buggers been?' We've got jobs coming out of our ears. John, you go with Gerry. There's a Silver in Falmouth to go up to London.'

The Silver was a really beautiful 65ft motor yacht. That would be a cushy trip with Gerry. He liked to pull in somewhere most nights, not like his brother who never stopped until he had arrived at the appointed destination.

'Scratch, you're with me. We've got an old Motor Torpedo Boat called the *Panorama* to go to Birkenhead. The engines are knackered, so we'll tow her to Liverpool with the *Linnet*.'

Five

FOG

There was no time for formalities, John was on his way back to Falmouth and I was on my way to Birkenhead. The *Panorama* lay in The Bag in Salcombe. She was around 65ft, but very boxlike and high sided. However, she towed remarkably well. We nailed plywood over all her windows for protection against any weather we might encounter. But, alas, it was fog that was to be our nightmare.

I asked Jeff if I could bring my girlfriend along. He wasn't too keen but agreed as long as we kept her down below and Lil didn't see her.

'Lil will go bonkers if she knows there's a woman on board.'

Marilyn Boarder was a beautiful tall, slim Australian girl who was in the UK on a working holiday. She agreed to lie low until we sailed.

We fuelled up the old *Linnet*, got the *Panorama* alongside and gently edged out of the harbour. Once clear, we dropped the tow astern and laid course for The Lizard and Land's End, about a fourteen hour steam at 6 knots. Rounding Land's End in the night, a course was set up through the Irish Sea, to the Hats and Barrels off the south west tip of Pembrokeshire. Half way across this stretch, the fog set in and it was pretty thick as well, with a glassy sea and no wind to shift it. The old *Panorama* had disappeared astern. The visibility was no more than about 20 yards. For eight hours we saw and heard nothing, but then Jeff instinctively knew we were approaching land. God knows how we survived without radar, but we did.

'Ease her back to 500 Scratch. Switch the pilot off and go on the wheel. I'll go up forw'd and listen. They have explosives on the Hats.'

I am sure I could just make out the shape of Jeff on the focs'le head. He was looking up rather than straight ahead. Then we heard the bangs.

'Hard a-starboard, Scratch,' yelled Jeff. 'Go back out at 160 degrees, otherwise we'll hit the *Panorama*.'

I put the *Linnet* over 160 degrees. Looking out of the wheelhouse window I saw the cliffs towering above us, yet nothing could be seen at sea level. I realised why Jeff was looking upwards, clever old bugger.

Jeff came running back aft.

'Ease her down to tick over, Scratch.'

The *Panorama* floated eerily down our starboard side like a ghost ship. The tow rope was now completely slack. Everything was silent as the old *Panorama* disappeared into the fog. Would that be the last we would ever see of her?

Jeff lay in the stern of the *Linnet*. 'Knock her out of gear now, mate,' Jeff almost whispered.

Everything was silent except for the gentle thud of the Gardner engine. At last the tow rope came tight.

'Thank Christ for that!' Jeff said, with great relief. 'Slow Ahead, mate.'

I put the *Linnet* back into gear and gradually increased to

400rpm. Marilyn came up into the wheelhouse and asked what all the fuss was about. 'Nothing, no problem,' she was told.

I altered course out to the west and by the late afternoon the fog had cleared as quickly as it had come down. The old *Panorama* was following us like a dog on a lead. I would never know how close she came to the Hats and Barrels, but it was close.

The rest of the trip was plain sailing. It took about four days before we entered the Mersey. We brought the *Linnet* alongside the *Panorama* and locked into Birkenhead Docks. We had a good run ashore in Birkenhead. The chap who had bought the *Panorama* was a nightclub owner and he took us around a couple of his clubs. Typically, Jeff sailed as soon as we were back on board and so leaving the Mersey was a bit of a blur.

It took about sixty five hours to get back to Salcombe. Lil was on the quay as we pulled alongside and so Marilyn once again had to hide down below. Jeff soon got Lil ashore and so all ended well, but I didn't see much more of Marilyn after that. I don't think she was cut out for life at sea.

Six

HMS WOLDINGHAM AND HMS PULHAM

Jeff was certainly busy that summer with yacht deliveries up and down the English Channel and across to France. I couldn't recall all the deliveries we made, but a few do stand out in my memory and it was in that same summer that we delivered two mine sweepers from the Royal Navy to Italy. That was to be quite an eventful voyage which took us about three weeks.

Once again, we steamed one and towed the other and once again, Roy was our engineer. They had twin Paxman diesels of about 800hp each. Both ships had been laid up for a year and so coaxing the old Paxmans back into life was not easy.

We sailed from Portsmouth in early August '67, with the two Ham Class minesweepers, *HMS Woldingham* and *HMS Pulham*. Both ships were clad in copper sheets, I suppose for anti magnetic protection, but that night, as we proceeded down Channel on a westerly course against the Atlantic swell, many of these large sheets of copper became unattached. As dawn broke, looking astern, *HMS Pulham* resembled an injured bird, with large copper sheets hanging from her sides, *HMS Woldingham* the same, but perhaps not quite as bad.

Jeff immediately saw an opportunity.

'We'll drop into Salcombe and get all this copper up to the scrapyard in Kingsbridge,' he said.

And that's the way it was. We brought both minesweepers into Salcombe, moored them up in the Bag and proceeded to strip down the copper plates, load them up in Jeff's launch and deliver them to the Noyce Bros scrapyard at Kingsbridge. We had a good night ashore that night in Salcombe to celebrate our unexpected good fortune. Jeff had insisted on a cash settlement from the scrapyard and so we all had money in our pockets. A good start to the trip.

Needless to say, we sailed again at closing time. Seventy two hours later we had crossed the Bay of Biscay and were slowly plodding our way down the Spanish and then the Portuguese coast The weather was good. We did lose the tow once due to chaffing in the thimble on the tow line. We had trouble with this chaffing, especially if there was a bit of sea running and the tow snatched. Theoretically, the tow should be in the water the whole time to avoid any snatch. We lengthened it using one of the old minesweeping hawsers and this helped quite a lot.

About seven days out of Salcombe we reached Gibraltar. Roy informed Jeff we needed to refuel in Gib. And so we entered Gibraltar and tied up alongside a naval ship and an Admiralty tug. Jeff then had another brainwave.

Our plan was to use the fuel out of the dead minesweeper to refuel the one we were using as the tug. All we needed was a big fuel pump – Royal Navy to the rescue. Jeff managed to blag a suitable heavy duty fuel pump from the Navy, not only that, but the crew came over to do the transfer for us – said it was too much of a job for us, they had better do it themselves. Fair enough. What a hoot, here was the Royal Navy pumping their own fuel into our minesweeper at no cost at all. Jeff would have made an excellent Prime Minister – very diplomatic when it was needed, very ruthless when it was not.

We all had a good run ashore in Gib. The old Bull and Bush pub was still going strong, and relieved us once again of hard earned money. Still, that's the sailors' way and I don't think it will ever change.

We headed the two minesweepers east out across the Mediterranean. We were looking at another seven days at least to cross the Med to Italy and the port of Leghorn, which was our destination. Two calm days passed and the Med was the Med as everyone dreams it to be – flat, calm, glassy seas and light winds. We passed the island of Majorca to starboard on the third day out. All was peaceful, but it was not to last. On the fourth day out the winds started to increase from the north.

'Not a good sign,' said Jeff.

Sure enough by the evening a full mistral gale was blowing from the north right on our port beam. The roll of these minesweepers was hideous. To cap it all that night we lost the tow again – same problem, the wire hawsers had chaffed through and we couldn't find the tow. So here we were, in a full mistral gale with a lost minesweeper adrift somewhere astern of us. Jeff decided to zigzag back on our course for an hour and then back again, but all to no avail. We did not want to leave our present position too much or we would never find the missing minesweeper. So he decided to lay there and just drift until dawn broke and hope we would find her in the daylight. And that's what we did. Dawn broke slowly around 4 am, but it was not a good, clear dawn. It was rain and mist, with a full, northerly gale still blowing. Our minesweeper was almost doing somersaults in this awful, short, sharp, Mediterranean sea. The sea in the Med in a northerly offshore wind is a very unkind sea, short and sharp with hardly any swell. For the first two hours of daylight we saw nothing, so Jeff started a big circle course about three miles wide.

After almost half an hour, a small voice was heard coming from back aft, 'There the bugger be!'. Ernie Edgecombe, who probably had the worst eyesight out of all of us, with his small milk bottle bottom glasses, had spotted her, but then she was gone again. 'Over there.' Ernie shouted. 'I'm sure 'twas 'er!'. Ernie was right, thank goodness, and as we approached to where he was pointing, she re-appeared amongst the heavy seas.

'Free beer for you when we get to Italy, Ernie!,' Jeff yelled above the storm.

Good old Ernie, he was as proud as punch that he had spotted her. He was not really a seaman, but used to come along as cook and bottle washer, so it really was a feather in his cap. All we could do for the next 12 hours or so, was to stand by her because to try and get anyone aboard in this sea would have been suicidal.

It was around mid-night that the sea finally gave up. Jeff brought the two ships together and in the dark Mick Halem and I made a leap aboard. Within a couple of hours we had her under tow again and resumed our course for the northern end of Corsica. The sea calmed off very quickly after the mistral wind blew herself out and five days later, we pulled into Leghorn Bay.

Jeff said he did not trust these 'Eyeties' to pay up, said they were all a load of villains. He had secured half the money for the delivery before we'd left the UK and was to get the other half on arrival in Italy. So we anchored one of the ships in the Bay and entered Leghorn with the other.

'A bit of security,' Jeff said.

We tied up in a small sort of naval dockyard, which was well patrolled by armed police, a little intimidating to say the least. Jeff told everyone to stay on board while he went onshore to secure payment. After about three hours we were beginning to get a bit apprehensive as to Jeff's wellbeing, when he suddenly made a pretty dramatic appearance in a big Mercedes car, swinging around a bag of cash. Payment after all had been no problem. The 'Eyeties' had paid him and got him half pissed in the deal.

We chugged out into the bay and brought the other minesweeper in. We tied them together alongside and all hands went ashore to party. That evening on our return to ship, one of the armed guards on the dock came aboard for a drink. Within a couple of hours, he was legless. We were drinking the Spanish brandy we had bought in Gib. The guard soon passed out and Ernie started to strip his gun down. Ernie, having been in the army, knew a bit about guns. However, it was duly reassembled a little while later and we disappeared into our bunks, only to be awakened by a lot of excited shouting on the dockside. The poor old guard who had left his post during the night was now at the double march around the square, rifle above his head, being shouted at by a very vocal sergeant. Heaven knows what happened to him in the end.

Seven

LEGHORN TO MONTE CARLO TO COWES AND BACK TO SALCOMBE

We left Italy that morning. All the others went straight home, but Jeff, John and I caught a train to Monte Carlo to bring home a 65ft Silver called *Trout*. She was a beautiful James Silver Motor Yacht, probably built in the 20s or 30s and she had to come back to Cowes. It was a pretty uneventful trip home, around twelve days I think. Her twin Gardner diesels pushed her along effortlessly at a good 9 knots. We briefly stopped at Gibraltar to refuel and load our cargo for Jeff's store in the park. Same procedure as *The Lady of Rudding*, slipping into Salcombe under the cover of darkness and up to Jeff's store with the contraband. It was old hat by now.

I remember that Jeff was in a brandy phase, so there were two cases of Courvoisier Brandy for certain. To our amazement, when daylight dawned, the customs rummage boat was tied up about three moorings away from us. It was a good job we hadn't woken them up as we came in. We took the *Trout* up to Cowes a couple of days later and brought back a Class One Ocean racer called *Firecrest*, which was skippered by one of Jeff's other brothers. I can't remember the name of the owner, but it was a very fine yacht. I think it had just won the Fastnet Yacht Race.

The yacht delivery business sometimes went like that. In the last four weeks we had gone from Portsmouth to Italy, to Monte Carlo, to Cowes and back to Salcombe. Jeff was always very good about wages and we were paid as soon as we got home. So John and I had a 'pocket full of tin', as the Maggie May song goes, only difference being we paid off in Salcombe and not the Port of Liverpool!

And so the summer of '67 had slowly slipped by. I did not fully realise just how much I had learnt since those days on SY *Norian* with Simon. This knowledge only becomes apparent much later when you put it into practice and then you appreciate all you have learnt – look up high in fog. Years later, during my fishing days, I lost my little dog overboard in some fairly snotty weather. He was a small Border Terrier called Diesel. I did manage to recover him but only when I put into practice what I had learnt from Jeff searching for the lost Minesweeper in the Med. I circled for a short period and then knocked her out of gear and just drifted. Sure enough, Diesel's little head came over the wave tops, no bigger than a tennis ball. I managed to grab him and drag him back aboard. He stayed in the wheelhouse in rough weather after that.

After one or two small deliveries along the south coast, by mid October it was time to head out to sunnier places. John and I both shipped out foreign, going with Union Castle to South Africa, this time on Liners – two trips down to the Cape and back, about a ten week run overall. The first one was SA *Vaal*, owned now by Safmarine, a subsidiary company. She was the old *Transvaal Castle* until Safmarine took her over. The second trip was on the *Edinburgh Castle*, same trip; Las Palmas, Cape Town, East London, Port Elizabeth, Durban, same ports homeward bound. It was the *Edinburgh Castle* we had passed and saluted from the *Richmond Castle* a couple of years before.

Eight

TWISTER

The *Edinburgh Castle*, *Eddy*, as she was affectionately known, was a very happy ship and I was up for doing another couple of trips, but John said he wanted to be back in Salcombe for Christmas, so home we went. I didn't go to East Portlemouth for Christmas but stayed with Jeff and Lil in their small cottage, 5 Market Street, in Salcombe. In fact, I didn't go back to East Portlemouth very much after I had left home. It seemed so dull and uninteresting, never a party going on, unlike 5 Market Street, where the party never stopped. Jeff was either working or partying. That was the life for me.

Between Christmas and New Year, a shipyard at Brixham called Uphams, contacted Jeff with a brand new wooden Twister to go from Brixham to Gourock on the Clyde, just down from Glasgow. A Twister is a wooden sloop, about 28ft, a well built sea going yacht that could take a lot of weather. Jeff agreed to take her up first thing in the New Year, but a few days before New Year, he was suddenly laid up with a stomach virus. Most unlike Jeff who never suffered from anything except hangovers. Too much Courvoisier over Christmas.

'You can take her, Scratch, if you want.'

'You reckon I can , Jeff?'

'Yes, sure, you'll be all right, you and John. You're the skipper, remember, John's the mate.'

Jeff was always very keen that a ship should have only one skipper.

'High pressure to the north, east south easterlies setting in – you'll fly up there like a greyhound.'

I felt both apprehension and excitement. I was a little over eighteen now and I was to be trusted with a brand new yacht, to be delivered in mid winter, through some of the most treacherous waters in northern Europe; the Western Approaches, Land's End, up through the Irish Sea and a 'starb'd hand into the Clyde', as Jeff put it. Simple!

Lil told Jeff he was daft for letting us do this.

'They're both too young,' she said.

But Jeff knew we were well capable. He said he had often brought the Thames spritsail barges back from London to Essex whenever the skipper was 'under the weather.'

Lil made up a mountain of sandwiches for the first day or two out. The trip would take us around four days, Jeff reckoned. We also took the usual delivery grub with us; tea, sugar, long life milk, a few tins of Fray Bentos stew, some tins of peas and potatoes – staple diet on Scott's Yacht and Ship Delivery Service. No one could cook, so we just hashed it all up into one big pan every evening. Delivery Stew we called it.

Ernie drove John and me over to Brixham. The Twister was on a mooring off the yard and old man Upham took us out in a launch. He did ask where Scotty was and we told him he was ill and that we were going to run her up to Glasgow. He didn't seem too concerned and trusted Jeff's judgement. The designer of the Twister was a fellow called Kim Holman and he was there as well. John and I climbed aboard and within a few minutes had the feel of her. She was a little beauty, everything brand new. I did not use the engine at all but sailed her off the mooring.

The wind was well in the east north east, not too strong, about a five. We bore away out of Brixham and rounded Berry Head and then down for the Start, the Lizard and the Irish Sea. The wind was kind to us the whole trip and as we rounded Lands End in the dark, it seemed to follow us round, letting a little more into the east south east. If this held, it would give us a broad reach right up through the Irish Sea. The wind did hold in that quarter and up into the Irish Sea we went. Unlike Jeff, I kept a course line on the chart using only dead reckoning and our favourite piece of navigational equipment of the day, a hand held Seafix Direction Finder, a brilliant bit of kit, often used by Jeff. A couple of fixes and you knew exactly where you were.

Forty hours out of Brixham and we were passing the Smalls and the Hats and Barrels off the south west tip of Wales. It brought back memories of the *Panorama* earlier that year. No fog this time, but a fair old sea running because of the Spring Tide. As we sailed further north, the next light we picked up was the Isle of Man. We sailed quite close to Peel on the west side of the island. We were tempted to go ashore, but didn't want to lose this good wind, so on we pressed and entered the Clyde four days out of Brixham. We sailed past Largs on our starboard hand, going like an express train, wind and tide right up our ass. We rounded up off Gourock Yacht Club around midday on the fourth day. We picked up a mooring, stowed the sails and turned in for a few hours.

Not long after that the owner came out to take us ashore. He was very pleased we had had such a good run up and took us into the Yacht Club for a shower and a big fry up. Boy, was that good! I phoned HQ to let Jeff know we had arrived with no problems. He said Lil would be pleased.

We didn't hitch hike home. It was January and bloody cold

in Scotland and so the luxury of a train ride took us down from Glasgow to Totnes. When I got home I felt I had taken a really big step forward. It had been my first run as skipper and taking that Twister to Scotland was a real milestone. Only five years ago I had signed on the *Norian* to peel spuds and shovel coal. It demonstrates how well you can do if you are studying the right subject.

Jeff paid me £50 for delivering the Twister to Scotland. That was a good pay off for four days work. I had sailed around the world for less.

And so 1968 dawned. It was to be the most tragic year of my short life so far.

We did a few local deliveries and honed our skills at tree felling. Jeff often did this at slack times of the year with a fella called George Greenwood. For the logging trade we had an old Fordson Major tractor and a couple of chainsaws. It wasn't good money, but it paid the bills. The word 'tree surgeon' had not been invented and George was about as far removed from any kind of surgeon that you could imagine. He was as wild as hell, but could handle a tractor and a chainsaw. In later life, he cut off half a foot, but he didn't seem too concerned about it.

Jeff, Lil and daughter, Jenny, at the Red Lion Inn, Chacewater. Harvest Festival, September 1971.

By the end of February that year John and I went back to sea, once again with Union Castle foreign going on the cargo ship, *Rustenburg Castle*. We did a ten to twelve week trip to South Africa for a cargo of apples and grapefruit. We were around two weeks in Port Elizabeth and East London. But we never made much money with all that time on the coast – too many subs to go ashore. On the Australian and New Zealand coast, British sailors could work at nights on the docks and this subsidised shore-going activities no end. But this did not apply in South Africa because of Aparthied and all the cheap black labour.

We sailed from Port Elizabeth to Copenhagen and unloaded part cargo, the rest for Southampton. We were concerned about the double header situation but that did not arise and we paid off in Southampton around Easter of that year. The usual night at Gatti's bar to say our good-byes to other crew members and then home to see what was on offer at Scott's Yacht and Ship. Jeff had done a few small jobs, very local, but had spent most of the winter logging with George. So he was itching to get back to sea.

Our first job was with the *Linnet*. We towed some concrete barges from the London River down to Poole in Dorset. They were going to be used to make a concrete breakwater for the Lilliput Sailing Club, the same Mulberry Harbour plan that was used in World War II for the D-Day landings. It was an easy tow with no problems. The *Linnet* was a faithful old horse. The 6L3 Gardner never missed a beat in all the miles we did in her. One fine day, I was standing on the quay in Dartmouth. It was 2012 and there she was, the *Linnet*, almost forty years since I had last seen her. She looked a little different but I still recognised her. She had been completely restored and her engine rebuilt by Hubbards of Brixham. I went aboard and introduced myself to the owner. He was very interested to hear all the old stories of her days with Scotty. She is now in beautiful condition and will sail for many years to come.

Nine

CANAL DU MIDI

In July we had quite a long job, a lovely old aft cockpit Hillyard built boat to go to Port Andrax in Majorca via the Canal du Midi. The three of us went, me Jeff and John. Really it was only a two man job, but Jeff thought we might pick up work on the way. Anyway, there was a 45ft steel motor yacht called the *Swarte Beer* to come back to Dartmouth from Alicante.

The Hillyard, *Corunna of Burnham*, was a cutter rig with a long bow sprit and two big head sails, with tiller steering. She sailed really well and we passed into the Bay of Biscay and up the Garonne River. Just after Bordeaux, we entered the Canal du Midi, mast down and bowsprit off for the long haul to the Med. Christ, it was hot – about as hot as the Panama Canal, but without the flies.

Twelve to fourteen days got us through to the Etang Lake. We saw the beautiful white horses of the Camargue and finally entered the Mediterranean at a place called Sete, re-stepped the mast and bowsprit and set course for Majorca. It was not too far across and the weather much better than the previous year with the minesweepers. At last, one fine morning, we pulled into Port Andrax. Jeff left John and me to clean the ship while he went ashore to find the owner.

The owner turned out to be a really fussy old bugger. He went through the inventory with a toothcomb but could not find the frying pan. John had thrown it overboard because it was in such a state, but with the water so clear it was easy to see sitting on the seabed just beneath us. I don't remember the final outcome, but I am pretty sure the price of the missing frying pan was deducted from the total payoff.

'Won't be delivering any more bloody yachts for him. Silly old sod.' said Jeff afterwards.

We caught a bus to Palma where we boarded a ferry for the Spanish mainland, direct to Alicante, and where Jeff was to show us a good trick for future passenger only ferry crossings.

'Stay there, you two, and watch this.'

He walked boldly into the lorry park where the lorries were queuing to board the ferry. He picked a lorry with one driver and offered him an English £5.00 note if he would board with Jeff as his driver's mate. The deal was immediately clinched.

'Bye-the-way, I have my two sons with me.'

No problem. John and I climbed into the back of the lorry driver's cabin and within a short time we were aboard the ferry

Of course, a good meal was included in the lorry driver's ticket and so we all piled into the restaurant, had a slap up meal and quite a few drinks. During the overnight crossing we became the best of buddies and next morning he even dropped us off at the dock where the *Swarte Beer* was moored.

The *Swarte Beer* was a Dutch built steel motor yacht of about 45ft. She ran on two diesels. I cannot remember what they were but they gave us a lot of trouble on the homeward voyage – dirty fuel trouble. We were continually changing fuel filters and bleeding them through. It was not a good trip home with fog and wind for the best part of two weeks, from Alicante to Salcombe. The gearbox on the starb'rd engine seized as we entered Biscay, so we did the final leg on one engine, a wing and a prayer.

Here was a major problem with yacht delivery. You never knew what you were picking up and you could never believe an owner's briefing. Sailing yachts were the best to deliver. Sails never let you down – motor yachts, always a problem mainly because they were never used enough and condensation seeped into the diesel tanks. Water and diesel do not mix. The result was always 'shitty fuel'.

We limped into Salcombe in the dead of night with our usual cargo on board, same old routine with a visit from Black Jake the following morning. He was very sorry to hear about our arduous voyage and shared a bottle of gin with us. He was a smashing old fella, Black Jake. The gearbox was fixed, nothing too serious, just loss of pressure, and then John and I took her on the final leg to Dartmouth a couple of days later.

Corunna of Burnham, Canal du Midi. summer 1968. We
saw the beautiful white horses of the Camargue.

Ten

_____

JOHN

It was by now mid to late August and things were quiet at home, which was unusual for that time of the year. Jeff had bought a small fishing boat and spent a lot of time hauling the few pots he had acquired. So John and I decided to ship out.

Down in the Plymouth Pool Mr Profit fixed us up with one of Everard's bigger coasters, the *Rosemary Everard*. We joined her in Manchester and loaded grain for Rotterdam. We wanted to stay Home Trade to increase our chances of doing any yacht deliveries that might come up with Jeff.

And so we duly sailed from Manchester bound for Rotterdam and 48 hours later we were locking into the huge grain berth.

It was late August, 1968.

Rotterdam is an enormous port and we seemed to be miles away from anything. The first morning, the Bosun, with another AB whose name I cannot remember, gave John and me the 'job and finish', as it was known, of painting the face of the Bridge. That meant as soon as the work was finished, we were off for the rest of the day. We finished soon after midday. It was sweleringly hot and after a quick shower the three of us headed ashore to find the nearest bar, which was not that far away. We went in, found a table, lit up, ordered three beers and started chatting. After a little while John stood up and announced that he was going to the loo.

That was the last time I saw him alive.

After some time, I decided to go out and see what he was up to, but there was no sign of him. We didn't worry too much, fully expecting that he had struck lucky with a girl. Even so, it was a bit odd. He usually told me everything. The afternoon passed into the evening and there was still no sign. By midday of the next day, I reported his absence to the Captain, but no-one gave it much attention. Seamen can go missing for days at a time in foreign ports, but by the following day I was really concerned. John always told me what was going on.

We were unable to get a berth immediately to unload our cargo and this meant that we were in Rotterdam for two and a half weeks. After ten days the Dock Police pulled a body from the water in another dock a few miles away. The Captain told me to go and identify the body.

It was John.

I can't describe how I felt – numb with shock and horror. The Police did not seem too interested. They took a statement about the day he went missing and that was that. They probably saw the same situation a dozen times a year and could only draw a line under it. But I knew he was murdered and they knew he was murdered. His young life had come to an end. John and I had been through a lot together. We were like brothers, but now he had gone.

Many years passed before I came to terms with losing John. We brought his body back aboard the *Rosemary Everard* and I paid off in Avonmouth. Coming home was terrible. Jeff and Lil were distraught. John was the second child they had lost. A daughter had also died as a youngster.

We took John's ashes to sea on the *Newbrook* and scattered them across the Bar. One of Everard's ships came in close and blew her whistles in salute and we said goodbye to a Salcombe boy, one of our own.

I had by now just turned twenty and I thought the best thing would be to get right away from everyone and everything.

I went to London and did two round the world voyages with the Shaw Saville Line. I came home again and did one more voyage on the *Freemantle Star*, eventually arriving back in the UK early in '69. I returned to Salcombe to see Jeff and Lil. Things had improved a little and they made a big fuss of me, treating me like a son. I did my best to help them in their grief, but there was a gaping hole in our lives. Jeff said he had decided to leave the sea. He and Lil were going to run a pub in Cornwall. They needed to leave Salcombe and all the memories, start a new life. And so the following year they left the little cottage in Market Street with the seashells around the door, where all those wild parties had taken place, and took on the Red Lion Inn in Chacewater, Cornwall. God bless 'em.

John Scott 1950-1968
We sailed many thousands of miles together. We were like brothers.

PART FOUR

MV CANBERRA STAR, DRAMATIC HOMECOMING AND CROSSROADS

One

FINAL VOYAGE, DEEP SEA, MERCHANT NAVY

I went back to London and joined a Port Line ship, the *Port Lincoln.* She was bound for New Zealand, but she was a terrible old ship, long overdue for the scrapyard, built in the 1930s and a survivor of Atlantic convoys in World War II. She sailed from London to Liverpool before outward to New Zealand and luckily I managed to pay off in Liverpool.

Across the Huskisson Dock was the *Canberra Star.* She was loading cargo for South Africa, Australia and New Zealand. And so I signed on the *Canberra Star* for what was to be my last voyage in the Merchant Navy.

We sailed from Liverpool for Australia via South Africa in late February 1969 with a general cargo. The outward voyage was mostly uneventful apart for some atrocious weather through the north Channel and out into the Atlantic. We had very low visibility and severe gale force winds for about 24 hours. Blue Star ships at that time carried no radar so we were down to Slow

MV Canberra Star at sea – pictured from top
foremast, spring 1969.

The Apple Station, Port Huon, Tasmania. Two British
cargo ships of the day.

Ahead, about 5 knots. There was a lookout on each wing of the
Bridge and one on the fo'csle head. The Bridge was tense and
quiet. With no radar, the Captain remained on the Bridge the
whole time. Twenty days later we called at Cape Town and then
Port Elizabeth, spending about a week in each port. We broke
out the big jumbo derrick in Port Elizabeth to unload heavy
electrical equipment before sailing across the Indian Ocean to
Albany on the south west tip of Australia.

I found Albany interesting because it was still a full-time whaling station for the Southern Ocean. On we sailed across the Great Bight of Australia to Melbourne where I visited the enormous and impressive Melbourne War Memorial.

When I was a small boy, my mother, relating a bit of family history, told me about the Gallipoli campaign that was such a disaster in World War I. My grandfather had fought at Gallipoli alongside the Anzacs, with the 5th Battalion Manchester Regiment. Mum told me the story of Simpson, a stretcher bearer with the Australian and New Zealand Army Corps, who repeatedly went across the lines with his donkey to bring back the wounded. My grandfather remembered having seen Simpson and his donkey. The story was related to my mother and so to me. It captured my imagination and stuck in my memory and now, years later, here was a chance to go and search for the little memorial in their honour, somewhere in that vast Shrine of Remembrance.

I found the bronze statue of Simpson and his donkey in a small wooded glade to one side of the main Avenue. I took a photograph with my little Instamatic camera that I always

I finally found the statue of Simpson and his donkey in the vast
Anzac Shrine of Remembrance, Melbourne, Victoria.

Myself in New Zealand, aged 20.

carried with me and I sent it home to my Mum. She was delighted. A childhood memory of her father had come full circle.

The rest of the voyage along the Australian coast was pretty uneventful and apart from a bit of a scare in Sydney Harbour.

I was over the bow with another AB, Paddy Brown, in an attempt to repaint the name, Canberra Star. The bow was very flared and so we had ropes leading down to pull us in close enough to do what we had to do. This made the stage on which we were standing hang at a very awkward angle. Suddenly, Paddy Brown froze and pointed down. In the water, directly beneath us, were six large sharks, circling just below the surface. I froze as well

'What do we do now, Billy?' said Paddy.

'Just sit tight,' I said. 'Don't move.'

Our lives depended on two ropes leading over the bow of the *Canberra Star*.

After what seemed an age, with the sharks not moving away at all, the Bosun, George MacKinnon, showed his head over the bow. He sized up the situation at once and very soon a small tug appeared, trying to scare them off. Paddy and I slowly climbed the rope ladder, back to the safety of the fo'csle head and we sailed for New Zealand the next day with only the word Star visible on the starboard bow. A pretty rough crossing of the Tasman Sea saw us arrive in Auckland where the missing word was finally added to the bow of the ship, giving her full name, *Canberra Star*.

MV Canberra Star in Port Huon, Tasmania, loading apples for the UK. My last deep sea voyage, Spring 1969.

The Canberra Star limps into Falmouth after its collision. 'You should look where you're going,' a voice yelled up from the harbour tug, *St Meryn*, - 'Doug Richard , a Cornishman and steam engineer.'

Two

MA GLEESON'S BAR

One of the most famous bars in the Merchant Navy world was Ma Gleeson's, Auckland. Heaven only knows why it was so popular because it was surely nothing special. It was situated on a street corner up a slight hill and just a short distance from the Auckland Dockside. Inside there was a very simple oval shaped bar with stools and a pipe that seemed to be coming out of the ceiling. This pipe produced nothing but cold lager beer. There was no choice, cold lager or nothing.

We were only to be in Auckland for a couple of days, so on the last afternoon a few other crew members and I were testing the lager in Ma Gleeson's. I don't know to this day what started it, but a free for all punch up suddenly flared. Minor scuffles and scraps were quite common between various crews, Shaw Saville, Federal Line, New Zealand Shipping Co., Blue Star and others, but this time it was full on. Even Ma Gleeson's Maori girls joined in. My lasting recollection of it was being locked in combat with an Irish fella, Tommy Murphy, from a Shaw Saville Line ship, the *Suivic*. I don't recall the final outcome, just that we scarpered up the gangway of the *Canberra Star* just minutes before we sailed. As we let go fore and aft and slipped out of Auckland, a feeling of relief came over me. I certainly didn't want a lot more of what Tommy Murphy was handing out.

If you're still alive Tommy and one day you happen to read this, 'Well done, mate. It was all good fun.'

Our voyage then took us back across the Tasman Sea to Tasmania. Passing across Storm Bay, we steamed south of Bruney Island and entered the Huon River. A few miles up the river was the apple station of Port Huon.

As we rounded the bend in the river, we passed the *Hobart Star*. She was sister ship to the *Canberra Star*, both built in Bremen, Germany in 1956. It was quite unique for these two sisters to come together, tramping the oceans of the world as they did, a chance meeting like this would probably happen once in a lifetime. As we came together our whistles blew in salute and then the *Hobart Star* disappeared astern of us, but what a meeting of two magnificent ships that was.

Tasmania is a very beautiful part of the world and reminded me very much of home and the Salcombe Estuary with its wooded banks and forests. There were no cranes at Port Huon so we loaded a cargo of apples with our own derricks in all five hatches. This was quite common practice. A lot of the more remote ports in New Zealand, Tasmania and Australia are no more than small wooden jetties. Derricks, guys, cargo runners and blocks had to be kept in good working order because they were often in use in that part of the world.

And so, with our cargo of mainly apples, we had one more call at Freemantle for wool. We did not go around the world again on this trip. Our homeward voyage brought us back around the Cape of Good Hope and up through the Atlantic. We were bound Freeemantle for Hamburg. After about thirty days out of Freemantle, we entered the Bay of Biscay. It was July 1969.

Three
_____

TWO DAYS OUT OF HAMBURG

We entered the Bay in flat calm weather, but soon the dreaded fog came down and it was thick. It was down to Slow Ahead with all look-outs posted. I was about to go on the 8-12 watch when three blasts were sounded from our foghorn. The powerful Mann Diesel was put Full Astern causing the whole ship to shudder from stem to stern. I ran out from the back of the accommodation to the front end of the No 5 hatch. And then there was a huge explosion.

Unless you have been in an explosion like that it is difficult to describe. The air all around seems to be sucked away, followed by such a deafening bang that you fear your eardrums have been blown out. The massive bow of a Monrovian tanker, *La Fleche*, was scraping down on our port side causing huge flames and explosions. Debris from the explosions flew in all directions across No.5 and No.6 holds. We were carrying two empty Beefeaters Gin Tanks as deck cargo and I dived under one of these to shelter from the flying shrapnel, probably saving my life. Looking back on all this now, I can understand and appreciate the horror of being torpedoed.

We disengaged from each other as quickly as we could. The last I saw of the tanker it was still exploding as it disappeared into the fog, now thick and yellow in the flames. I then made all haste to the Bridge. My emergency station was on the wheel.

I spent the next fourteen hours on the wheel. We had fires in No.1 and No.2 holds. The forecastle head was also in flames. These were difficult to extinguish because they contained wool. The Captain had been injured with flying glass and the Mate had assumed command. He turned us 50 degrees to starboard to bring us inside the main shipping lanes between Finisterre and Ushant, which was a good move. One of the lifeboats from the tanker was perched on our forecastle head. Our two port lifeboats were on fire and so I wasn't sure what I would do for the best should we have to abandon ship. Fortunately, it didn't come to that. We managed to get the ship under full control again after twenty four hours. We were bound for Hamburg, but limped into Falmouth a day later.

Lo and behold, the tug right under our bow was the *St Meryn*, and sure enough, there by the engine fiddly, was Doug Richards, Steam Engineer, rolling up a fag. I yelled down to him, but he did not recognise me.

'Billy, *Norian*.'

He recognised me then.

'Christ Almighty! What have you been doing?' he shouted back, looking up at our bent and twisted bow. 'You should look where you're going.'

When we finally docked I went down aboard the tug. It was really good to see Doug after all these years. We had both changed. I had a good few pints with him that night but I never saw him again.

Concrete was poured into our damaged bow a few days later. The *Canberra Star* was repaired and became the *Buenos Aries Star*. She was eventually broken up in Taiwan in 1982.

We finally discharged our cargo in Hull. I paid off the *Canberra Star* and my days in the Merchant Navy had come to an end.

Four

THE HAND OF FATE

It was not the dramatic incident on the *Canberra Star*'s homeward voyage that made me decide to leave the Merchant Navy. It was really an accumulation of things. I had turned 21years of age on that voyage and had come a long way since signing on the old *Norian*, but I didn't have a penny to show for it. Perhaps that was the price I paid for my education. Jeff had gone ashore and so the deliveries had finished and I knew that my life had reached a crossroads. I could have easily stayed on in the Merchant Navy but the chance of any further promotion was nil. I would never sit for a Mates Ticket because of my poor ability in Maths, so to become a Captain along that route was impossible. If seamanship was all they desired, I would pass with flying colours, but, of course, that was not the case and I had to be realistic. Having just paid off in Hull, I had £30 in my pocket after a six month trip.

It is strange how fate takes a hand in your destiny at times. As I waited for a train to take me home, I walked aimlessly into a small dockside pub. There was only one other bloke in there and I soon started chatting to him. I told him I had just paid off a six month trip with thirty pounds in my pocket. He laughed and said he had been in the Merch but now worked on oilrig supply vessels for an American company.

'You want to get your ass down to Yarmouth. You'll get a job easy with an AB's Ticket.'

So here I was at the crossroad and it was up to me to choose which road to take.

Looking around I saw a lorry parked directly in front of me. It had the name of the haulier and Great Yarmouth across its sides. Into practice came one of Jeff's old tricks and in no time I had blagged myself a lift down to Yarmouth. The driver was happy enough with the twenty Rothmans I gave him from the two hundred with which I had paid off the *Canberra Star*. He wished me good luck and we said our good-byes.

And so here I was in Great Yarmouth, thirty pounds in my pocket and somehow I had to get a berth on an oilrig supply vessel. The first thing I did was book into a small Bed and Breakfast at a rate of about £3.00 a night. This gave me a week to acquire a berth, otherwise it was back to Hull as quickly as possible.

The first three days were hopeless. I went into office after office along the river at Yarmouth. These offices were portakabins that had been assembled to accommodate the needs of the various oil companies. With only a couple of days left in my digs, it occurred to me that maybe I should try the drilling companies and get work as a roustabout on the rigs. There were as many drilling company offices as there were oil supply vessel offices and so this opened up a new range of opportunities with many different companies, mainly from the Southern States of America: Texas, Louisiana, Florida, Oklahoma. I was now getting desperate and more than a little disappointed. Surely someone must need an AB from the British Merchant Navy. The money had almost run out. I had decided to give up this idea of life as an oilman when I spied a small portakabin I had not seen on my previous rounds. Above the door it read, International Drilling Company, Houston, Texas. I was sure I hadn't been in there before. Anyway, here goes. Knock, knock and in I went.

Joe McCoy sat at a desk at the far end of the portakabin and can only be described as a long tall Texan, Stetson pushed back on his head, leaning back in a chair, feet on the desk and wearing the fanciest pair of cowboy boots I had ever seen. The only thing missing was the Sheriff's badge.

'What do you want, boy?' came the opening words in the strongest Texan drawl you can imagine.

'I am looking for work as a roustabout on a drilling rig,' I said with all the confidence I could muster.

'God damn it son, we've got roustabouts coming out our ass,' once again in that Texan drawl. 'What we all need are British Seamen.'

I pulled my Discharge Book out of my back pocket and pushed it across the table towards him. He picked it up, took a quick glance inside, snapped it shut and said,

'Pull up a seat, son.'

Some people strike oil but I struck gold. The road to Yarmouth had been the right choice.

PART FIVE

IN THE MONEY

One

'HERE COME THE YANKS!'

'Joe McCoy's the name.'

'Billy Hitchen,' I said and we shook hands.

'Now then,' said Joe. 'listen up. We all got us a brand new rig just been built at John Brown Shipyard on the Clyde. She has got to go to South America, Argentina, but she has to sail there under the British flag, so that is why we need British seamen. Once we get her to South America, the world's your oyster. You can sign on the drilling crew or we will give you an air ticket home or anywhere in the world.'

"Where do I sign, Joe.'

'Right here, Billy. Now then, where are you staying?'

I explained about my humble little B & B.

'God damn it,' said Joe. 'We all stay in the Grand Hotel.'

Joe then asked for my bank account details. I explained that I didn't have a bank account and that I kept all my money in my pocket.

'Lordy be! We'll open an account for you in Jersey in the Channel Islands. That way you don't have to pay no tax. We all don't pay tax.'

Smit Lloyd tug, *Scaldis* stands by in full Atlantic storm.

Out in the wild Atlantic bound for South America. Heavy weather for the first ten days.
Smit Lloyd tug, *Scaldis* stands by in case of problems.

Offshore Mercury - sailed from the Clyde to South America in 120 days - probably the first self-propelled rig to take on such a journey. Here, it finally takes up position off Southern Argentina to start drilling.

Joe got me to sign a contract to deliver Oil Rig, *Offshore Mercury*, to Bahia Blanca in Argentina where the contract would expire. He informed me that my pay would be £250.00 a month. I felt sure he had made a mistake. I don't think even the Captain of the *Canberra Star* pulled in that much each month. The wage I was getting at that time was £48.00 a month. Could this really be true?

'Right, you got any money?' said Joe.

'Not much,' I replied.

He went to a safe and took out a wad of notes and gave me £100.00.

'That should buy you a few beers,' he said. 'Now, get your ass down to the Grand and book yourself in. We'll all get together tonight for dinner.'

Two

GARE LOCH TO ARGENTINA

I went back to my humble abode hardly able to believe what had just happened. I had a job, £100.00 in my pocket and was about to check into the poshest hotel in Great Yarmouth. That night with Joe at dinner, as he called it, I felt incredible. I had gone from rags to riches in a few short hours and this was to be just the start. Everything in the hotel was on the company and did those Texans know how to live on a company expense account.

Joe explained that a helicopter would take us up to Glasgow in a couple of days time, so, 'Have a good time while you can, Billy. It's a long way to Argentina.'

Joe was not wrong. I got on well with the other American boys in the hotel who were also going to make the voyage and three days later we were flown up by helicopter to the rig. That was the last time my feet touched dry land for a hundred and twenty days.

The rig was moored in the Gare Loch near a small town

called Helensburgh. The loch is very deep just there so the rig could slide its huge legs up and down without touching the sea bed. The other crew members were a mixed bunch: Dutch, German, Danish and of course, American. There were four British sailors on board, including myself. The Captain was Irish – Kavanah was his name. It was a self propelled rig and that is why it was registered as a British ship for the voyage out. All that would change once we got to South America.

We soon fell into shipboard life. There were two watches, twelve hours on and twelve hours off. I didn't mind the long hours at all, not for £250.00 a month, tax free. That was a fortune in 1969. We sailed from the Clyde in mid December and it would be mid March before we arrived in South America. It was the longest passage I had ever done. I used to think the thirty five days home from New Zealand was a long haul.

We encountered heavy weather in the North Atlantic. A Smit Lloyd tug, the *Scaldis*, escorted us for the first two weeks until we got into the warmer weather and then she left us and returned to Holland and we were on our own. The best we could make was 5 knots, but with any head wind, that was very much reduced. Christmas passed and the New Year of 1970 dawned. We were all kept very busy preparing the rig to start drilling as soon as we arrived off Bahia Blanca, just south of the River Plate.

Finally we arrived on location and jacked the rig up. We must have been a good fifty miles offshore, well out of sight of land. Almost immediately everything changed to oilrig mode. A helicopter arrived and out jumped Joe McCoy.

'Howya all doin'?'

'OK, Joe.'

'Right, who's goin' and who's stayin' ?'

Out of all the boys who came down on the rig, I was the only one to stay on and join the drilling crew. It had been very tempting to take the air ticket home, but on the outward journey

I had learned to drive the big Koehring cranes. A crane operator could earn another £100 a month on the drilling crew. Joe signed me up right away as crane operator. The only bit of experience I'd had was on the docks in Australia and New Zealand with the *Freemantle Star* and her two small cranes.

Once again, it was twelve hours on and twelve hours off, but the catch was, it was three weeks on and two weeks off and my three weeks on was just about to begin. It was the longest I had ever been at sea, but I knew that when I did get ashore I would be rich. I learned from the Americans the work ethic that has remained with me for the rest of my life: never be beaten by a job and always do more than the next man, without showing him up. The Yanks really knew how to work, but let it be said, they also knew how to play.

Three

DERRICK MAN

I didn't know anything about drilling, but during that first three weeks I think we drilled four wells. Finally, my three weeks were up and it was time to go ashore. It was a strange feeling. When it was time to get on the chopper, I was almost scared to leave the rig, but I did.

Almo Payne stood about 6ft 6ins tall. He came from El Paso in Texas, not twenty miles from the Mexican border. He was a driller and had taken me under his wing. He had been in the oilfield since boyhood on the East Texas Oilfields and didn't know anything else. He called me Limey and we struck up a good friendship from day one. So Almo and I arrived in Bahia Blanca for two weeks 'hell raisin'', as Almo called it. We checked into a fine hotel on the seafront which was commandeered by the Company. Everything was on the house in what was at least four star accommodation. I hadn't touched any wages since Joe had given me that £100. Every month a bank statement came through from Jersey, all monies having been paid in by the First National Bank in New York. I was sitting on about £1,200 when I went on leave with Almo.

'Christ Almighty,' I thought. ' At this rate, I could buy the *Canberra Star* next year.'

Life had really changed for me in the last four months and thank the Lord I had walked into that portakabin in Yarmouth and met Joe McCoy.

We certainly did some hell raisin' during the two weeks ashore. Almo gave me some pills called Bennys to keep me awake, able to visit more nightclubs. Two weeks quickly passed and before I knew where I was we were back on the rig, twelve hours on and twelve hours off for the next three weeks.

As the year moved on and we moved further south, the weather became pretty bad. We were doing exploratory drilling and as we pushed our way down into the Southern Hemisphere, winter set in. We were drilling quite well south by now, off a place called Comodoro. The weather by this time was awful. Gales form the Andes sent driving snow down and across the sea, but the drilling continued regardless.

At one time we were a derrick man short. The job of the derrick man was to stand on a small platform at the top of the derrick, clip the 90ft lengths of drill pipe into the fingers that stick out on the inside of the derrick and then to unclip them before they go back in the hole with the huge kind of scissors called an elevator. It sounds easy, but apart from the driller, a derrick man is one of the most highly paid men on the rig and I was about to find out why.

'Hey, Limey, you could work the derrick this next shift – another forty dollars a shift. Git yer ass up there.'

Bubble Head Grimes, the tool pusher from Oklahoma, also agreed with Almo. It was well within my capabilities to work the derrick. So clad in a thermal suit, wearing goggles and gloves, up I went.

I don't know what the temperature was up there, but it was bloody cold. I got to the top and looked down. The driving snow made it almost impossible to see the drill floor almost 90ft below. Almo started his descent back down the hole and I was on my own. Up the derrick, the huge block, about the size of a Mini motor car, came screaming past as the wires ran through. It stopped just above my head and the enormous elevators swung towards me. I had to lean away from the platform on the safety harness with a 90ft section of 8 inch drill pipe in one hand, get this into the elevators, clamp them shut and then pull back to the platform to get the next length of drill pipe ready. I wasn't afraid of heights, I never had been, but I soon realised I was out of my depth. I managed about ten lengths of pipe and then tried to yell down to Almo. It was no good. It was too much for me. It wasn't about physical strength – technique was the key.

I remember little else about that night, but I know I used up one of my lives. When I came to, I was hanging in the harness 90ft above the Drill floor with a broken nose and a fractured wrist. The elevator had knocked me clean off the platform and I was swinging in the harness, snow driving horizontally across me, turning red with blood as it poured from my nose and mouth. My days as a derrick man were over and how anyone ever did that job I shall never know.

Four

HOMEWARD BOUND

I stayed in my crane for the rest of my time in South America. Almo Payne and I remained good buddies all that time. We always spent the same two weeks off together and so I saw a fair bit of Argentina. Sometimes we would have a fortnight in Buenos Aires. It was a beautiful city with plenty of night clubs. On one two week break, Almo announced that we were going skiing.

'What are you talking about?' I said.' I've never been skiing in my life.'

'Neither have I,' said Almo.

And so it was that we took a bus to a little place in the foothills of the Andes called Bariloche. I believe it has now become a pretty posh ski resort, but it certainly was not posh when Almo Payne and I arrived. It was just a small hick town up in the Andes. To get any height on the slopes, a donkey would pull you up as far as it could, you skied back down and that was that. I believe it is a bit more refined now.

We did a couple of skiing holidays in Bariloche. Our skiing

did not improve that much. The snow was always a good 3ft deep, but it gave me a basic knowledge which has come in useful on holidays in the French Alps forty years later.

While in Bariloche one day, I happened to see a small tobacconist on a street corner. It looked pretty scruffy and deserted, but rumour had it that Adolf Eichmann used it as a hideout when on the run in South America after the Nazi defeat at the end of the Second World War.

It was December 1970 and another chapter in my life was finally coming to a close. I was on no fixed contract with International Drilling Company who owned the *Offshore Mercury* and I could finish whenever I chose. That time was approaching. I had money in the Bank. I was rich. It was time to go home. Almo also announced that it was around time he hauled ass and headed back to El Paso. And so, in the December of 1970, we both handed in our notice and prepared to leave.

We caught a plane from a small place called Doro, I think, well down in Southern Argentina. We walked out across a grass runway and boarded an old Dakota, a relic from WW2, I am sure. Still visible was the shabby camouflage paintwork and faded red white and blue circles of the RAF. We boarded through a side door about half way down the fuselage. Inside a bench seat ran around both sides. It was full of peasant farmers taking their livestock to Buenos Aires; chickens and ducks in small cages, pigs and goats, all somehow tied down, made up the rest of the passenger list. This was quite the norm in southern Argentina at that time. The DC Dakota was one of the safest aircraft that has ever flown and thank God for that.

Looking up through the fuselage to the cockpit, a curtain suddenly drew back and a character with a Jimmy Edwards handlebar moustache appeared like a magic show.

'Three stops to Buenos Aires. Hold tight on take off and landing chaps. Tally ho!'

I can't remember the pilot's name, but Almo and I had a few drinks with him during the flight. Reluctant to give up his beloved aircraft, he had flown the Dakota to South America after the war and had started up his own small airline. As we flew up through the Andes towards Buenos Aires, it was just like an Indiana Jones movie and he probably imagined himself right back in the Second World War.

We could not climb over the mountains, so we flew through them. Pigs, chickens and ducks were going in all directions. Finally, after three landings and three take offs, we arrived in Buenos Aires.

'Tally ho, chaps! Hope you fly with me again.'

I never did, but what an experience.

Almo and I had a last night out in town. Next morning we said our goodbyes, Almo on a Pan American flight to Houston, Texas and me on Iberia Airways to Madrid and London. I never heard of or saw Almo ever again. We were ' ships that pass in the night', but maybe one day he will read this book.

I chatted up the very attractive air stewardess on my homeward flight but, surprisingly, without much success. I was rich and homeward bound and maybe a bit too much champagne had passed my lips.

Five

_____

JACK THE LAD

I arrived back at Heathrow a year after I had paid off the *Canberra Star*. My outlook on life had changed a lot and I had money in the bank. I didn't have to look for the next ship out as soon as possible. It was playtime. I hired a car at Heathrow Airport, a Triumph Dolomite, and drove home to Salcombe feeling a real Jack the lad.

Back in Salcombe, I met up with all the old buddies with whom I had grown up. I had been away from Salcombe for eighteen months – the longest time I had ever spent away from home.

'Where the bloody hell have you been, Scratch? We thought you were dead.'

'No, came close a couple of times, but scraped through.'

Salcombe was not the same. Jeff and Lil were missing. It was only two years ago that I had lost John. After a few days of partying in Salcombe, I decided it was time to go down to Cornwall and visit Jeff and Lil. It was about a two hour drive to Chacewater, the small village where Jeff had taken over The Red

Lion Inn. I stayed with them for a few days. They seemed to be doing quite well. The pub was busy with tin miners. Jeff didn't appear to keep very strict hours and tin miners were coming and going most of the day and night, some coming off shift and others about to go on. But things were never going to be the same for Jeff and Lil, although they did seem to have moved on. I had moved on and so had Jeff, but I remember thinking what a waste of his seagoing talents to end up pulling pints behind a bar. But this was his new life, away from the sea and all the memories it held.

After a few more days back in Salcombe, it was time to think once again about my new found career in the oilfields.

Almo had told me that the real money was to be made working for big offshore construction companies as a pipeline welder. He wrote down a couple of names for me to follow up: Brown and Root of Houston, Texas and J Ray McDermott of Morgan City, Louisiana. The only problem was, I was not a welder. A qualification in welding requires a full training and a ticket to prove it before you flew half way round the world on contract. Brown and Root were offering a fully coded pipeline welder £25,000 pa, which back in 1970 was an incredible amount of money. Almo also told me that they always needed heavy equipment operators for overseas contracts because most of their workforce did not want to leave the Gulf of Mexico. Having operated many different heavy cranes in Argentina, my title on leaving International Drilling was Heavy Equipment Operator.

I finally located the London offices of J Ray McDermott in Curzon St., Mayfair, about four doors away from the Playboy Club, which I thought was quite handy. In I went, up a couple of floors on the elevator and there it was: J Ray McDermott, Offshore Construction, Louisiana, USA.

I was greeted by a lady at the reception desk, twice my age

but very attractive. She looked fantastic and I told her so, which I don't think did my future prospects any harm. I introduced myself and explained that I was a Heavy Equipment Operator, had been working in South America for the International Drilling Company and I was now looking for an overseas contract in construction.

'Well,' she said, in a smooth Southern American accent, 'you have come to the right person, but you need to be in Louisiana to hire out overseas. We will get you a flight to the States as soon as possible. Meantime, check into one of our suites in the Connaught Hotel, Park Lane.'

*

I had to pinch myself yet again. How far removed this was from the British Merchant Navy that I had left just over a year ago.

I duly checked into the Connaught. I was not given a suite, but a very smart room overlooking Park Lane and I remember thinking so clearly, all those years ago, that I was now important enough to be wanted by this huge American company.

In the bar at the hotel I soon met up with other McDermott employees. There was the usual banter about overseas contracts. The Far East, Libya and Nigeria seemed to be where most of McDermott's offshore work was, but everyone agreed that Nigeria was the best paid.

Once again, remembering my days on the old *Newbrook*, you don't get anything for nothing and it was not long before I found out why.

That night, a group of us went out to the Playboy club in Curzon St.. I still had plenty of money in my pocket, so could afford it. It wasn't cheap and afterwards I felt it was a bit overrated. Yes, the scenery was beautiful, but don't touch, unless you were a millionaire.

Next morning, an early phone call summoned me to Head Office. There was gorgeous, looking just as good as any of the Bunnies from the night before, but I didn't tell her.

'You're booked out on tonight's flight to New Orleans, Billy. Here's your ticket. Go straight to our main office in Morgan City and hand them this envelope. It explains everything.'

I felt like James Bond with Miss Money Penny. .

'And, good luck.' she said, but there was no kiss.

That night I flew Pan American to New Orleans. After landing, I made my way to Morgan City which was about thirty miles to the east. On arrival I entered McDermott's main office and handed over my introductory envelope. I was soon checked out and given an intensive medical examination. I was then told that I could 'hire out', as the Americans called it, in Morgan City Yard until an overseas contract could be found.

'Any preferences about where you want to go?'

'Nigeria,' I replied.

The recruiting officer smiled.

Three days later a vacancy in Nigeria was secured. My contract would run for twelve months. I would do six months on location, have two weeks leave, followed by a further six months to complete the contract.

It was early February 1971 when I signed the contract and apart from a two week break in the Canaries half way through, it was mid to late February 1972 before I returned to civilization. There were no days off, it was twelve hours on and twelve hours off, seven days a week. A good part of the salary was tied up in a Contract Completion Clause which meant that I had to be sure that I could stick it out in order to leave with the £7,800 that was offered. I was twenty two years old. Could I do it? Yes.

Six

WARRI

Almo had been right and I was about to earn every penny. There would be no skiing holidays in the Andes or two week breaks in Buenos Aires. It was nose to the grindstone time, but in dreadful conditions. Snow and wind were replaced by heat and exhausting humidity, flies, mosquitos and finally malaria: West Africa, the white man's grave and they weren't far out.

In New Orleans, I teamed up with two pipeline welders from Texas, both on the same contract and together we flew back across the Atlantic to Amsterdam. There we boarded a KLM flight to Nigeria and finally landed in Lagos. The aircraft door was opened and Christ Almighty, it was like stepping into an Aga. The oppressive heat wrapped around me like a blanket. The smell was foul, horrible and pungent, the smell of decay and waste. This was Africa in the raw. Oh, well, only twelve months to go.

After a three mile taxi ride that took two hours, we arrived at our hotel, a bit different from the hotels I had become used to, but by Lagos standards, right at the top. We spent only one night there and were then taken to board a Widgeon Seaplane for our journey to Warri. It had six passenger seats and two pilot seats. We took off from somewhere in Lagos harbour and headed out across the Niger Delta and the endless green jungle that became my home for the next year of my life.

We flew through a bad electrical storm which shook the small Seaplane like a rag doll. The pilot yelled over his shoulder, 'Hold on tight boys! This isn't too good.'

Very comforting, I thought. Many of the pilots with McDermott in West Africa were ex Vietnam fighter pilots and loved to put the fear of God into 'greenhorn pipeliners', as we were called.

Finally, the pilot announced, 'There she is, boys: Warri, city of sin,' and then banked off into a very steep turn before lining the old seaplane up on a fairly straight stretch of Warri River. We made a terrible landing, at least, I thought it was. As we were about to nosedive into the water he brought her up level, just seconds before touchdown. Splash, bang, spray and water everywhere! Finally, we rounded up to a halt.

'Big Red' handling connected pipeline in the swamp.

Big Red 100 ton crawler and drag line, my crane for six months on Lay Barge 21.
Henry and myself.

'Sons of bitches to fly, these goddam Widgeons,' said the young pilot.

He was not much older than me but had obviously done his stint in Vietnam and I think revelling in scaring the pants off his passengers. Six months later I was to take another flight in the Widgeon, but at that time the pilot was a little older and a little wiser, thank God.

On arrival in Warri, we were taken to the main yard for the final transit to location by helicopter.

Warri Yard was roughly five miles square, situated on the banks of the river. It was a hive of industrial activity, constructing the huge oil platform jackets for offshore production. Work in the oilfields went on twenty four hours a day, seven days a week. At night it was like a huge firework display with all the welding, cutting and grinding going on. It seemed to be even hotter than ever at Warri, but the jungle was to be even worse.

Laying the 42 " pipe in the bush swamp.

Eventually, the rat tat tat of the chopper was heard and we began the final leg of our journey to a small settlement on the banks of the Burutu River called Escravos, a Portuguese word meaning 'slaves'. Strangely enough, Burutu was a name that would have much significance a few years later.

Well, Escravos was interesting to say the least. I was really surprised to discover the remoteness of these African villages: deep in the jungle, unchanged in a thousand years, small groups of mud huts alongside the river bank, just as early Portuguese navigators, slave traders and missionaries had found them. Children played in the water and ran to hide behind a tree whenever a white man entered their village. There was no currency and no electricity. The population lived by fishing and hunting, but were in the twilight of a dying age. Oil had been discovered in their jungle and for the simple life they led, the game was up. These were the early days of a gigantic shake up for

Deck view of *Lay Barge 21* being towed down the Escravos River. The big crane at the rear is back towards us.

the Niger Region and today Escravos is a major oil production terminal.

A small tug, *Jaramac Four*, transported us to our final destination. Round a winding tributary of the Burutu River, *Lay Barge 21*, half aground, half afloat, lay in a hot steamy clearing. This was to be my home for the next six months. No sir, you never get anything for nothing.

Seven

HEAVY EQUIPMENT

I soon met up with another Heavy Equipment Operator, Ace Kolan, from Galveston, Texas. Ace turned out to be a good bloke and I shared a cabin with him for the next few months. There was a mixture of nationalities on *Lay Barge 21*, not all of them good guys. It was a man's world and a harsh environment, far removed from the almost luxurious life I had left behind in Argentina.

Ace soon explained my duties to me. I was to operate all heavy equipment on site:

- 4 x D8 Caterpillar Bulldozer Tractors, 2 fitted with side booms
- 3 x Heavy Crawler Cranes
- 3 x American 92 – 99 Crawler Cranes
- 1 x 150 Ton Crawler Crane – a Manitowoc 4,600, Dragline Crane

42" pipe ready to be laid in the jungle. My weight dropped to twelve stone.

The large Manitowoc crawler crane was mounted on a barge and fitted with a dragline which dug the huge trench in which the 42 inch pipeline was laid. This line would eventually carry oil from a well approximately 60 miles inland out to sea and to water deep enough for an oil tanker to pick up.

And so, Ace informed me that my first shift would start at midnight and run until midday the following day – 'twelve on, twelve off'. Only three hundred and sixty four shifts to go – no sweat.

You soon fell into the way of life on *Lay Barge 21* – you had to. On most shifts I operated the dragline, digging the trench for the pipeline. We were surrounded by swamp-land and as soon as the pipeline was welded together, it disappeared under water into the swamp. The pipeline came in 60ft lengths. Each length weighed in at 40 tons. The thickness of the steel pipe itself was roughly one inch, encased in a further four inches of concrete.

Christmas Day 1972. Twelve hours on, twelve hours off. It was good to just get into the air conditioned portakabin away from the oppressive heat.

I soon discovered why the welders were the highest paid operators on site. Their twelve hour shift was spent 'burning rods' and their heads hardly came up for a breather in all that time. As soon as they burned one rod down, a Nigerian helper, as they were known, would be there with the next rod to burn. Their eyes were red and constantly inflamed, but they continued to work, shift after shift, twenty four hours a day, seven days a week. The only respite for the welders was if the trench caved in or if there was a problem laying down the pipeline. Every joint they welded was x-rayed for a bad weld, but there was hardly ever a bad weld.

Unlike the 'dry' oilrig life offshore in South America, alcohol was around, although it was not supposed to be – a Nigerian beer called Star Lager and a local Nigerian whisky. The whisky was terrible, but the beer was drinkable as long as it was well

4000 Manitowoc crawler loading jacket, Warri yard.

chilled. Alcohol never got in the way of any work procedure and was never the cause of any trouble. The company turned a blind eye. There was all sorts of stuff to smoke and I did have the odd puff. Fortunately, it did nothing for me and I stuck with the Marlboros.

Slowly, the weeks and then the months slipped by. Ace finished his contract and left us to go back to Texas. I was given promotion and put in charge of all the heavy machinery. Promotion in the oilfield was like that, no exams or courses, there was no time. If you could do the job, you got it, right up to the top man, a fella' called Ernest Lee Span who was Barge Superintendent, or Barge Captain, as he preferred to be known. He was from Baton Rouge, just outside New Orleans, claiming that he hardly ever went to school as a kid but 'grew up on the pipeline'. He could drive any of the equipment and weld by the time he was ten. I felt this was an industry in which I could go far, but, eighteen months later, fate intervened and I never followed that particular road.

At last, six months was up and my two weeks leave was due: chopper and Widgeon back to Warri and then Lagos.

The base section of DB9/400 ton pedestal crane.

Eight

JU JU MAN

I returned to the UK for this short break. It would be Regatta Week in Salcombe. The Canaries was a popular destination, but I was looking for cooler weather and chose the British summer, a wise move. It was a brilliant two weeks at home, sailing all day and partying every night. I raced the Salcombe Yawl, Y35, in the 1971 Regatta with my old chum, Wills, who by this time was running his parents' restaurant, the Creep Inn, in Russell Court. I would go out and rig up the Yawl, Y 35, sail it off the mooring and in to the Ferry Pier picking Wills up at the very last minute. He would crew the race in his waiter's uniform, usually with a can of beer in one hand. We never won, but were never last. I hadn't raced much before, but I could sail. Wills had done neither, but we got through. It has changed a lot and is now, maybe, a bit too serious.

Before I knew it, two weeks were up. In no time, I had sobered up and was on the helicopter, heading back to *Lay Barge21*. Things had not changed much, humidity and oppressive heat made worse by the onset of the rains. It rained twenty four hours a day and made life a lot more difficult and dangerous. The entire area became a huge swamp. The bog was ready to suck up heavy equipment and materials deep into thick, heavy mud. We lost a Caterpillar, a huge 40ton Bulldozer, to that mud. It just disappeared – the price paid for bringing down heavy crude oil to the coast.

When I returned, there were roughly twenty miles of pipeline left to lay before reaching the coast. It took almost the next six months, the ground becoming softer and more swamp like by the day.

I had made good friends with two welders. Don Bridges stood around 5ft 2in and we nicknamed him 'Mini Welder'. The other was Roland Wilson from Corpus Christi, Texas. Roland was a big man, a bit of a hard case. I am sure he had a very checkered career. Two fingers were missing from one hand and he was minus one ear. ' Bar room brawls,' Roland claimed, but I think there was more to it than that. But still, the three of us got on well together.

For quite a long time I'd had some warts on my hand and they were really quite ugly. It didn't matter out there in the jungle, but when I was at home they were a bit embarrassing. One day, one of the Nigerian boys noticed them and said he would take me to the Ju Ju man who would cure them. I took it with a pinch of salt to start with, but Mini Welder and Roland said I should give it a go. So one day the three of us set off into the jungle with our Nigerian guide to find the village where the Ju Ju man lived. I had tried all sorts of treatments to get rid of these warts, but all to no avail, so my last hope lay with the witch doctor.

We trekked for about three hours along various jungle paths until we came to a clearing and a very small village of only eight or ten huts. Abraham, our guide, told us to wait. After ten minutes or so, he took me into a dark, smoky hut. By now, I was feeling apprehensive and beginning to wonder what I had let

Where the Ju Ju man lived. The villages around us were just as the
early Portuguese navigators, slave traders and missionaries would
have seen them.

myself in for. The hut was tiny, but in the gloom I saw the Ju Ju
man. He must have been over a hundred years old. Anyway, he
certainly looked it. He took my hands in his and he muttered
some mumbo jumbo for a few minutes before giving me a small
carved wooden pot, indicating that I was to put the contents
of the pot directly on to the warts. He had no English and I
certainly couldn't speak whatever language it was he spoke, but
we had understood each other and that was good enough.

Back outside, Mini Welder and Roland were also looking a
bit worried, realizing the fact that we could never find our way
back to *Lay Barge21* without Abraham, who had disappeared.
I showed them what the witch doctor had given me, but they
didn't seem too impressed. It was getting dark and, 'God
only knows where we are,' said Roland. Thankfully, Abraham
suddenly appeared out of the darkness. Within the space of
about three hours, we were back at the barge.

That night I opened the small pot and rubbed the creamy
white paste into my warts. Within twenty four hours the warts
had dropped off, leaving small white dots where they had been.

I couldn't believe it. It was a miracle. Abraham later told me that it was a 'goat's tooth muti'. Christ only knows what it was, but it certainly worked for me and the warts never ever returned.

Enormous investment was one thing, but the cost of getting oil out to the coast, in terms of men and machinery, was also high. A pipeline barge is a dangerous place. Hands, fingers and limbs were often in trouble. Four men were killed during that twelve month contract: two Nigerians drowned in the swamp, one American was electrocuted, one German was run over by a reversing bulldozer. It was a freak accident and, thankfully, I was not the driver of the bulldozer. He went right under the track on the huge wooden pads that were used to prevent the bulldozer from sinking into the mud. Had it been softer ground, he may have survived.

Nine

JAKE PORTER AND THE MILWAUKEE WELDERS

The days and weeks dragged on, twelve hours on, twelve hours off. The pipeline was going down slower by the day, or so it seemed. With the softer ground came more problems. After about a month back on the barge, I seem to remember a dispute setting in with the welders. There was a bit of unrest because McDermott had employed some Lebanese welders at a much cheaper rate than the Americans. Quite a few Americans demanded to be returned to the US. They were duly repatriated and this left quite a hole in the welding team. There was great excitement on the barge as the Barge Captain, Ernest Lee Span, announced that Jake Porter and the Milwaukee welders would be arriving in a couple of days.

We all tried to imagine just what Jake Porter and the Milwaukee welders would look like and pictured some sort of jazz band appearing out of the jungle, trombone playing Jake at the head, leading his group to *Lay Barge 21*. The arrival didn't quite match up to the image. In fact, Jake Porter turned out to be, 'a real mean son of a bitch', as Roland called him. But the pipeline was soon moving again, much to Ernie's delight.

The sun never shone in the jungle and if it wasn't raining, it was overcast. The heat was very hard to live with and there was always plenty of bug life. One day I found a 6 ft black snake coiled up, fast asleep on the operators chair in the crane. A Nigerian boy came and removed it, killed it and then fried it up to eat. He kindly offered me some, but I politely refused.

At night, the huge crane boom was lit up like Blackpool Tower in order to illuminate the working area. Looking up at the boom you saw a living mass of flying creatures; mosquitoes, moths, flies, every winged bug imaginable, all attracted by the bright lights. It was always a great relief, after every shift, to get back into the air conditioned interior of the Barge, put down a couple of cold lagers and hit your bunk.

The last few weeks of my contract were slowly passing. I was almost there. When my Contract Completion day arrived, we were still about six miles from the coast, but I had done it. There were many times when I thought I was not going to make it, but I had: twelve months in the sodding jungle. Oh my God. I was so glad it was over.

I said my goodbyes to all my mates on the Barge and pretty soon it was back to Warri and the seaplane for Lagos where I spent one last night before boarding a Caledonian flight, homeward bound.

It was late February 1972 when I finally touched down at Gatwick. The door of the aircraft opened. It was raining and cold – just beautiful.

I walked slowly across the tarmac and breathed in the cool, clean English air and let the cool, clean English rain run through my hair and down my face. People turned to look at me as if I was mad, but after the sweltering jungle of Nigeria, I was in heaven. I was home.

PART SIX

JANE

One

PARTY, PARTY

I hired a car from Hertz, a Granada or a Zephyr, I can't remember which, but money was no object and I was about to start spending after twelve months on *Lay Barge 21*. I didn't have a suitcase. I had given all my belongings to the Nigerian boys on the Barge. All I carried was a brief case containing my necessary documents, my photos and papers about my contract.

Among all the papers was the very important bank statement from Jersey telling me just how much I was worth. I was worth a little over £8,500, which in 1972 was a fortune. 'A fool and his money', etc. and although I had come to terms with earning serious money, I was yet to learn how to manage it.

I drove into London to buy clothes and visited the trendy boutique shops in Knightsbridge and King's Road. They soon relieved me of some hard earned cash and after a couple of nights in an expensive hotel and time out in several West End night clubs, I was suddenly several hundred pounds down. At last I sobered up and came to my senses. It was time to head home to Salcombe.

Benny Fairclough and myself - the last of the 'Pawnee Indians' from Wigan.

From left to right its myself, Wally, Benny and Dan in Warri yard ready to go off shore.
Big jacket in background.

The massive jacket arrives on location waiting to be launched into position.

Top: Deck view of DB9 looking forward, showing the 92/99 crane on deck with helicopter pad behind it.

Left: The jacket is positioned on the seabed. Note the main hoist block weighing about 20tons, the size of a large transit van.

DB9 positioning the jacket over the well.

The structure is gently lowered down to fit on top of the jacket.

The huge slings are attached to the DB9 crane.

In early March that year, 1972, I finally arrived back in Salcombe. I rented a flat in Devon Road just above the park where we used to stash all the contraband when I was with Jeff in the good old days. I soon hooked up with my mate Wills who had opened up a restaurant called Creep Inn in Russel Court.

Accommodation structure arrives alongside DB9.

Job completed, DB9 moves away.

I was to spend most nights for the next six months in that restaurant – as a customer of course.

The other main attraction in those days was the Galley Restaurant in Fore Street, run by the late Charlie Yabsley. Charlie certainly was a one off. He stood around 5ft 2ins and the ruder and coarser he was with the lady customers, the more popular the restaurant became. By the late 1960s and early 70s the Galley

Two giants in action, DB9 and DB15, gently lower structure into position.
My crane is on the left.

was in its heyday: booking a table for 8pm, you were lucky to sit
down by 11pm. But the people kept pouring in. There was never
such a thing as closing time. Customers would often drive all the
way down from London in their expensive cars in the hope of
getting a table. It was the place to be seen but not for its culinary
fame, more for the groping, dancing and drinking. I spent many
a happy night in the Galley that summer.

Two

MY KAYHAYLEN

Six months in Salcombe, from March '72 to August '72 was just one big party. It was a bland time for me, looking back, no real adventures, no highs, no lows, but by the end of August I had met two people who would influence the rest of my life. It wasn't another crossroads because I didn't have a choice. It was a bridge and I was about to walk across.

One noisy night in the Galley, Charlie introduced me to a rather distinguished looking fella called Jimmy Maybank. We immediately hit it off together. Jimmy was a waste paper millionaire from Charleton, SE London. He was around sixty, I suppose, slim with dark glasses and well dressed in a smart suit. He had started as a rag and bone man and in twenty years had made his fortune. He now owned a large waste paper factory on the banks of the Thames. He was staying at the Salcombe Hotel about three hundred yards up the street from the Galley and insisted that I join him there for a drink. We could walk to the hotel, but oh no, we had to travel the three hundred yards to the Salcombe Hotel in his Rolls-Royce stopping at the King's

Arms on the way for another few drinks. We parked up on the kerb and entered the King's Arms, which was in full swing. Up against the bar, as usual, was Stan Crow talking to Gerry Scott, Jeff's brother who had retired from the sea and was living in Salcombe. As Jimmy and I entered the pub Gerry caught sight of us and immediately yelled out, 'Scratch will skipper your yacht, Jimmy.' Gerry had brought Jimmy Maybank's yacht down to Salcombe from London but was not interested in skippering it for the summer and so without any choice in the matter I was skipper of the *MY Kayhaylen* Jimmy's motor yacht. In a way it was a good thing. It gave me a bit of purpose and responsibility. But skippering Jimmy Maybank's yacht was a new way of going to sea. We didn't really go to sea, but spent most of the time tied up at the Salcombe Hotel. One drinks party just led to another and so on. I really just looked after the *Kayhaylen*. Jimmy would come and go up to London for a few days then he would be back down again. It suited me fine and he treated me like a son, not an employee.

The summer was slowly passing. I was certainly having a good break from the pipeline industry. Some Saturdays Wills and I would race Y35 with the son of her owner, a fella called Graham Cottle. Graham was studying law but had taken a summer job at Wills' restaurant, the Creep Inn. He also did a few shifts in the King's Arms and I got to know Graham well that summer. In years to come he became a good family friend.

One fine day, Jimmy arrived back in Salcombe and announced that he was having a big party in Paris the following week and could we get the *Kayhaylen* over there in time? I didn't see any great problem with that so agreed to meet him in Paris the following week. I thought about taking her over on my own, but a fella called Chris Winter turned up with the son of a London River pilot, Jeff, a mate of Jimmy's. So we left Salcombe bound for Paris – simple, across to Le Havre and up the Seine to Paris. After a good trip we were informed that the party had been cancelled and could I take the *Kayhaylen* back to London. About turn, back down the Seine and London bound. I must admit I got it a bit wrong on the Varne bank. There was a strong west wind, not a gale but just enough to make it a shit with the hard ebb spring tide. You live and learn.

I took the *Kayhaylen* up to a pier at Jimmy's London factory. Jimmy was very grateful and gave me a good night out in London, his home patch, and he knew where to go. Next day, after a couple of Bloody Marys in his office, I caught the train back to the Westcountry and duly arrived in Salcombe. It was late July, a week before Regatta.

Three

RICHARD

And so it was back in Salcombe that late July in 1972 that I first met Richard. Graham introduced him to me one night in the Galley and I remembered him vaguely from childhood days back in East Portlemouth. He was, however, from the next village, East Prawle. Richard was six years older than me and that is a huge age gap when you are a kid. Rich had had a pretty colourful life since leaving school, but I think he was an engineer at heart. He could fix anything. In 1972 he had about two years fishing experience under his belt and owned a crabber called the *Ibis*. Rich and I became lifelong friends from that day on. I told him I was going to return to Africa for one more contract when the summer was over and also of my hankering to go fishing. My great uncles, Lancashire men, had manned the square riggers out of Birkenhead and Liverpool that had carried those brave immigrants to the New Worlds of Australia and New Zealand, during the latter part of the nineteenth century. Although it had skipped a couple of generations, the sea was in my blood. It had been in the back of my mind for some time that I could eventually make my livelihood from the sea and what was in it.

'If you want to come in with me, mate, just say the word.'

Before twelve months was out, I would hold Richard David Murray to exactly that.

And so the crazy, playboy of a summer rolled on. I had bought and sold a few cars. They were an expensive passion and were taking a toll on the Jersey bank account. Phil Dumont, a tall Brummie who had come to Salcombe and bought the restaurant at the top of the Ferry Steps, then called The Ferry Corner, had a beautiful 4.2 midnight blue Jaguar for sale and I had to have it. We did the deal in the Ferry Inn over a few pints. I think I got a good deal, anyway we were both very happy. That afternoon I set off in the Jag to arrange some insurance in Torquay. On the way home it happened.

Four

JANE

Suddenly, there she was, the girl with whom I would spend the rest of my life.

Driving up the hill out of the small market town of Totnes, I saw her – Miss World, thumbing a lift.

I couldn't believe what I was seeing. Was I pissed?

In a daze, I managed to stop the Jag about fifty yards on. Through the rear view mirror I saw a vision of long blonde hair, 60s flower power bell bottom trousers and a flowery top running up to the car.

'Salcombe?' she said.

'Yes,' I said.

If she had said Manchester I would have said yes. I was in a trance.

She climbed into the car and I drove off hardly able to speak. She kept the conversation going all the way to Salcombe, while I did my best not to put the beautiful Jag into the hedge. She said she was joining her parents who were on holiday in Salcombe. They were staying in a flat opposite the Salcombe Hotel. Christ, I thought, I wonder if they know Jimmy Maybank? I duly dropped her off outside the flat, said goodbye and drove on. What an idiot. Would I ever see her again?

I soon met up with Wills and Graham and told them all about her. 'You'll see her again, Scratch. Don't panic.' A few stiff whiskies in the King's Arms for Dutch courage and I was off up Fore Street to where I had dropped her off. I met her coming the other way. The whiskies had kicked in.

'Hello, again.' I said. 'Would you like to come for a drink?' Very original but it worked.

So we had our first drink together in the Shipwrights Arms. I wanted to keep her away from the Goon Show down the road at the King's Arms. I didn't want to share her with anybody and I knew my life would never be the same again.

I had just met Jane Louise Robinson.

She was five years and five days younger than me, from Shepperton in Middlesex and she was looking for a new life. She had met the right man and I think we both fell in love that first day. If you are very lucky, it happens that way and the feelings are still there forty five years on, love turning into friendship and like two swans, we are best mates for life.

Five

'YOU'VE GOT A FRIEND'

Jane, at that time, was working for a secretarial agency in the West End of London. Within forty eight hours she had phoned the agency to say she would not be returning to London. Within a couple of days she had secured a new job in Salcombe through a friend of mine, Simon, who we called Garfunkle. Garfunkle worked for a local sailing institution, Blue Water Charters up South Pool creek. He was launch driver and general dog's body but easily managed to get Jane a job aboard their headquarters ship an ex Thames sailing barge, the *Violet Sybil* .

I drove Jane back to London to get clothes and some belongings. Her parents seemed very good about it all. I honestly don't think they had much choice. Jane had chosen her new direction in life and Shepperton didn't feature.

Garfunkle's girlfriend at that time was a tall elegant girl called Sue Mattthews who also worked for Blue Water Charters. She and Jane became good friends for many years afterwards.

There was just August and a bit of September left before I was to return to Africa and so Jane and I made the most of it. One day she was a bit shocked when I took her racing in Graham's Yawl and turned up wearing smart velvet shirt, plumb coloured trousers and patent leather boots; dressed to impress, or so I thought.

I told her all about Jeff and Lil and their little pub in the Cornish countryside. We drove down to visit them for a couple of nights, but it turned out not at all as Jane had expected. She imagined a cosy little country pub, oak beams and open fires. Instead, it was full of pissed tin miners, twenty four hours a day. She took it all in her stride and spent most of the time in the kitchen making toasted cheese sandwiches for hungry tin miners.

Lil gave me a hot tip one night. She whispered in my ear, 'You want to marry 'er, boy.' Good old Lil!

Back in Salcombe I received a letter from McDermotts asking me if I would sign up for another twelve month contract, beginning in mid September of '72. I decided it was time to return to the real world and get back to work. But what about Jane? How could I possibly go back to Africa now? We sat down together and talked it through and decided that I should do one more contract and then come home for good.

I couldn't imagine spending twelve days without Jane, never mind twelve months. We left Salcombe in mid September and drove up to London. Jane said she would work in London while I was away overseas and I signed a new twelve month contract in West Africa.

The departure was awful. She came to Gatwick to see me off but I had never, ever felt like this before in all my travels around the world. We said goodbye with heavy hearts and I boarded the plane.

PART SEVEN

UNEXPECTED EXIT,
A TASTE OF CITY LIFE
AND BILLY

One

THE SHOW MUST GO ON

On arrival back in Lagos, I was greeted with at least a little good news. I was to go to Tema in Ghana to finish off the refit of a Lay Barge that was in dry dock. Tema was a large coastal port and cooler than the Nigerian jungle I was so dreading. Unfortunately, the refit was completed in about five weeks, but during that time we were housed in a comfortable hotel. The barge was relaunched and we were towed back around the West African coast to Cameroon on the Gulf of Guinea. Christ, that was hot! I was then transferred back to *Lay Barge 21*, by now about two miles off shore and continuing to lay the pipeline out to deep water and the Single Point Mooring where the oil was discharged, through a network of hoses, to the tanker. At least, I was not in the jungle.

I slowly settled back into life on *Lay Barge 21*. There were a few old faces, but most of the crew were new. I shared a cabin with a deck foreman, Benny Fairclough from Pensacola, Florida. Benny was quite a character, short and stocky, claiming to be descended from the Pawnee tribe of American Indians.

With a name like Fairclough, I reckoned his descendants more likely came from Wigan, but I never told Benny. He was very happy thinking he was a Pawnee! Benny and I struck up a good friendship for the rest of my time on that barge and although we were off shore, he could always put his hands on beer and whisky from somewhere.

The weeks slipped by and at long last we had reached deep enough water to be able to lay the SPM bouy for the tankers to pickup and *Lay Barge 21* had completed her task. There had been many problems and setbacks on the way. I think the line was almost a hundred miles long, stretching from the jungle interior to the SPM through very difficult terrain. I can only say how much I admired the Americans' approach to any problem we encountered – nothing ever got the better of them, no matter how big the obstacle, the show must go on, the pipeline must go through. Of course, money was no problem and equipment that got wrecked was quickly replaced. That was all part of the pipeline experience, alongside the danger of injury and fatal accident, which was commonplace.

Lay Barge 21 was towed to Tema for a big refit after the completion of the line and she was ready for it. I never saw her again, but I had spent well over a year of my young life on that old barge. You never get anything for nothing.

Two

A CLOSE CALL

During the tow, I was picked up by a helicopter along with a few welders and transferred to a construction barge at least twice as big as old 21. *Derrick Barge 9* must have been around 6,000 tons. She was like an aircraft carrier. She could lay pipelines, but her main purpose was construction, the building and erection of the huge oil platforms that pumped the black gold of Nigeria's wealth to waiting tankers and then distributed around the world.

The one good thing about this contract was the fact that I was experiencing plenty of variety on location, by contrast to the wearying twelve months in the jungle on *Lay Barge21*. I was very homesick, though, or was it lovesick? Both. I was missing Jane terribly. We had about two letters a week going backwards and forwards but I knew that after this contract my travels would be over.

Up until the time I joined DB 9, all my crane operating experience had been on steady platforms, but now, working in any kind of swell or a running sea, it made the operation very awkward, both platforms rising up and down independently, sometimes with as much as a six to eight foot drop between them in a see saw effect. This made picking up heavy loads of 50 tons or more extremely dangerous. Simply put, the crane could have a full load of perhaps 80-100 tons and the barge from which it was being lifted could suddenly come up six feet or more on a swell. The weight was then off the crane and she would go down, but the full load of 80 plus tons was swinging around in front of you. Combine trying to control the swing and the tremendous side pressure on the boom, operating the crane suddenly becomes extremely dangerous. It was in such a situation that I was about to use up one more of my nine lives.

The crane was an American 92-99, 100 ton crawler, used mainly in Warri yard, but DB9 had two of these on deck. The 92 – 99 was a good and well proven machine with a very wide track base, giving good stability. A dumb barge had been towed out to us from the Warri yard by one of the McDermott tugs. On its deck was a piece of generator type electrical equipment, weighing around 50 tons. This had to be plucked off the dumb barge by the 92-99 crane. The amount of swell movement ruled out using the huge 500 ton pedestal crane that was permanently mounted on the back of DB9. It was too far too slow and unwieldy to be used for this particular operation.

We waited two days for the swell to decrease and then the Barge Captain decided to go ahead with the lift. I positioned the 92 – 99 on the very edge of DB9, tracks facing forward, track lock well engaged. We could have chained the crane to the deck, quite common practice in calm seas, but not today. It was necessary to boom up as high as possible before accepting the enormous load. I boomed up and started to lower down the big block, the size of a forty gallon drum. It was a six fold block and this made the lift slow, but soon the Nigerian deck hands, working on the dumb barge, had connected the huge slings to the load. No signals are given to you in the crane.

You have full view of the operation from up there in the cab and you make your own decisions. I gave the hoist lever full stick and I could hear the powerful Detroit diesels screaming away behind me. The entire length of the boom shuddered. The crane 92 – 99 tilted forward and the back left the deck, but the load was airborne. I thought we had it in the bag, but I was unable to lift fast enough. The dumb barge came up on a swell and took back the weight while my crane sat down once more on the deck of DB9. Within seconds I had the full load again but this time with a hell of a snatch and I just could not slack off quickly enough. The crane and its load were doomed. Sparks flew in every direction and with steel crashing in around me and to the terrifying noise of crushing metal, I leapt through the cab door. I remember thinking how nice and warm the water was. Thank God it wasn't the North Sea, I would have been dead in minutes and thank God I hadn't landed on the deck, I would have broken my legs. I was floating around in

Not much left of the cab I was sitting in. I remember thinking how nice and warm the water was. '…another life used up'.

the sea between the two barges. Someone on the dumb barge threw a rope and I scrambled aboard, unhurt but a bit shaken. Both the generator and the crane were wrecked and had to be towed back to Warri on the dumb barge. For some reason I went back to Warri with them. I think it was for a medical check. I was okay, but a few hours later I felt very shaky. Within a week a brand new generator and crane were on their way to DB9. That was the off shore oil industry for you. Nothing got in its way.

And so Christmas '72 dawned and New Year, '73, arrived. Very early in January I was yet again transferred, guess where? Yes, back into the bloody jungle! *Dredge 10* was a small barge with two portakabins on it. She was used to keep parts of the Escravos River dredged. She had on her deck a big 4,600 ton Manitowoc crane rigged with a dragline. Life on *Dredge 10* was dreadful – back to the heat and the flies, bugs, flying insects and mosquitoes. Ironically, fate was to take a hand in a way remarkably similar to the way in which it had done on the *Newbrook*, almost ten years previously.

It started with a few dizzy spells and then came the bad stomach, the raging fever and throbbing headaches and then the shakes: Malaria. I was sent back to Lagos for a full medical and the result was that McDermott did not want to continue taking the risk of having me with them in Nigeria any longer. They offered me another contract in the Gulf of Mexico but there was only one place I wanted to be and it wasn't Mexico. It was early February 1973. My career on the oilfields was at an end and my travels were over.

Three

WHERE I WANT TO BE

Jane was at Gatwick to meet me. I came through Customs and Immigration and I saw her immediately. She looked like a film star, wearing the beautiful suede coat with huge fur collar that I had bought for her before I went back to Africa. She still has that coat today. It's a bit out of fashion, but I know she would never part with it. I was back with Jane and I was in heaven. I knew I would never leave her again, at least, not for the oilfields. Separations from now on would be short and in home waters. We took a taxi to her parents' house in Shepperton where Chris and Robbie were very pleased to see me. I think they had approved of me from the start, but had only ever seen me at play and were reassured to see another side to me.

Jane was still temping in the West End and was able to be pretty flexible, so we took a few days off to collect the Jag from my mate in Bridport and head down to Salcombe. It was great to be back. Wills was still running the Creep and the Galley was still in full swing. Graham had gone back to University and Rich was fishing with the *Ibis*. Stan Crow and all the usuals were still propping up the bar at the King's Arms. Things hadn't changed much.

Jane and I returned to London. What now? I suggested to Jane that we get a flat and move in together.

Her reaction was, 'I won't move in with you, but I will marry you.'

'Okay.' I said.

And that was that. We got married a week later on 26th February at Hampstead Registry Office. We managed to find two witnesses – Sue Matthews and an American friend of mine, Don Jesse. Jane's dad, Robbie, organised a party at the Bamboo Club in Mayfair where there were nine of us including Jane's younger brother, Stephen. It was that simple.

That night Mr and Mrs Hitchen went home to a tiny one bedroomed flat, 26 Norfolk House Road, Streatham, which I had rented the previous week.

What to do now, I wondered the next morning when Jane had left for work. At the back of my mind was Rich's offer to go fishing. But, oh no, not yet. I was about to spend a very interesting and informative six months in the big city.

First up was a meeting with Jeff Winter, friend of Jimmy Maybank. He was a River Pilot and it was Jeff's son who had sailed with me to Paris with *Kayhaylen*. I helped Jeff for several weeks in the Piloting Trade and learnt a fair bit about the London River. But there was not enough work to keep me on full time. The work was patchy and the hours were very odd, mainly due to tides and being able to get to certain docks.

After a few weeks, I happened to bump into Don Jesse once again and he introduced me to a fella called Gerald Moon who was an actor. During the course of the evening I said that I was looking for any kind of temporary work and asked Don if he had any ideas. Gerald chipped in and said, 'Why not do telly commercials?' I told him I knew nothing about photography.

'No,' he said. 'you'd be at the other end of the lens.' He gave me a short introductory note and told me to go to an agency called Ugly in Tottenham Court Road and ask for Julie.

The next day I went to Ugly and asked to see Julie. She was very nice and told me she could get me some work that very week, but I really needed a portfolio.

Back to Don Jesse who was a good photographer and within days I returned to Ugly with my portfolio. Julie was very pleased and got me work immediately, mainly cigarette and beer commercials; Kensitas, Marlboro, Embassy, several for beer and one for Scotch Whisky called Scotts Mac, another for Dunlop Tyres in a shoot on the motorway dressed in a gorilla suit, clutching a half naked blonde in hairy arms. In another one, again for cigarettes, I went to the south of France for two weeks. We did several shoots for Marlboro in the French-Spanish border region of Perignon. My co-worker was a gorgeous model who was sometimes required to enhance the desirability of her cleavage with the use of sellotape.

Summer 1973. A job with an advertising agency, Ugly.
But it wasn't my world.

Her name was Chipples and I thought Chipples was okay without the sellotape. But there you go.

Just around the corner from Ugly on Tottenham Court Road was a shop that sold all the latest records and music and where I loved to go and browse when I had a bit of time between shoots. It was owned by a tall, lanky fella with long hair called Richard and his little shop was called Virgin Records. Richard has come a long way since then.

The weeks of summer '73 slipped slowly by. Jane continued working, but for some reason we decided to give up our little flat in Streatham and move to Harrow on the Hill. Work was coming in regularly now with Ugly, but I wasn't happy. They were a different breed, all phoney show-bizz, 'dahling' this and 'dahling' that. Ugly wanted me to join Equity, the actors' union, so that I could take on speaking parts. But it was an empty way of life and I knew I could never fit in.

One evening Jane came home from work and I said to her, 'Let's go home.' Her eyes lit up, 'I wondered when you would say that.'

I had sold the Jag and bought a spanking new Audi which we loaded up with all our possessions. Two days later we left Harrow on the Hill and motored due west. Life in the big city was over and my fishing days were about to begin.

Salcombe Harbour looking seaward. 'I felt a great sense of homecoming.'

EPILOGUE

1973

As we dropped down into Salcombe I had a great sense of homecoming. I could see the Estuary slowly spreading out around us; East Portlemouth and Ditch End, South Pool Creek, Snape's Point, the harbour and the Bag, the farms and villages and little grey churches, 'wooded coves and white sandy beaches.'

'Gone to sea on *Norian*. Be okay, Billy.'

Billy was home.

THE FISHING YEARS

THE INVISIBLE PREY

PROLOGUE

'*Burutu, Burutu – Kastel Paol, Kastel Paol.* You getting me, Scratch?'

'Aye aye, Scruff. Got you fine. Yeah.'

'Don't bother trying to come into Alderney. It's well north west now. You would never get in through the breakwater end. The outer end of the breakwater is buried. We are in Bray Harbour, dodging. We can't get alongside. Wing Nut and Battle of Britain have just come away from the Quay. They can't get alongside.'

*

After receiving the news from Scruffy, I had to reappraise the situation. Cherbourg lay about eighteen miles south east. I turned the *Burutu* another 20 degrees and lay a course for the western entrance of Cherbourg. This put the storm directly behind us. *Burutu* liked that a lot more and settled into a surfing motion down the giant waves. Rich and Long Hair entered the wheelhouse from the galley end.

'What's the crack then, Billy Whizz?' asked Long Hair. I never knew why Long Hair always called me Billy Whizz, never Scratch.

I told them that Alderney was a no goer so we were going to run to Cherbourg, now about fifteen miles away to the south east. Richard's first comment was, 'Bugger, I haven't got any French money.' Long Hair said no problem, we could sell a few lobsters. Rich then disappeared and came back with a bottle of rum, de-corked it and threw the cork out of the wheelhouse window into the raging wind and snow. All three of us had a good belt of rum and Long Hair produced three Villager cigars. The wheelhouse was soon filled with the rich smell of rum and cigar smoke: eight miles to run.

The radar screen was dotted with dense snow showers, but they seemed to be passing mainly to the west of us. Every so often a huge sea would come crashing over our quarter and run up the deck, at least clearing the snow. I had a last look at the chart. It was simple enough to run into the western end. The purple A.74 lane on the Decca ran straight into the entrance. Two miles to run and the bottle of rum was well down. Long Hair produced three more cigars and we lit up.

'Half a mile to go, boys,' I said. At the same time I noticed, taking up the bottom half of the radar screen, a huge snow shower, dead astern. I could see that it would be upon us as we hit the entrance.

Snow had completely blocked the radar and the screen was blank.

I had to make a quick decision: turn into this roaring tempest or run on for the entrance blind.

I think she would have turned in that sea, but I remembered at that moment that the Decca A.74 lane goes straight through the entrance.

Caught up in this sudden blizzard, visibility was down to nil, the forward mast disappearing into the night and the driving snow.

So I steered her in on the Decca needle.

I estimated that we were roughly 500 yards from the entrance when the radar had gone blind. Five minutes later, with the gale still raging and the snow horizontal, the sea began to calm.

We all looked at each other. 'I think we're in,' I whispered.

PART ONE

KENAVO

1973

One

OUT OF SALCOMBE
WITH *IBIS*

Coming home after being away on my travels for ten years, came as quite a shock to me. But I knew my wandering days were over and apart from fishing all sea areas from Dover to Rockall, I would never leave Salcombe again. Now married to Jane, I was ready for the change in lifestyle and the new responsibilities that came with that. We soon found a small place to rent in a little road, just above the Church, called Lakeside. From here was a most wonderful view of Salcombe Harbour, the place of my childhood, the place where I grew up.

I had only recently met Richard Murray but we shared much in common and I soon set up a meeting with him to discuss the future. I told him that I was home for good and within a few days I was signed up as crew on his Crabber, *Ibis*. And so began our lifelong friendship.

Who else should be working on the *Ibis* but Ears, my old childhood friend from East Portlemouth, Rick Stead.

The *Ibis*, Customs Quay Salcombe, 1969.

It was a good Autumn on the *Ibis*. The fishing was plentiful, as it always is in the fall of the year. We were fishing about twelve miles off Start Point in an area on the Decca charts known as the Cs. Fishing areas were divided up alphabetically. The areas in G were about forty five miles off, over a huge trench, the Hurd Deep, that runs from east to west along the English Channel. But C was far enough for the old *Ibis* .

The previous summer, Richard had teamed up with another local Skipper, Barney Powlesland. It was Barney who was one of the survivors of the firework battle at Whitestrand car park in 1961. His boat was called the *Frances* and they had ventured as far as the Hs and Is, about 65 miles out of Salcombe on the eastern edge of the Hurd Deep. There they found good fishing, large cock crabs and good lobster. They also met up with some Jersey fishermen who told them of big catches of lobster to be made off Scotland's west coast. A huge fella called Mo de

Buchier, who had a boat called the *Finnarbed*, had ventured that far north the previous Spring. He had put ashore some excellent catches that Autumn.

Richard retold the stories of Mo and his big catches and this certainly fired up my imagination no end. No one in Salcombe had fished even as far afield as Barney and Richard, who had made it as far as the Hurd Deep. Going up to Scotland we would become an important part of Salcombe fishing history and so the die was cast.

Of course, a few problems stood in the way, the biggest of which was, we had the wrong boat. It was well outside the capabilities of the *Ibis* to undertake such a voyage. We had to have a bigger boat with accommodation and facilities to hold 6 – 7 tons of live shellfish aboard for at least a fourteen day trip. She also had to cope with the type of weather to be encountered in these northern sea areas.

Mo's boat, the *Finarbed* was a Frenchman, built in Brittany. She was about 50ft, but her magic was that built into her was what the French called a vivier, a holding tank in which shellfish can be kept alive at sea. We had to have a vivier boat if we were going to undertake deep sea voyages to Scotland.

Two

PREPARATION

Just before Christmas that year, Richard and I went to Plymouth and boarded what I am now sure was the first ever Brittany Ferry. She was carrying mainly cargo with just a few passengers in a Portakabin on deck. We duly arrived in Roscoff and set off under the guidance of Monsieur Tuorilly, a local boat broker, who drove us to several ports down in the Bay of Biscay. After looking at several boats, we finally found the *Kenavo* in Camaret in the Finisterre region of north western Brittany. Her last voyage was Tunny fishing off the Azores, but she had done many trips to Morocco and Mauritania off the coast of Africa for crayfish. Her seagoing credentials were good, but most important of all, she had the magical 8 ton capacity vivier hold which would be the key to our success in Scotland.

We soon decided she was the right boat for us and did a deal the next day with the old skipper, Monsieur Cornec, a proper old Breton fisherman, who, I am sure, slept with a Gauloises cigarette in his mouth. I never saw him without one.

We arranged to pick up the *Kenavo* early in the New Year

Kenavo steaming down Loch Indaal, Islay, 1974.

and then sail her home to Salcombe. We felt very pleased with ourselves.

Christmas was good that year, the first Christmas I had been at home for many years. We were all very excited about what the coming year would bring. Richard and I had formed a small company called *Kenavo* Fisheries. *Kenavo* Fisheries is still going today and is the oldest established fishing company in Salcombe.

And so in the New Year of 1974, Rich and I took our young wives with us to bring *Kenavo* back to Salcombe. Richard's wife at the time, Beatrice, was French, so she was able to help a great deal with the final transactions of the sale which were very complicated. At least eight people had shares in the *Kenavo*, but at last everything was completed and we were ready to sail.

Aged 24, ready to sail into the unknown. *Kenavo* in the background.

That afternoon Rich and Beatrice met up with a French woman who was a fish merchant, Fanny Backrope. She had heard that two Englishmen had bought the *Kenavo* and was keen to handle our catches of lobster from Scotland. That night before we sailed , she took us out for a slap up meal at the best restaurant in Camaret. I went for the steak, but the other three had Lobster Armoric, a sort of lobster stew, which they would all three regret next day on the voyage home.

Fanny Backrope never did handle our catches from Scotland. Sadly, a few weeks later, she fell into a vivier and drowned.

A twenty hour run home from Camaret brought the *Kenavo* back into Salcombe. That day was quite a big piss up. All the other fishermen came aboard to have a look around. Many remarks were made, the best from an old salt, Les Cook. 'Well, mate,' he said to his brother, Terry, 'Scratch and Richard have bought a bloody aircraft carrier to haul pots.' Les had never been further than Prawle Point in his life.

The scene that greeted Richard and I in Cameret, Brittany where we found the *Kenavo*.

The *Kenavo* was 60ft long, 15ft beam and drew 12ft. She weighed around 60 tons and was powered by a Baudouin diesel engine, air start only, but an excellent engine. It never let us down. A good fisherman always looks after his engine as a number one priority. Richard carried on the tradition and looked after that engine like a baby and it ran like clockwork.

In mid January, we took the *Kenavo* back to a small port in France, Granville, near St Malo, to have a new winch fitted and a tripod put on the foremast. We hauled our pots in a different way to the French, hauling in from the starboard shoulder of the boat. This enabled us to haul in more tide. The French never hauled in much tide and so worked amidships.

By the end of January we had returned to Salcombe. Jane came across to join me for the return trip across the Channel. She was very seasick as we rounded the SW Minquiers light buoy. She visited me a few months later in Scotland with quite a bump on her tummy and completely unplanned, our little girl was born nine months later.

The following six weeks was spent in preparation for our forthcoming voyage to the West Coast of Scotland and the wild North Atlantic. Were we biting off more than we could chew?

My fishing experience was really quite limited. Apart from my baptism of fire on the *Newbrook*, it was practically nil. But my seamanship was good and on that front I had no doubts. Richard, on the other hand, had about three years fishing experience behind him, combined with good engineering skills. We were both young, but both confident the voyage was within our capabilities.

Fishing is a different way of going to sea. The fisherman's approach to navigation and seamanship is a world apart from that of a yachtsman or a merchant man. Their job is to get a vessel from one port to another. The job of the fisherman is to make a living from the sea between the ports, hunting and catching a quarry he has never seen. Fishermen, from the deck upwards, naturally all become very good seamen. They spend 90% of their lives on a heaving deck, continually fighting wind and tide, often up to their knees in water that cannot drain off the deck quickly enough. I saw many men come and go during the next thirty five years of fishing. You could usually tell by the way they walked on deck for the first time if they were going to make it. Many fell by the wayside within a few hours, but the few to whom it was second nature, they carried forever the superb skill of being at one with the sea and all it could throw at you.

By early March 1974, we were ready to sail. We had been very busy during our final preparations. We had made up another one hundred pots to add to the two hundred and fifty we had from the *Ibis*, making a total fishing effort of three hundred and fifty pots. It was all we could load on the old *Kenavo*. With 3 tons of bait, full of fuel and stores, the *Kenavo* was well down in the water, with only about 2ft of freeboard in the quarters.

Three

INTO THE UNKNOWN

We sailed from Salcombe at midday on 5 March 1974. We rounded up off the Ferry Inn and I gave the horn a good farewell blast to the girls in the pub, sitting on the wall. It was the first time we had used this powerful air horn and we didn't realise that it had a plug in it to keep the weather out. The blast shot this two inch wooden plug right across the Ferry Inn garden, but thankfully didn't hit anyone. Jane and Beatrice waved us farewell and we were off.

I felt good heading down to Land's End. The four of us on board were good mates. Wills had decided on a career change and gave up the restaurant to become a fisherman. It didn't take him long to pick it up and later on he became a successful fisherman himself, never returning to the catering trade. Wills was never without his camera and it is thanks to him that we have a photographic record of those early years. The other crew member was, of course, Rick Stead, my old childhood mate from East Portlemouth. He had joined Richard on the *Ibis* two years previously.

The weather was good. We called into Falmouth briefly to have the compass swung. It was miles out. We rounded Land's End and the Long Ships and headed the old *Kenavo* northwards into the unknown as far as fishing was concerned. Looking back on it now, forty five years later, it was all very primitive. Our navigational equipment consisted of a paper echo-sounder which showed the depth of water underneath the keel and the type of seabed over which you were sailing – rock, sand, mud; a Decca Navigator that received a grid of radio beams giving your position; an old-fashioned French direction finder that would home in on a lighthouse beyond the horizon. We weren't too sure how to use the direction finder because it was French. The *Kenavo* had no auto pilot but a very heavy chain and link steering. She was also assisted with main, jib and mizzen sails. We did not know at the time, but we were slowly leaving behind yet another iconic age, the age of sail in the fishing industry. Apart from oyster dredging in Falmouth in Cornwall, to my knowledge, sail is no longer used in any form of commecial fishing in the United Kingdom.

Rick Stead and I steaming north on *Kenavo*, Spring 1974. Note wire and cane pots.

After rounding the 'end of the land', as sailors call it, a good west-south-west Force 5 set in, so we hoisted all sail and eased the throttle back to conserve fuel. This made a big difference and certainly checked the roll of the ship. If the wind was on the beam, the French would always use the sails on their long voyages to the Azores and Mauritania and we kept the sails on the *Kenavo* all the time we owned her.

We steamed a good seventy six hours from Salcombe ,to the fishing grounds north west of Islay for which we were heading. Islay was a good place to fish from. It had seventeen distilleries, all of which, over time, we were to try.

Now, at last, was the moment of truth and we were ready to shoot away the gear. To the west of Islay the seabed is pretty rough. It runs out from the coast for about two miles at 15 fathoms and then slowly drops away to 30 fathoms – (one fathom equals 6ft). It was down these western slopes that we shot away all 350 pots in strings of 50, each pot 15 fathoms apart, so that each string of 50 pots was roughly three quarters of a mile long. The big super shellfish boats of today work about 3,000 pots, so you can imagine how many miles of rope they have aboard.

With all the gear shot away, it was time to sample some of Islay's malt. Port Ellen was our first run ashore and we certainly did sample the whisky. Next morning was pretty much a blur. Thank the Lord the weather was fine.

Four

'JACKPOT!'

We duly arrived back on the west side of Islay. Now for the real moment of truth. I was operating the winch or capstan as it was called, Wills was on the roller, Rick was also on the rail waiting to bait and stack the pots, Rich was in the wheelhouse keeping us on the gear. Suddenly there was a yell from Wills on the roller, 'Jackpot!,' he yelled. The first pot had four lobsters in it and so it went on, pot after pot. We weren't fully prepared for a catch of this magnitude. There were lobsters and crayfish walking all around the deck. Rich dived out of the wheelhouse to shut all the scupper doors, so nothing was lost overboard. We finally got control of the situation with plenty of wet sack to keep the lobsters quiet until we could band up their claws. We fished on and on for the next twenty four hours and only then took a break. We hauled the gear almost continuously. In four days we had two and a half tons of lobster and crayfish aboard. We stopped fishing after the fourth day and went into a small port called Port Askaig in the Sound of Islay with the island of Jura to the east. Rich made a phone call to Beatrice to tell her the good news.

Beatrice had made contact with another Frenchman called Raymond Squarnack, (we immediately nicknamed him Square Neck) who was top shellfish buyer for a big shellfish company in Brittany called Primel. We were to land to Primel and Square Neck for the next six years , but it would result in many battles with Square Neck about price. Square Neck arranged for us to land in Mallaig the following day. Although Mallaig was roughly an eight hour steam north of Islay, we thought we had better get there as we weren't too sure how much crayfish and lobster we could mix in the vivier. Crayfish have very sharp horns and would kill a lobster with banded claws. We stopped fishing at just the right time. We had a dozen or so dead lobsters that had fallen to the aggressive crayfish. Some of the crayfish weighed in at around 4.5 kilo, so they were big old boys and sold for a good price.

We grounded the *Kenavo* alongside the town pier at Mallaig, not a stone's throw from the Central Bar, which was obviously the main fisherman's pub. That was handy.

We started to land our catch at low water. The *Kenavo's* vivier tanks had to completely drain out before we could get down

A happy crew after landing record catch in Mallaig.
(l to r) Richard, myself, Wills, Rick April 1974.

to the seething mass of lobster and crayfish. We landed just about smack on two and a half tons in total through Burgons of Eyemouth which was then transported overland down to Brittany and Primel. We made the local newspaper and were interviewed by *Fishing News International*. Mallaig had never seen a catch that size before. Richard and I were very relieved indeed. We had made a really good grossing for the trip. In fact, we paid for half the boat on that first landing. Perhaps old Les Cook was right, we did need an aircraft carrier after all.

After we finished landing it was all hands to the Central Bar to celebrate. Our celebrations, however, were cut short. Two little faces appeared at a window. Jane and Beatrice had driven about eight hundred miles in a little Morris1000 to be with us. It had taken them twenty hours to drive from Salcombe to Mallaig. Jane hadn't yet passed her Driving Test and there were L plates up on the front and back bumpers. That is what you call true love. It was really great to see them, especially having just landed such a good trip. With our new found wealth, we booked into the best hotel in Mallaig, The West Highland, for two nights. Jane's bump, as she called it, was now a little more noticeable. It did suit her though and she looked wonderful.

So after a stay in Mallaig for three days, the girls said their goodbyes. We refuelled the *Kenavo*, salted down 2 tons of mackerel for bait and with stores and provisions aboard, set sail for lobster grounds once more, with a belly full of beer and fish and chips. We arrived back west of Islay the following morning. The lobsters were still abundant, but the crayfish had moved on. They are a migratory species, but I was to find out in time where they had gone. We fished on for another five weeks, making around six more landings in Mallaig, all through Square Neck. We had been lulled into a false sense of security, however, with the weather. A huge high pressure system had planted itself right over the top of Scotland. There were days of endless calm. We could well have been in the Mediterranean. For almost six weeks we saw hardly a ripple on the sea. Huh – this is easy, we thought, but we were about to get a rude awakening. This certainly was not the Scotland I remembered from my days on the old *Halcience*, carrying coal to North Devon.

I think we finally came home in early May of that year. We left the *Kenavo* in Mallaig and travelled home on the West Highland Railway from Mallaig to Glasgow. That was a beautiful run across the Highlands. Catching the overnight sleeper from Glasgow to Penzance, we arrived at Totnes the following afternoon, where we were picked up in, yes the Morris 1000. The only difference was there were no L plates. Jane had passed her driving test, bump and all. It was wonderful to be home. Jane and I moved into a new house in which we would stay for the next four years until we managed to put a deposit down on our own house. It was good to see all the other fishermen and tell them about all our adventures.

Richard Cove, the old skipper of the *Newbrook*, had also bought a Frenchman, the same as the *Kenavo*, called the *Kastel Poal*. He also tried a trip to Scotland, but with not much success. He had gone further north than us and fished to the east of Barra Head. He also knew Mo de Bouchier, but on reflection, I think Mo had sent him on a fool's errand. The ground where he was fishing was far too sandy and soft. Not good lobster country. Covey steamed back to Salcombe with about six hundred lobster on board and never left Salcombe again. He sold the *Kastel Poal* the following year to Scruffy Ingram of Jersey, who fished her well for the next six years.

We returned to Scotland in early June. A week later, Rick was offered a job skippering a boat for a fella called Tom Epps who lived on Islay. Rick moved on, but he was ready to skipper and he did well for Tom Epps for several years. He finally came ashore to run a pub in Plymouth. Rick never made old bones and must have died in his early fifties.

Five

GOON IN TROON

Richard, Wills and I continued to try to work the boat three handed, but it was no use, we had to have a fourth hand. Enter Goon, full name, Arthur Seekings. Wills gave Goon a call and he agreed at once to join the crew. We arranged to pick Goon up in Troon a few days later. Goon was a good lad, about 6ft tall with a shock of blonde hair and a big blonde beard. Sure enough, a few days later, we pulled into Troon on the River Clyde, and there was Goon, standing on the end of the pier. We didn't stop, we just picked him up and headed back to the gear.

Coming back down the Clyde, basking sharks began to appear around the Isle of Arran and Sanda, just to the south east of the Mull of Kintyre. I had never seen so many basking sharks at one time in my life. There must have been hundreds of them and you had a job to miss them. Goon was sharpening up the harpoon that we carried to catch a couple, but Richard said they didn't make very good bait. The flesh was too mushy and would disintegrate in the pots. So we stowed the harpoon. We rounded the Mull of Kintyre or the Puffers' Cape Horn as it was

Goon.

known locally and arrived back at the gear soon after midnight. The moon was full and it was a beautiful night. It only really gets dark for a couple hours around midnight at these latitudes at this time of the year, but alas, storm clouds were gathering out in the Atlantic. The big high pressure had slipped away and tomorrow would be the last calm day that we would experience for many weeks. We went around the gear once with Goon and then headed to Port Askaig for stores.

It was a week before we got out again. A deep depression had approached from Rockall Sea Area and there was a storm Force 10 from the west for five days. At last, it eased to a Force 6 and we felt that we had to give it a try. We sailed up the Sound of Islay and rounded the North Light as we called it. Then we opened up the Atlantic to the west. I could not believe the size of the swell. The *Kenavo's* engine changed note as she climbed the huge swells and picked up again as we descended down the other side. We looked at each glumly, but pressed on. What on earth state would the gear be in with this sea running? We were soon to find out – a disaster.

Usually pots and nets shot in over 20 fathoms are pretty safe, but our gear was all shot in 10-15 fathoms. Not good – and this

Goon and me on *Kenavo*, St. Kilda 1974. 'We went to Troon to pick up Goon.' - Arthur 'Goon' Seekings, a good hand, RIP.

had been a full Atlantic storm with nothing between the west coast of Islay and the Nantucket Light off New York.

We circled around where we had shot the gear for an hour or so. The tide finally slacked off and we found a few of the dhan buoys that marked the pots. Slowly, all that day, we recovered what remained of our gear, but it was in some mess. The nets and the bridles on the pots were all badly chaffed up. There was only one thing to do, take everything ashore to Port Askaig and start repairing and mending the damage. So that is what we did. It took a good week to get fishing again, but we managed it. The pots had all been badly shaken up. Poor old Goon had missed all the good times that we had experienced in the early summer of '74. It never really came good again that summer. The weather was continually poor and the fishing around Islay slacked right off. So we spent many weeks moving around looking for the ever elusive lobster.

We rounded Barra Head and ventured as far north as the Monarch Isles and the Flannan Isles, but it was a pretty inhospitable stretch of coast with not many ports to run into for shelter. In late July we at last landed a hard earned catch in Mallaig, tied up the old *Kenavo* and returned home for a couple of weeks. It was great to be home again, but, in retrospect, looking back, we should have loaded all the gear and steamed home then. Financially, it would have been a much better bet.

Six

A CAN OF BAKED BEANS
AND A TEA TOWEL

We returned to Scotland for another four weeks but encountered
bad weather combined with poor fishing. By mid September the
decision was made to load the gear and return to the English
Channel for the autumn crab season. As we loaded the gear
aboard spirits were suddenly high with smiling faces to be seen
all around the deck. We were homeward bound at last. We had
a good northerly gale blowing which meant that as soon as the
last pots were loaded aboard, we could turn and run with the
the gale, much more comfortable. But just as the last pots were
loaded, *Kenavo* took a very nasty sea aboard over the starboard
quarter. She was now very heavy in the water with the weight
of all the gear. The heavy green water crashed down, tearing
open the wheelhouse door. The wheelhouse was suddenly full
of water, washing everything overboard and soaking all the
electrical equipment. The worst thing of all was that our charts
and books were gone, including our seaman's bible, Reed's

Nautical Almanac. Finally, the last pot came aboard. I was wet through and cold because of the soaking from the freak wave and I quickly turned south to run with the gale.

A quick damage report revealed all charts gone. The only electrical equipment still working was the ship to shore radio and the direction finder, but the direction finder was no use without the Almanac to find out the frequencies of the lighthouses. Here we were on the borders of Rockall and Malin with a 1,000 mile steam in front of us and no means of navigation. I ran south for several miles. I knew it was roughly the correct course for Barra Head and the North Channel down into the Irish sea. Then I remembered in the galley we had a scruffy old tea towel showing a complete map of the British Isles. It was a tea towel showing all the lifeboat stations around the coast.

I washed all the old stains out of the tea towel and put it to dry on the top of the engine. When it was dry I laid it out on the main table down in the cabin and placing a baked bean can down on it, just north of Northern Ireland, about where I thought we were, I carefully drew around the can and produced a perfect circle. On it I marked the points north, south, east and west and then magnetic north and all the quarter points below east and west. I had my compass rose. This would get us home.

We were making good speed, around 8-9 knots with this northerly gale behind us. Richard cooked up a good meal which we washed down with red wine. We had enough food, fuel and booze aboard for the long run home. The navigation side should not present too much of a problem as long as I could recognise some of the lighthouses along the way. It was a great pity we had lost the Reed's Almanac. Reed's has all the information you need for basic navigation without any charts. In the last of the darkness, the following morning, I recognised two lights that I had become familiar with in recent months, Inishtrahull Lighthouse on the northern tip of Ireland and Rhinnes of Islay

Lighthouse on the south western extremity of Islay. I managed to get a quick fix on both lighthouses and we sailed safely down into the North Channel between the Mull of Kintyre and Belfast.

During the next few days, I took courses off passing ships, guessing as to where they were bound. Once again, what Jeff Scott had taught me years before now came into its own. Jeff wouldn't have needed any charts, so why should I? During the homeward voyage, Richard got a link call to Square Neck from our big radio, through Port Patrick Radio, to arrange a landing of our catch. The best Square Neck could offer was to go straight on to Roscoff or to land in Penzance four days later. With our navigational problems, we opted for Penzance in four days time. And so, on arrival in the Celtic Sea, we had to wait four days before we could land. On the tea towel it clearly showed the island of Lundy off the north Devon coast.

'Do you think we can find it, Scratch?' Rich asked. 'If we can, we'll get in another three days fishing before we land at Penzance.'

'We'll find it okay,' I replied .

After rounding the Smalls I put another 20 degrees east in the course. I remember heading for Yelland Power Station in the coal boat days on the old *Halcience*. After rounding the Smalls, on the south west tip of Wales, *Halcience* always left Lundy on the starboard bow and sure enough, Lundy finally loomed up on our port bow. It was dark when we arrived, so with no charts, we left shooting the gear away until first light next day. Our echo sounder had returned to life with a bit of Richard's magical tinkering. I remember it was a Kelvin Hughes MS 39 paper sounder. I will never forget the name of that sounder. I spent so many hours staring into it.

Dawn next morning and we gingerly shot the gear away, hoping there were no off lying rocks. The seabed looked good and rocky – good lobster country. We fished all around Lundy

Rolling home in *Kenavo*, myself in the wheelhouse. You can tell by the size of my hands!

for the next sixty hours, anchoring now and then for a break. Fishing was good. It was well worth the stop, but now we were running short of everything, bait, fuel, food and the drinks cabinet was completely dry. We loaded the gear and started the last leg of our voyage down the north Cornish coast, around Cape Cornwall, Land's End, past the Tater Du Light and into Penzance to land. We dried *Kenavo* out in Penzance and landed one and a half ton of prime lobster and crayfish and three quarters of a ton of large cock crab from Lundy. We spent the rest of the day and most of the night in the Swordfish Pub on the quayside in Newlyn. I reckoned we deserved a good session.

Square Neck paid us a good price and we made a good grossing. The whole catch then went by lorry to France. The following day we departed Penzance and headed the old ship back east up the English Channel, the final leg home. We ran into a nasty short sea that a fresh east wind always gives in the Channel, but we finally rounded Bolt Head and steamed into Salcombe Harbour. We had been away for almost six months and had clocked up many thousands of sea miles. The *Kenavo* had never missed a beat. We had not let her down, and she had not let us down. Our first trip to distant waters had been a success.

We were soon ashore, leaving the *Kenavo* on a deep water mooring. It was many years later that the new fish quay was built. In those early days everything was taken to and from the boat by the net boat, a small 16ft clinker built dinghy. There was nowhere in Salcombe that we could ever get alongside. We had a good week off before Rich and I met to discuss future fishing plans. Wills and Goon both paid off. Goon went on to skipper a small boat called the *Boa Pescador* out of Salcombe and Wills changed mode and went to work on a scalloper called the *Bucky*. All good sea going experience.

The first thing Rich and I had to do was to make about 150 new pots. Whether fishing is good or poor, overheads are always the same – bait, gear and fuel come top of the expenses list. We had only about 200 of the 350 pots we had originally taken to Scotland and the remaining 200 were not in the best of condition. Many were made of cane and wire and didn't take kindly to being raked around rough seabed in bad weather. With new rope as well, we were looking at roughly £3,000 to get all the gear back up to standard again. That was a lot of money in 1974. We both got stuck in and within a month were ready to go to sea again.

Seven

A NEW CREW

Two new crew members joined us on the *Kenavo*. Colin Brander was an ex merchant seaman who served his time as an apprentice with Houlder Bros. on the South American meat run. He had arrived in Salcombe, made it his home and just went fishing. With our Merchant Navy background, we soon struck up a good friendship and have remained friends ever since. He was to crew for me many times during the next thirty five years. We always knew Colin as CB. The other new addition to the crew was an old school mate of mine, Bimbo Distin, also a survivor of the Whitestrand firework battle. Barry, or Bimbo as everybody knew him, had joined the Royal Navy on leaving school, but really always wanted to go fishing . He definitely ranked among one of the best hands I ever took to sea, totally reliable. It all seemed so natural to him, but he came from a good sea going family, which must have helped.

By the end of October '74 we loaded up the *Kenavo* with 350 pots and headed for the Fs around forty miles out of Salcombe. Not lobster this time, but brown crab and plenty of it, average

Kenavo at Whitestrand, Salcombe, landing a catch from Rockall and Malin,
November 5 1974.

November 5 1975, *Kenavo* at Whitestrand , Salcombe. We put ashore two and three
quarter tons of lobster, three quarters of a ton of crayfish and one ton of large cock crab
from Rockall and Malin. A record catch that still stands today. *Kenavo* looks a little
weather beaten after her eight month voyage.

catch rate of 2 tons per haul with very easy fishing as well. Crab are always found on a soft, sandy, muddy bottom and so the pots survive much better than they do on the rocky bottom where lobster is found. We were also fishing in forty fathoms of water, so the gear was always safe from any storm, but not from Belgium and French trawlers. These trawlers almost put us out of business two years later with the damage they inflicted on our pots.

November 17th of that year and Jane gave birth to our first child, a little girl. We called her Sarah Jane. She was a little beauty. I got to hear about her arrival in quite a novel way. It was before the days of fathers being at the bedside holding hands. We were fishing about fifty miles offshore and I told the local coastguard at Prawle Point that my wife was likely to give birth any day and so it was agreed that he would call me on the radio with a prearranged signal to give me any news. If he asked me what my red Decca coordinate was, it was a girl, if he asked what the purple coordinate was, it was a boy.

We were two days into the trip when, soon after midnight, Richard called me in my bunk.

'I'm not sure what's going on Scratch, but Prawle Point keep asking us what our red Decca coordinate is reading.'

I jumped out of my bunk and shook his hand.

'It's a girl!' I yelled.

He looked at me as if I was bonkers and I then explained the arrangement I had set up with the coastguard.

'Crafty old bugger,' he said and we drank a bottle of Scotch together to celebrate the birth of Sarah Jane.

Eight

SCRUFFY

We stayed in the Fs until late January, which was very late as the crab usually finishes a couple of weeks before Christmas. By February 1st 1975, thoughts of Scotland were returning. Richard detected some problem in the main engine, so we steamed across the Channel to Granville, near St. Malo for a quick top end overhaul. During our visit to Granville, a small, scruffy little crabber from Jersey pulled alongside called the *Stalingrad*. She had previously been owned by the Communist Mayor of Audierne in Brittany, hence the name *Stalingrad*. She was now skippered and owned by a Jersey man called Graham Ingram. His nickname was Scruffy. He was not a big fella but quite stocky and already losing some hair, but all boy. I don't think he could ever complete a sentence without it being half swearing, but that was Scruff. It was easy to see why Scruffy and his crew all fitted the boat so well. They looked like they had been at sea for about two years. I wasn't even sure what colour the *Stalingrad* was supposed to be. It seemed to be just one big rust colour, but looks can deceive and Scruffy, only about twenty years old at the

Scruffy's *Stalingrad*. He just made it back to Jersey and sank.

time, was to become one of the most respected shell fishermen in the English Channel.

I shall never forget the first night ashore with him and his crew. They all had Dover Sole on the bone. After the meal, Scruffy pulled all the Sole bones on to his plate and scoffed the lot! He must have had the constitution of an ox. As the night wore on and the wine and the beer flowed, Scruffy told me he had heard of our success in Scotland the previous year and was going to give Scotland a try this coming summer. I knew what he was after, the locations of our lobster grounds west of Islay. I gave nothing away and told him our best fishing was north of Barra Head, towards the Monarchs and the Flannan Isles. He seemed to swallow this story, but I am sure he was not totally convinced. The last thing we wanted this coming spring was to get back to our golden ground and find the *Stalingrad's* gear all across it.

Graham 'Scruffy' Ingram - top shell fisherman of his day - RIP.

Scruffy's *Kastel Poal*, loaded with pots, resembles the *Kenavo* when she hit rocks in the Sound of Harris.

Two or three days later our engine was ready. We said farewell to Scruffy and his crew, 'We'll see you in Rockall or Malin,' and after that, Scruff and I became pretty good friends. I stayed at his house in Jersey a couple of times. Sadly, we lost him to the sea a few years later.

Nine

'OOT, OOT, OOT
MA HOOS!'

By early March of '75, we were ready to sail for the west coast of Scotland once again, Richard and me, Bimbo and Colin. This would turn out to be a very different summer season from the previous one with Wills and Goon. Once again, the old *Kenavo* was laden down with stores, fuel, bait and a total fishing effort of 350 pots. Our new pots were made of plastic and were very strong. Gone now were the days of wicker, wood and wire.

We had a lousy trip north to Scotland, hugging the Irish coast all the way up through the Irish sea because of strong westerly gales. It was also considerably colder each day as we headed north. It took us a good eighty five hours steaming to arrive at the fishing grounds. We managed to shoot away all the gear in atrocious weather. As soon as it was all over the side we ran away to the north east and took shelter in Scalasaig, the small port on the island of Colonsay. A solitary old gentleman on the quay kindly took our ropes as we pulled alongside the pier. We chatted for a few minutes and he asked where we were from.

'Salcombe, South Devon.' I said and I shall never forget his reply.

In his slow Western Isles accent, he said, 'My goodness, boys! It's a long way to come for a few lobsters.'

Those wise words stuck in the back of my mind for the rest of that season.

It started to snow. Had we been too impatient and sailed too early in search of the illusive blue lobster? On reflection, we had, but life is one big learning curve, and there we were in Scotland. We had established ourselves and now we must make the most of it. Bad weather combined with the sea temperature hindered our fishing effort, but we soldiered on. By May we had made three or four landings in Mallaig, not the big catches of the previous summer, but because of the bad weather, the price of the lobster had almost doubled.

It was after our fifth landing in Mallaig, we had finished landing our catch at about six thirty in the evening and all hands gathered in the Central Bar on the water front. The forecast was, as usual, pretty poor and the Central Bar was heaving with the crews of many boats who were taking shelter for the night. One of these boats was called the *Minnie MacLean*. Her skipper was locally known as Crazy Horse. I think the name MacLean was a well known local fishing family. As the evening wore on, Crazy Horse announced that his missus had gone to Glasgow to see her mother and do some shopping, so there would be a ceilidh at his house on the Mallaig waterfront after the Central Bar kicked out. The news of the ceilidh was well received by all hands in the bar and carry outs were quickly purchased from the local Off License. By midnight, Crazy Horse's house was wild with raucous singing, dancing and drinking. Not long after midnight, what can only be described as a mini tornado swept in through Crazy Horse's front door.

Crazy Horse's wife was not a big woman, but she could pack a punch. She was not due back until the following afternoon, but her plans had changed. I think she had heard the weather forecast and knew that Crazy Horse would be ashore.

All I can remember was, 'Oot! Oot! Oot o' ma hoos!'

She was laying into any fisherman she could with her bags of shopping. Men were climbing out of windows, finding any escape route possible to avoid the wrath of this little lady. Crazy Horse himself ran for the quay where the *Minnie MacLean* was tied up. Engines were started, crew were aboard, ropes let go and the *Minnie MacLean* was gone out of Mallaig Harbour, gale or no gale. To be at sea was the safest option.

The next day we all sailed and Crazy Horse's ceilidh was all the talk between boats on the radio. I am not sure how long Crazy Horse's trip lasted, but he had returned to face the music and the *Minnie MacLean* was tied up in Mallaig next time we landed.

Ten

ST KILDA

In June we rounded Barra Head and headed north to find better fishing. This we found to the west of Toe Head at the western entrance to the Sound of Harris, but the fishing was still patchy. Forty odd miles out into the Atlantic beckoned the tall, mystical island of St Kilda. We had nothing to lose and everything to gain. Fishing is always a bit of a gamble. We loaded *Kenavo* with 200 pots, leaving 150 shot away south of the Monarch Isles.

St Kilda can only be described as a mysterious, magical, sad place. It was inhabited until the 1920s or 30s when, because of disease and famine, the dwindling population was relocated to Glasgow. As we approached St Kilda on that beautiful summer evening in late June, the top of the 1800ft cliffs were shrouded in mist and it reminded me of that first visit to South Africa when I saw Table Mountain for the first time. It hardly got dark at all now in midsummer at theses latitudes, so we got all the gear away that evening and finally anchored in Village Bay on the eastern side of the island, where there were the ruins of a small street. It was obviously where the last inhabitants had lived. After supper we ventured ashore in a small dinghy we carried. There was a proper creepy feeling in this small abandoned village. Suddenly, across the coarse grassland an army Land Rover appeared and four soldiers jumped out. They greeted us like long lost brothers. Unbeknown to us, the army had a radar tracking station at the top of St Kilda. I think it was manned by soldiers who were not too good at behaving themselves on the mainland. They made us most welcome and took us to a small pub they had built called the Puff Inn, all at NAAFI prices. I don't think we really turned in that night. It was broad daylight again by 1 am. We just went back out and started hauling the gear.

'Jackpot!' as Wills had shouted out the previous season. The first pot came up full, five or six good lobsters. And so it went on. The best thing was the gear was only shot away about ten minutes steam out of Village Bay, so we would go out and do the gear in the morning, in for lunch or an hour or so in the Puff Inn, then out again in the afternoon and the lobsters were there again. I don't think any lobster gear had been shot around St Kilda for many years. The French were the last fishermen to visit in the late 1950s.

A high pressure system had settled across Scotland with fine endless calm days. We were lucky. You would never fish St Kilda in any sort of weather. The fishing was dangerous in that you had to get very close in. With a 60ft boat drawing 12ft, you were bound to hit rocks, and we did. The first time was quite a fright, but in Camaret they built strong boats. They had to be for this sort of fishing. Hitting the first rock, we came down on it so hard I bit my tongue and it shook the boat as though we had been torpedoed, but the most dramatic rock dodging was yet to come. After about a week we had as much lobster and crayfish as we could carry, so headed back towards the west coast of Scotland and through the Sound of Harris to Mallaig to land. Square Neck screwed us down on the price, saying the lobsters were too big, but the crayfish sold well. The French loved them. They are known in France as 'rouge royales' and always make a good price.

Through July and August we started a sort of rota system with crew so that we could all have a week at home without stopping the boat from fishing. It worked quite well. The fifth hand to join us was Long Hair or Tony O'Reilly as he was christened. Long Hair was a good hand, always quite cheerful, with a big smile, but we also nicknamed him Wheelhouse Willie. He was always leaving the deck and coming into the Wheelhouse, asking questions about our fishing positions etc. but as a deck hand, he couldn't be faulted. He later became a trawler skipper after sailing with me many times on both my big boats.

We made a very good grossing from that trip to St Kilda, but now, with September approaching, it was time to head back to the English Channel for the autumn crab season and not to leave it as late as we had done the previous year.

Eleven

_____

DIRTY PIRACY

We left Mallaig and steamed past the Hebridean islands of Rhum, Muck and Eigg, across the Minch and back out through the Sound of Harris and into the Atlantic. The first job was to pick up the 150 pots we had left at the Monarchs. We duly arrived back at the Decca co-ordinates at which we had left them. Alas, no sign of a dhan or float of any description. This was not right. The weather had been good and finding the pots should not have been a problem at all. We crept for the pots for about 24 hour hours.

Creeping for lost gear is a nightmare many fishermen have to face, going gently ahead over the Decca co-ordinates of the lost gear, towing a heavy grapnel called the creep. On a sandy bottom, it is pretty easy. The creep just pulls through the sand, but on a rocky seabed, it is much more difficult as the creep hangs and bangs across the seabed.

Our lost pots were all on a rocky seabed.

Finally, after about twenty four hours, we lost the creep as well, but Richard and I were now convinced the pots had been stolen. It was about five years before we were to learn the truth about the fate of our 150 pots. A gentleman from Tiree, who had recently bought a vivier boat from Jersey, had come across them and helped himself. He is long gone now and shall remain nameless, taking his secret to the grave.

Piracy still abounds.

Twelve

'THEY BUILD STRONG SHIPS IN CAMERET.'

With a worsening forecast from the west, the last thing we wanted was to be trapped on a lee shore west of the Outer Hebrides. So we soon loaded up our remaining 200 pots and headed back north from the Monarchs to pass back through the Sound of Harris and into the Minch for shelter to start our long steam home. But, it would be several weeks before we arrived back in Salcombe. We were about to put the *Kenavo* through what I would imagine was going to be the toughest ordeal of her life. I said they built the ships strong in Camaret, I had no idea that they built them that strong.

We had passed through the Sound of Harris several times that summer and thought we knew it quite well. We didn't actually have a chart of the Sound, but I knew from experience that there were many unmarked rocks in these remote places that only local knowledge knew about.

We entered the Sound of Harris at six o'clock in the evening

Kenavo at Ditch End mooring, 1975.

with a full westerly gale behind us and about 4 knots of tide with us. So we were probably doing around 11 knots over the seabed or over the land, as they say. Richard was in the wheelhouse, but was completely blind because of the haystack of pots on the deck in front of him. I went up and sat on top of the pots to call back directions to him.

'Starboard – 10, Port – 10, hold it, Starboard easy.'

Richard was following these directions exactly. All looked well. Then, just off the small village of Leverborough, where the channel was at its narrowest, to my horror, in the raging, turbulent grey water, not fifty yards directly on the bow, I saw kelp breaking the surface.

'Christ, Rich! Hard over!'

Kelp is a long strandy seaweed that grows on rocks just beneath the surface. We were doomed. We didn't stand a chance. Doing 11 knots, we struck the rock like hitting a mine. I held on like a limpet to the foremast and was lucky not to have been thrown overboard into the raging tide and sea. Another life used

Burutu on a calm day in Salcombe, 1982.

up. The Kenavo almost came right out of the water and then fell on her port side, masts horizontal to the sea. The haystack of pots spewed over the port rail into the raging water. I looked back aft towards the wheelhouse to see Richard crawling out of one of the side windows. He hadn't even had time to knock her out of gear and so the propeller, now half in and half out was thrashing the water around the stern into a white foam, like some mad whale that had just been harpooned. She was taking in water fast through the engine room hatch and the fore hatch and I really thought this was the end. We were in a bad situation.

Bimbo and Colin, who had gone to their bunks when we started steaming, soon appeared out of the same window from where Rich had escaped. At least, we were all on deck, but the life raft was mounted on the engine room hatch and was buried in pots. Then a miracle happened. An extra large wave, combined with a bit of tidal surge, came through the Sound from the west

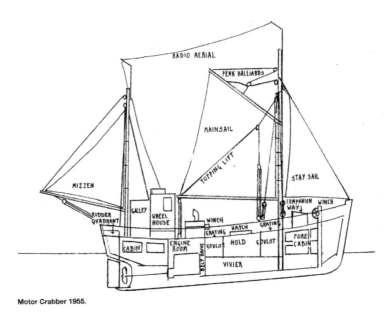

Motor Crabber 1955.

Kenavo, built 1947, Cameret, Brittany.

and spun the *Kenavo* round like a rag doll. With this, she popped upright and came clear of the rock.

All four of us were clinging on to whatever we could grab. Being afloat again, but with no one in the wheelhouse, she started steaming at full speed towards the village of Leverborough. Bimbo managed to get back through the window into the wheelhouse and knock her out of gear. The engine room was flooded, the big flywheel throwing water and hot steam everywhere. We got things under control and limped into the calmer waters of the Minch. By now, it was dark. We reckoned we must have damage under the engine room. The pumps could just keep up with the intake of water, so we headed north up the Minch to Stornaway for an out of water inspection and repairs.

We managed to keep her afloat that night and by midnight the ingression of water had eased. We pulled into the tiny port of Rodel for a breather, making Stornaway the next day and were immediately slipped at the boatyard on Goat Island.

The keel was not a pretty sight. An area right under the engine room had taken the worst battering. It was almost through to the garboard plank (the first plank that adjoins the keel). Had that plank gone, we would have all gone. It took the shipyard at Stornaway about five or six weeks to repair our keel, so we all travelled home for an unexpected good break.

Thirteen

'THEY BUILD STRONG ENGINES, TOO.'

We relaunched the *Kenavo* at Goat Island shipyard, Stornaway, in late September or early October of 1975. Loading our remaining pots, we sailed south to our original golden ground west of Islay, trying for a catch to land back in Salcombe: not a good move. The winter weather had set in on the west coast of Scotland giving just one gale after another. We could work in a gale of wind but the huge Atlantic swells killed the fishing off. I expect the lobsters and crayfish were just hanging on to any rock they could find down there and not many were going into our pots. By the end of October, we finally had a decent catch aboard and were homeward bound.

Unlike the year before with Wills and Goon when we had a northerly gale behind us, this time we faced a southerly gale. The southerly wind held all the way to Land's End, right on the nose, but, at least this time, we had charts. The old *Kenavo* made heavy weather of it, taking the best part of 36 hours to get down to the Isle of Man.

With the Isle of Man now about 30 miles astern of us, we were faced with another crisis.

Bimbo had just come off watch at midnight. Coming off watch, it was always your duty to go into the engine room and pump up the diesel header tank for the main engine. This task only took five minutes but it meant that someone went into the engine room every two hours and would notice any problems, such as a split pipe, a diesel leak or a water leak. This system was a French idea and in my opinion, was good practice.

Bimbo entered the engine room but was immediately driven back into the cabin by steam, hot water and smoke.

'*Christ, Scratch, we're sinking!*'

Richard was out of his bunk in a second and dived into the engine room, in his underpants, disappearing into the fog of the engine room. I raced up to the wheelhouse and immediately turned her 180 degrees to run with the sea. The old ship settled down much better running with it. Rich had managed to get the big emergency bilge pump working and within half an hour, the engine room was pumped dry but the big main dynamo, which provided all our electrical power, had been underwater so we were now running on batteries. How the main engine had kept going, I shall never know. Rich said the water was not far from the main air intakes,

'They also know how to build engines in Camaret,' was his remark.

With our electrical power about to run out, we decided to return to Peel on the Isle of Man to repair the dynamo. The odd thing was, once we had pumped out, she stayed dry. We never knew where the water in the engine room had come from – a mystery we would never solve. Maybe it was something to do with the rocks we hit around the Sound of Harris, but we never found out.

Twenty four hours in Peel and Rich had got the dynamo

charging again – clever old bugger. But he did get a good electric shock from the radar while testing the system, turning half his beard green. He did look comical – black beard, green highlights.

The weather was a little better when we left the Isle of Man and headed south again, on down through the Irish Sea, past the Tusker Rock and into the Celtic Sea. About twenty hours out of Land's End, a little voice came squeaking over the radio,

'Kenavo, Kenavo, Stalingrad, Stalingrad, Channel 6. Anybody about?'

It was Scruffy. He was about two miles to the west of us and had recognised us, a big Frenchman plodding along on the same course. The Stalingrad was smaller than us and still hadn't had a coat of paint, so she was difficult to see but we slowly converged on each other. He was also homeward bound, to Jersey. We stayed in company together around Land's End and all the way up to the Lizard. Scruff's course then took him more south east to Jersey and so we parted company. I had several good chats with him on the radio. Unbeknown to us, he had been fishing at the Flannan Isles about sixty miles north of St. Kilda and the Monarchs and had done quite well. I told him about our Sound of Harris drama.

'Yea,' he said, 'I think I have altered the underwater shape of the Stalingrad quite a bit as well.'

Scruffy managed to make it back to Jersey by the skin of his teeth. The Stalingrad was barely able to get on to the slipway at Jersey before she sank. But Scruffy put a good catch of Flannan Isle lobsters ashore at low water the next morning. I don't think the Stalingrad ever sailed again and Scruff came to Salcombe after Christmas and bought the Kastel Paol from Richard Cove.

Fourteen

BACK TO THE ENGLISH CHANNEL

We finally arrived back in Salcombe on November 5th, 1975. It was evening and fireworks were lighting up the harbour. We had been away for eight months and once again had steamed thousands of miles. I felt the *Kenavo* had looked after us perhaps more than we had looked after her on this voyage, but we were now, all four of us, safely home.

The following day, Square Neck sent a lorry over on the Roscoff ferry to Salcombe. We landed at Whitestrand and dried the *Kenavo* out in front of the town where the rocket fight had been staged against the Salcombe-ites only fifteen years before.

We landed two and three-quarter tons of lobsters and crayfish – another record to go into the archives of Salcombe's fishing history.

About a week or so after that landing, we steamed forty miles south out into the English Channel to the Fs and shot away our remaining 200 pots to catch the end of the hen crab season. Fishing was good. Being a vivier boat we could keep our catch aboard for a six day trip and then land in France, making a good price, unlike the day boats from Salcombe and Dartmouth, landing every night at their home port to the crab processing factories for a fixed price.

And so, Richard and I pioneered the shellfish export trade from the south coast of England to Europe.

Within a few years the penny dropped and more and more vivier boats arrived in south west ports.

Christmas came and went and 1976 arrived. By mid-January the hen season was over and we slowly moved further east up the English Channel, our main quarry being large cock crab and lobster. They are abundant in the spring, on the harder rockier ground between Cap de la Hague and Portland Bill. We came across a large Jersey and Guernsey fleet of about fifteen boats, all juggling for good ground. Among them was Scruffy aboard his newly acquired command, the *Kastel Paol*.

Most nights we would all tie up in Braye Harbour, Alderney for a few hours. January, February and March of those late 1970s and early 1980s would often see as many as fifteen vivier boats a night in Alderney. I can only leave to your imagination the scene in the Divers Inn and the Sea View Hotel on Alderney seafront each night with all those fishing boats tied up for a few hours. The landlord of the Divers Inn at the time, a fellow called John Allen, told me one night he made more money those three months than for the whole tourist season.

Most trips to the grounds north of Alderney that winter usually lasted for about seven to ten days. They were filled with many dramas of one sort or another: engine failures and the need to tow each other in, very difficult working conditions through gale after gale. Calm days are very few and far between at that time of year in the English Channel – the further east, the stronger the tide and the rougher the sea bed.

Creeping and looking for lost gear was an on-going problem. Our boats were not really powerful enough to cope with the strong tidal flow. All of us could have done with an extra hundred horsepower to keep up over the tide when hauling, but somehow we always managed to get a catch aboard and secure a good grossing.

Fifteen

VEHICLE TRADING AND RUSSIANS TO WINDWARD

In Alderney at that time vehicles were not subject to MOT tests and so to help ease the expenses of a trip, we sometimes loaded a couple of MOT failures on deck to be sold in Alderney on arrival. This trick often paid for the bait. Alderney was always very keen on the import trade and Scruffy would also frequently start his trip from Jersey loaded up with building bricks. Many deals were clinched in the Divers Inn and one particular trip stands out in my mind.

There was an old Bedford van and a Morris 1000 van that we had for delivery to Alderney. We laid scaffolding planks across the deck of *Kenavo* and using these, we shoved and pushed our load carefully on board. Leaving Customs Quay we returned to our mooring at Ditch End where we tied them down securely, ready for the trip across the channel. Unfortunately, unbeknown to any of us, the hand brake on the Morris 1000 failed and the poor old van gently wheeled over the starboard side to a watery grave. Often, when I am on the Ditch End mooring, I think of the Morris 1000 van that sits underneath us, probably home to a few lobsters and conger eels today. If anyone wants a Morris 1000 engine, I know where there is one.

Another incident about that time also sticks in my mind. It was a typical nasty day in late March'76, grey, blowing a gale and raining. We had just hauled a string of 80 pots and had them aboard ready to shoot away, when it seemed from out of nowhere appeared a large Russian factory trawler of about 2,000 tons. She wasn't fishing, just gently cruising along on the same course that we wanted to shoot away our pots. She was about 300 yards to windward of us, forming a huge sort of breakwater. Ideal, I thought – a bit of calmer water in which to shoot away our gear.

It was looking good. Smiling faces looked up from the deck, all enjoying a small respite from the gale. Unfortunately, the Russian factory trawler was moving slightly faster than us. Many members of her crew were lining the rail looking down on us, probably in amazement as we weren't much bigger than one of her lifeboats. They must have thought – 'Crazy English'. Disaster was about to strike. As her stern finally cleared our bow a huge freak wave the size of a house was revealed.

Long Hair yelled, '*Hold tight everyone!*'

I turned the *Kenavo* as hard as I could, trying to put the wave behind us, but no chance – we were buried.

I remember looking forward, out through the wheelhouse windows. It was like being under a huge waterfall. The whole deck was completely flooded, pots everywhere. We had taken such a huge surge forward on this giant wave, the backline, connecting all the pots together, had snapped like a carrot. You don't often part off the gear while shooting away. The biggest disaster of all was that the shithouse, situated behind the wheelhouse, was obliterated, lying in pieces all around the deck. Life would never be the same. As the old *Kenavo* surfaced and shook the water from her decks, a huge cheer came from the stern of the Russian trawler as she disappeared into the gloom. We never did rebuild the shithouse. After that, it was 'bucket and chuck it.'

By the early summer of that year, we moved back to the hen crab ground further to the west, about fifty miles south of Salcombe all along the western end of the Hurd Deep. We reckoned we'd had our money's worth out of Scotland over the previous two years, so we did not return north in the summer of '76 but just kept plodding away on the hen crab. I always found hen crab fishing pretty boring and monotonous but it was steady money and Jane was due to have our second child.

Sixteen

CLOSE CALL FOR TONY

It was during the summer of '76 hen crab fishing that Bimbo paid off the *Kenavo* for domestic reasons. His place on the crew was quickly filled by a fella called Tony Lyle. Tony had spent most of his working life farming and building and was in his late twenties. A tall, slim guy, strong and very willing, he always hankered after a change of career and wanted to spend some time at sea. He had signed on the right boat but it would be a near fatal accident with Tony that alerted me to the very real dangers of shooting away the gear.

The weather was good. Deck accidents often happen in good weather, mainly because men drop their guard and relax a bit. A good mate of mine, Winkle Parsons, had his arm completely severed by a winch just a couple of miles off Salcombe in good weather. It's not always the horrendous weather that catches you out.

Tony was on the starboard rail of the *Kenavo* shooting the pots away when he slipped and one foot went into a coil of rope that was snaking over the side. In no time, the rope came tight around his ankle and he was pulled down the deck to what we call the shooting bar. This two inch diameter steel bar guides the rope over the starboard side of the boat to keep it clear of the propeller. I quickly grasped the situation and dived out of the wheelhouse with a knife, cutting through the backline and releasing Tony who fell to the deck with a great look of relief on his face. A fatal accident had been averted. After that incident we concentrated a great deal more whilst shooting away, especially on calm days. A few years later, I lost a fella over the side on the *Burutu,* but weather conditions were very different that day. Tony stayed as crew on the *Kenavo* and then went to work on oilrig supply ships in the North Sea before returning home to spend the rest of his working life as a builder.

Throughout that summer we were landing all the crab directly into France at the Port of Primel on the eastern entrance to the Morlaix river. The usual battles with Square Neck about price occurred most landings, but we usually kissed and made up and he almost always took Rich and me out for a good lunch after each landing. I am sure we were good business for Primel. Since the spring of '74, we had landed hundreds of thousands of pounds worth of shellfish to them. Poor old Fanny Backrope, she could have had all that had she not fallen into the vivier and drowned, but it was not to be.

Seventeen

SERIOUS FRACAS WITH BELGIAN TRAWLERS

And so, we had landed in Primel as usual, but on our way back across the channel, disaster was once again about to strike.

We would always haul the gear once on the way home and then have a few days off. It was still dark as we approached the gear, located around mid-channel, but we began to see what appeared to be a city of lights – not a good sign at all. As daylight broke it revealed about twenty large Belgian side-winders. A side-winder is a trawler that hauls nets over the side. More modern trawlers of today haul in over the stern – they are stern-draggers.

To cut a long story short, we recovered about 20 of our original 380 pots. In a few hours the Belgian fishermen had obliterated our gear along with our livelihood. The 20 odd pots we did retrieve weren't worth keeping – they were battered and broken. We rounded up alongside a few of the trawlers holding up pots and broken rope but to no avail, they didn't want to know. They were in a fishing frenzy for some valuable species that they had stumbled upon, probably squid, and the last thing on their minds was an English boat's pots. The situation became quite heated and by midday we had resorted to throwing missiles at wheelhouses, but we were no match for them. They were twice the size of the *Kenavo* and had just as much right to fish there as we did.

We could only assume the Belgian fleet was not made up of gentlemen. No good honest fisherman knowingly tows through another man's gear out of sheer greed. In an effort to salvage what we could, we attempted to creep amongst the trawlers but it was really quite dangerous. In a collision situation, we would have definitely come off worse.

We pulled into Salcombe about twenty four hours later. It was futile looking for any more pots; we were wiped out.

Eighteen

SALCOMBE PILOT

I walked up the hill to our little house at Lakeside and told Jane the bad news and 'Gosh,' she said, 'another baby on the way and no pots.' Fate, however, was about to take a hand once again: 'better born lucky than rich' as the saying goes. The following day the Harbourmaster phoned and asked if I would pop into his office to see him.

Jim Blazeby had taken over from Laurie Prynn after Laurie's retirement. He explained that a large Spanish trawler, about 120ft long and drawing about 20ft and which was converted for carrying shellfish live, wanted to call at Salcombe to pick up a cargo of live shellfish for export to Spain. Did I think it was possible to get her in and out of Salcombe and, if so, would I be the official Salcombe pilot to bring her in and take her out again? I knew it was quite important to all the local fishermen that this ship, the *Natalie*, should make the visit. The spider crab season was in full swing and this was a much needed outlet for them.

The *Natalie* drew about 20ft, roughly 6ft more than the

Kenavo and I felt sure I could get her in, but it would be leaving that may present a problem. The Salcombe Bar slopes upwards as you go out. I had caught the sand a few times with the *Kenavo*, but a quick bump and you are in. When leaving, however, there is a hill of sand to climb in order to get over the shallowest part. I felt pretty confident I could bring the *Natalie* in along the western side of the leading marks in the slightly deeper water under Bar Foot, as it is known locally. It is a rockier bottom, but a fair bit deeper than where the leading marks bring you in. On the strength of this, I took up Jim Blazeby's offer and became the Salcombe Pilot.

The following day, at around 7.30am, right on the top of a spring tide, I boarded the *Natalie* and brought her safely into Salcombe Harbour where I moored her up on a deepwater mooring at Snapes Point. I don't think her echo sounder was working too well. According to the information it was giving out, we were aground – never put all your trust in electronics. The *Natalie* took a good few tons of spider crab all that day and I returned her safely back to sea on top of the evening tide. She was probably the biggest ship to enter Salcombe Harbour since the arrival of the big American ships involved in the D Day landings in 1944.

Nineteen

TRANSPORTING BEGINS

The *Natalie* returned to Salcombe only a couple more times. The fishermen were not happy. There were always disputes about payment and other problems of a financial nature. But her absence heralded three good years for Kenavo Fisheries at what could not have been a better time, after our recent mauling by the large Belgian trawlers.

Late one hot afternoon, during the early summer of '76, Griff pulled alongside the *Kenavo*,

'Ere Billy, why not load up the *Kenavo* with all our spiders and run them across to Square Neck in France? That bloody *Natalie* ain't never coming back and us'll be stuck with the buggers,' or words to that effect.

Griff was one of those real old Salcombe characters, a stocky, middle aged man with a Beatles' haircut and one of the strongest Devonian accents you have ever heard. He was a good fisherman, coxswain of the lifeboat, top euchre player and, for some reason, always called me Billy. He was a great one though for christening people with nicknames that invariably suited the victim down to a tee. Sadly, Griff was hauled overboard by his own gear nine years later and drowned.

It was Griff who got us into the shellfish export business.

Richard called Square Neck and told him the plan. A fixed price was soon agreed and within twenty four hours, the *Kenavo* was loaded with about 15 tons of prime spider crab for the Spanish market. We were way overloaded – our vivier for spider crabs was around 7 tons but we loaded another 8 tons into water tanks on deck. This made her a little unstable but the weather was good and it was only twelve hours across the Channel to Primel. We arrived there early next morning and dried the *Kenavo* out to unload on the morning tide. Square Neck asked us if we could bring another 15 tons that same week. Things were looking good.

Homecoming was via St. Peter Port, Guernsey, where we filled the boat up with cheap diesel – we were in business. We did at least one trip a week to France until well into the autumn of that year and the bank account started to look good.

The summer of '76 was very hot. Poor old Jane had to wait until the twelfth of August before our son, Robert, put in an appearance. Once again I was not present for the birth but I did take her in a bottle of Scotch much to the amazement of the other new mums who had to put up with flowers, chocolates and fruit. I'm sure I drank most of the Scotch, but she had produced a fine son, God bless her.

During that winter and into the spring of 1977 we did many trips to France, carrying lobster and hen crab but the price differential was quite small. However, it kept the wolf from the door. By April '77 the spiders had started again and two trips a week to France was not uncommon. We opened up our buying ports and loaded at Cawsand in Cornwall and Dartmouth. A good week was 20 tons.

It was always a big day in Cawsand with the arrival of the

Kenavo to load spiders for France. The two main fishermen in Cawsand, at that time, were Tony Jago and Mike Henwood. They were a partnership and over the years owned several boats. Both were good fishermen in their day and landed many good catches to us.

The real excitement came from some of the local schoolboys, average age about nine to twelve years. There were six or seven of them and they had somehow acquired clapped out little rowing boats and two or three crab pots each. All week, after school or before, they would haul up their pots and store their few crabs in a storage cage ready to land them to the *Kenavo*. So each week I would have an envelope for Sam, Tommy, Shane, Bobo and so on. Sometimes there would be £20 to £30 to come. I remember one week, one of them turned up with a small outboard engine he had bought with his earnings. He was Jack the lad in Cawsand. When I see youngsters today, addicted to their phones and i-pads, I do feel sorry for them, but this is their world. I am sure the kids of Cawsand had much more fun catching those crabs and those were, without a doubt, the final years of freedom.

Twenty

T'WAS THE DEVIL

In Dartmouth, one of the local fishermen, Grey Lynn christened us the 'Cog Tycoons' – a cog being the local name for spider crab. So in June of '77, the bank account was looking quite healthy and Richard wanted to return to fishing again but this time with his own boat. We amicably dissolved our partnership and I bought Rich out, so I was now the sole owner of Kenavo Fisheries. Rich went his own way and bought a fine 40ft crabber called the *Silver Spray* – another Frenchman but with no vivier. He wanted to do day trips to the Alderney grounds as he had done with the *Ibis* in the early seventies and I continued with the spider exporting with no problems until mid-July.

We were loading spiders in a small port called Hope Cove, just a couple of miles down the coast from Salcombe. Here lived John Jarvis, another fishing character about the same age as Griff, a proper one for the ladies with a big shock of whitish blonde hair. Always good for a laugh, was John. John's father, Jack, also a fisherman but in the twilight of his fishing years was known locally as the Devil. I never knew exactly why but had a good idea. Even his son, John, always called him the Devil.

I had anchored in Hope Cove the previous evening to start loading spiders at first light the following morning. Slowly and silently, at first light, out of the fog appeared the Devil. He ghosted alongside and in the same strange silence passed me up a medium sized basket with six of the largest spider crabs I had ever seen. His boat didn't even stop alongside the *Kenavo* but as silently as he had arrived, without a word, he disappeared into the swirling morning fog. Usual practice was to weigh the crab and tell the fisherman his weight, but too late, the Devil had gone, seemingly uninterested in any sort of formal transaction. By about 9.30am, we finished loading at Hope Cove and I didn't give the incident any more thought.

And so I set sail for France with a good cargo aboard. Unbeknown to me, that evening a huge super tanker, the *Amoco Cadiz,* had run aground on rocks at a small village called Portsall on the Brittany coast, about 20 miles west of Primel, spewing its black cargo of death all along the Brittany coast in both directions. In the early daylight, we entered Primel. The French unloading gang were already on the quay waiting for our arrival, but as I pulled alongside they began pointing down to what was a huge black oil slick all around our white waterline. Unknowingly, during the night, I had steamed through a large oil slick from the *Amoco Cadiz*. Oil had entered our vivier and begun to kill our precious live cargo.

We wasted no time and started to discharge our load, but the oil had already started to take its toll. Oil floats on top of water and the 8 tons of crab we were carrying, was lying about 4ft deep in the vivier. The crabs lying in the top half were dead, poisoned by the oil. The bottom 2ft had survived, but half our catch was dead. We only managed to land about three and a half tons live. Thank you, *Amoco Cadiz*; not much profit in that trip. The disaster with the tanker caused chaos and big pollution problems along the Brittany coast for many months to come, forcing us to land much further east at the Port of Paimpol until well after Christmas that year.

A fortnight or so later we were again loading at Hope Cove. The Devil's son, John Jarvis, pulled alongside with another good catch of beautiful quality spider crab. He came aboard after we had finished loading and, over a mug of coffee, I told him the story of the trip two weeks ago and the *Amoco Cadiz*.

'Ah,' said John, quick as a flash, 'You shouldn't have taken them crabs off the Devil.'

I had honestly forgotten about the Devil coming out of the fog that morning two weeks ago, but John was convinced it was the Devil who had sent the *Amoco Cadiz* off course and on to the Brittany coast.

'No need for a Board of Trade enquiry,' said John, 'T'was the Devil's work.

Twenty-One

RULES AND REGS

And so the summer of '77 slipped by. Until about August of that year, my whole life had been free from government bullshit and regulations, but the net of bureaucracy was about to start closing around me and haunt me throughout the rest of my working life.

The biggest problem was that all the new rules and regulations the government and all its departments started to throw at us were invariably made up by people who had no experience of the industry for which they were making up the rules; master mariners from the Royal Navy and Merchant Navy making up rules of safety for fishing vessels. A master mariner may well be very capable of taking a ship around the world to Australia and back – no problem, but that is light years away from doing a ten-day trip on a trawler or shellfish boat in bad weather.

It is still the case to this day and we just have to do the best we can to steer around all the restrictions and rules that they have the power to impose but which can actually cost lives. I almost lost my life and that of my crew in 1991, strictly following the letter of the law. It was solely due to having a bit of equipment aboard that saved our lives, something the ministry would never have thought about in a thousand years.

This could well ruffle a few feathers, but the truth should be known. I have yet to meet a skipper, inshore or deep sea, who would not back me up on this.

By now, Black Jake, the Customs Officer for Salcombe had retired and a really nice fellow called Phil Andrews took over. He was completely bald so was very quickly given the nickname Kojak after Telly Savalas of the TV detective series fame. We had just about finished loading our cargo of spider crab when Kojak appeared at the rail of the *Kenavo*.

'Bad news I'm afraid, Scratch. It's my duty, as Her Majesty's Customs Officer, to stop this ship from sailing because you are not a fishing vessel but a British cargo ship operating without a load line or plimsol line.' (A plimsol line is a line that shows the depth of the ship when laden.) He was very good about it and seemed almost embarrassed to be the one to have to stop us. He knew the importance of this trade for the South Devon fishermen.

Jealousy is an ugly thing. We had been shopped – reported to the customs for this infringement of the rules by a sad fellow who has now departed this life and shall remain nameless. As I was fully loaded, Kojak, agreed to let me sail this one last time but, before we could get clearance again, we must carry a load line. I chugged across the channel that night pondering how I could get around this huge problem. To apply for a load line and go through all the bureaucracy would cost an absolute fortune and then, to captain a ship with a load line, I would require a master's ticket. The whole situation looked pretty bleak.

We discharged cargo in France as usual but I told Square Neck about the problem that faced me. He said, 'You want to see a good marine lawyer when you get home.' That seemed to make good sense.

Twenty-Two

SCROGGSY

I steamed the old *Kenavo* back to Salcombe and there were all the boys waiting again to load their spiders. 'Hold on,' I said and told them of the problem that now faced us and also what Square Neck had said about a marine lawyer.

'Scroggsy's the boy for you, Scratch,' said Tommy Preston, one of the fishermen who, in the past, had had some dealings with marine law.

And so it was. One hot sunny August afternoon, I managed to locate Scroggsy's office: Ken Scroggs, Marine Law, The Plains, Totnes. I entered Ken's office to be greeted by his secretary. 'Oh,' she said, 'Mr. Scroggs is in court but he shouldn't be very long. Would you like to wait in his office?' and I was shown through. His office was just how I imagined – definitely not Canary Wharf.

I waited for about half an hour, I suppose. The silence was broken by a bit of noise in the outer office, then the door burst open.

'And what's your bloody problem?' were his opening words.

Before I could answer, he walked around the back of his desk, sat down, loosened his tie and pulled it to one side, produced a bottle of Scotch and two glasses and said, 'Christ! what a bloody day that was.'

Things had probably not gone well for Scroggsy that day in court, but I knew I had found the right man. He pushed a large glass of whisky across the table to me and then just said, 'Good health.' We both drank. You don't get lawyers like that today. I explained my problem to Scroggsy, who, without consulting any marine law books, solved the problem in an instant, whilst pouring two more large whiskies.

'Simple,' he said with great authority. 'Just get all the fishermen to buy a £1 share in the *Kenavo*, then they are carrying their crab on their boat.' And that's how we got around the load line problem. Ken Scroggs, attorney in marine law, never even gave me a bill but accepted two large cock crabs as payment a few days later. Good old Scroggsy. I would say things are a little different today if you have a problem with marine law.

I drove back to Salcombe and told Kojak the good news. 'I'm so pleased,' he said, 'I knew there would be a way around it.' That night we loaded the *Kenavo* again with a full cargo for Square Neck. Everyone was happy except for the grass who had shopped us to the Customs. He smoked a pipe and was bald. That is all I will say.

Twenty-Three

DINO SOBERS UP

Because we were not fishing, I only had one other crew member aboard the *Kenavo* to stand a watch during night crossing of the channel. When fishing, there were four of us. A fellow called Tony Crunch, an ex-fairground wrestler, was crewing for me at this time. Not a man to tangle with, but he was a good lad, not a true seaman, although I soon taught him enough to keep a watch. About an hour before sailing one trip, he had some big problem that had just come up but said, 'Don't worry, Scratch, I've organised a replacement crew member.'

James Dean Barratt was slumped over the bar at the Fortescue. 'There he is, Scratch, he will sail with you, at least he said he would before he passed out.' Dino, as we always knew him, was the last of a dying breed of seaman cum fisherman. He was around twenty two years old then and had been at sea all his young life. To say alcohol ruled his life would be an understatement. He was ex merchant navy but also had worked on trawlers and oilrig supply ships. He stood around 6ft, quite well built with a mop of blond hair. He had a scar across his left cheek and his left eye was missing; he lost it talking when he should have been listening and had a broken bottle pushed in his face in a friendly Glasgow dockside pub. His party piece, when funds were low, was to drop his false eye into someone's pint at the bar. 'Aye, aye there, I've got an eye on your pint,' which was then claimed by Dino when the victim invariably didn't fancy any more.

Dino came to.

'Mine's a gin and tonic,' he said, 'make it a large one, I've got to go to sea with Scratch tonight, so I'd better sober up.'

'I am Scratch,' I informed him.

'Christ, so you are. What time are we off?' 'Now,' I said, 'forget the gin and tonic.' I helped Dino out of the Fortescue and within an hour, we were on our way. Although Dino had had a big alcohol problem all his life, he was trustworthy and reliable – well, almost. He worked for me many times after that and was generally a good all round hand.

Twenty-Four

MORE BUREAUCRACY

In October 1977, Jane and I had finally managed to save enough money to put down a deposit on our first house. It was quite a milestone really, and we are still in the same house forty years later. We moved three miles away from Salcombe to the small village of Malborough and bought a thatched cottage, with a modern extension on one end, called Bridle Cottage. The old part of the cottage dates back to 1620 and was built to house the labourers who built the church all those years ago.

By November of that year, the dreaded net of bureaucracy had another squeeze. All British fishing vessels over 50ft, had to go through a very stringent examination to check for so called seaworthiness. A whole host of senseless rules were made up. There were some good rules but many were just bureaucratic, inappropriate and silly. These rules made up by the DTI sent many honest fishermen bankrupt. They did not apply to Channel Island registered boats, so a quick trip to Guernsey and I re-registered the *Kenavo* in St. Peter Port. She was registered GU 5116 and so I gave up the UK registered number of SE 61 that old Black Jake had given us, but at least we were still in business.

PART TWO

BURUTU

One

J 633

By the spring of '78, the old *Kenavo* was starting to show her age. It was time to look for a newer, possibly bigger vessel. Raymond Square Neck to the rescue. After one particularly long, lazy, boozy lunch, having landed the cargo, Square Neck told me about a Camaret registered boat called the *Burutu*, which had just returned from a voyage to Morocco for crayfish. During the trip, in some bad weather, her skipper, Monsieur Moodinear had taken a heavy fall and damaged his shoulder quite badly. Being hundreds of miles at sea and in some considerable pain, his crew had administered morphine to him. French boats at that time all carried morphine in the medical chest. Perhaps a little too much morphine, washed down with a little too much red wine had spelled the end of Moodinear's sea going career, hence the *Burutu* was now lying in port waiting for a new skipper.

The following day Square Neck drove me down to Camaret, the port where Richard and I had bought *Kenavo* five years before. As soon as I saw her, I knew she was the right boat for me. She was all-round chunkier and bigger than the *Kenavo* –

Burutu lands a well-earned catch on Ditch End Beach, from NW of the Scillies and SW approaches 1981.

Burutu dried out on Ditchend Beach, from where I sailed on a telegraph pole when I was a kid.

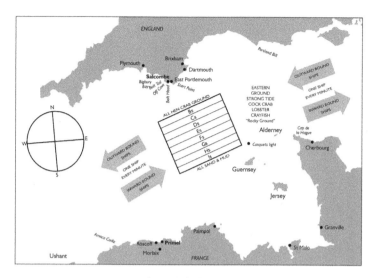

The English Channel.

Burutu loaded with 600 pots, about to sail for the west coast of Scotland, 1980.

Burutu J633, an all-weather ship, 1980.

more horse power, ten foot longer, four foot wider, deeper and almost twice the carrying capacity – what you could call an all weather ship and I was certainly going to put her through all weathers over the coming few years. Within a month, she was mine and I had an enormous feeling of pride that day I steamed her out of Camaret, around the Brest peninsula, up through the English Channel and brought her into Salcombe. She was the biggest shellfish boat in the UK. For several years to come we pioneered the scene, which would eventually set up the multi-million pound shellfish industry in the UK and which thrives today on export and foreign markets. The super crabber had arrived. Today, modern ships, the same size as the old *Burutu* and bigger, now fish all sea areas around the UK and as far north as the Shetlands.

I registered the *Burutu* from day one in Jersey, her registration was J 633 and we soon acquired the nickname '633 Squadron' among other vessels with Jersey registration.

During 1977-1978, vivier lorries started to cross the English Channel by ferry. These lorries had huge tanks in them able to carry 8-10 tons of shellfish live from south coast ports back to the continent where the big markets were. This situation spelled the end of my days transporting fish across the channel, and so by Christmas of '78 I very soon fitted out the *Burutu* with 500 pots and returned to fishing.

Two

<hr>

GOOD-BYE, OLD FRIEND

The old *Kenavo* languished in Salcombe harbour for about six months before I managed to sell her.

She had deteriorated quite badly, not being used, but I managed to get £1000 for her from an old coaster skipper from Bude in north Cornwall. Jane made me get him to sign something to say he had only bought the engine and the boat was scrap. We never imagined he would get her around Land's End but he did, steering her with a large spanner because I told him I wanted to keep the wheel. He phoned me when he arrived and all was well. It was sad in a way to see the old *Kenavo* go but, alas, she was surplus to requirements. However, she had been a lucky old ship, she had certainly been through some close scrapes with Richard and me in the early '70s but some vessels do lead a charmed life.

*

Within three years she had moved to Bristol from Bude and was bought by a filming company who spent hundreds of thousands of pounds on her. She was put back to sea as a fully rigged schooner, then crossed the Atlantic to do film work in the Caribbean. Returning to the UK in the early '90s, she was lost in the Atlantic west of Ireland. They changed her name to *Carrie* – perhaps she didn't like that. I kept the clock and barometer as well as the wheel and they now adorn my house. Had I not done that, everything of *Kenavo* would be lost – at the bottom of the Atlantic.

Three

EMERGENCY AT SEA

Back to the fishing and the first couple of trips on *Burutu* were not too profitable due to trouble with the engine and the fishing gear. I was very wary of trawlers after being wiped out on *Kenavo* by the Belgian vessels. Trying to keep clear of trawlers, we were fishing north east of Cap de la Hage off the Cherbourg peninsula in far too much tide. The gear was continually getting damaged. Fishing is not easy. Crew members on those early trips were Colin Brander, who had come to Scotland with me, and Spud Cudd, a very good old seasoned hand. Spud sailed with me several times on and off during the next ten years. The third hand was a youngster called Rabso Preston. Rob Preston, or Rabso as he was known, was the son of Tommy Preston who had told me to go and see Scroggsy, the marine lawyer back in the spider crab days.

During the second or third trip, Rabso suddenly became very ill. I seemed to think it was meningitis, but no, it was encephalitis. I got him into hospital in Alderney from where he was immediately flown back to the UK. The doctor in Alderney told me later I had done well to get him in; it was a bit touch and go. However, Rabso survived but he never went deep sea again yet went on to become probably the best inshore fisherman Salcombe has seen in many years.

Four

FISHING TRIP TO CHERBOURG

It was mid January and the tide had cut away to under 5.2 in the Salcombe book. It was time to head the old *Burutu* back up the English Channel for another ten day fishing voyage. I found it harder and harder to leave home. The children were just getting to an interesting age, but somehow you manage to get yourself together and you're off again.

Richard and I nipped into Kingsbridge to get the stores. I had loaded the bait the previous day and gone through the boat checking all was ready to go. Weather was invariably bad in the Channel in January and February and the tide would not really ease for another two days.

Long Hair was on for another trip and the fourth hand was a rooky called John Stephens. John was studying Marine Science at University and turned out to be a really nice fella.

We slipped out of Salcombe just after midnight. The weather was still and calm. I set course to 30 miles north of Cherbourg.

With the tide up our ass we were looking at about a six hour steam to get us back into the gear that was shot in a 14 mile square north of Cap de la Hague. We would arrive at first light. The small 6 inch buoys left on the gear at the previous springs had to be replaced by our big 40 inch dhan buoys and our first task would be to 'dhan-up.'

When gear is left on a building tide, the big dhan buoys are removed and replaced by small 6 inch buoys which go 'to tide'. As the tide goes over the springs they lie down on the sea bed and the gear comes to no harm. Every six hours, with the slack water, they reappear on the surface, but as soon as the tide runs again, down they go. To find all sixteen 6 inch buoys in one slack water demands being pretty slick. In bad weather it is often only possible to get half of them in one slack, which means waiting for the afternoon slack to finish the job. But by that first evening, all the gear should be fishing again.

The first haul was quite good: a slack ton of mainly cock crabs, 250 lb of mixed lobster and two crayfish, a fair bit of cod and mixed fish. We were in high spirits that night on the *Burutu*. Richard left his post on deck and soon the wonderful smell of cooking drifted across from the galley. Rich had always been a bit of a 'foody', and in all our time together at sea, he would get together the evening meal – almost a ritual.

The wind had increased a bit from the west throughout the day. This made an awkward sea with the west going tide, but it did improve when the tide turned east. St Peter Port had given out gale warnings for most of the day, but this was not unusual and a gale force wind was no reason to stop fishing. We had ten days to get a trip in and we certainly did not want to lose a day.

The door to the wheelhouse from the galley swung open and Rich passed through a bottle of sherry.

'Have a belt of this, Scratch, before I drink the lot.'

I grabbed the bottle and took a long pull. Boy, it was good.

'They've been giving out gales all day from St.Peter Port,' I said.

Rich just grunted, 'So what's new? They've got a record in there that they keep playing over and over.'

Long Hair and John were just about finishing off on deck and they both looked pretty knackered, but were still chirpy. I handed them a bottle of rum through the window. Long Hair took a good slug and passed the bottle over to John who politely declined. He'll learn, I thought. Of all the green hands I ever took to sea, John Stephens stands out above all the rest. This voyage would turn out to be a tough one but John had the guts and determination to see it through, at times staying on deck for as long as eighteen to twenty hours, often knee deep in water.

Fishing is one of the most dangerous occupations in the world. It requires a tremendous amount of stamina, concentration and will power to survive on the deck of a fishing vessel in bad weather. Work on a trawler is very repetitive: haul in the trawl, empty it out, shoot away. By the time you have cleared the decks, the whole procedure starts again, hour after hour, day after day for as many days as the trip lasts, the weather is immaterial. In daylight and in darkness, no good looking at the clock, keep going.

The shellfish boat works in much the same way: haul a string of 80 pots, clear, bait, stack them, turn round almost immediately to shoot away once again.

Shooting away a string of 80 pots on a strong tide has to be done with speed in order to stretch them out; 6-8 knots is common. This is the time when a shellfish boat crew are at great risk. In roughly fifteen minutes, almost a mile of rope snakes out over the side. The deck is a very tense place. One mistake and someone is overboard. Combine this with bad weather and great concentration is needed from the skipper down. Then, as soon as the last pot goes over the side, a good skipper is almost rounding up to the next fleet of 80 pots and it starts all over again

The life and work on a fishing vessel can never be fully appreciated. People see a fishing boat tied up alongside the quay only as something quaint and picturesque. Little do they know of the hell that goes on 24 hours a day when they are at sea.

Our trip had now moved on to day five. Fishing was still pretty good. We had 5 tons of crab on board and the lobster had taken off. Rich told me that we were running short of fresh milk and alcohol and so on the sixth night, I decided to head into Alderney. We radioed through our provisions list to the Diver's Inn. Eileen, the landlady was very good and her son, Tim, would run up town to get what we needed. I spoke to my mate, Scruffy Ingram on the *Kastel Paol*. He told me most of the Jersey and Guernsey fleet would be in that evening, so stand by. We finally pulled alongside in Alderney at about 6.30pm. We tied up alongside the *St Sylvair*, owned by another Jersey skipper, Stewpot. Scruffy pulled in alongside us in the *Kastel Paol*. I knew Scruffy's game. He always wanted an outside berth so that he could be first away in the morning. Scruffy at that time was rated as possibly the most successful shell fisherman in the English Channel, but sadly he was not to make old bones. He was lost overboard and drowned a few years later.

Rich had the grub ready as soon as we pulled alongside: all hands down below and two bottles of wine later the meal was over. A quick wash and clean up, all hands ashore to the Diver's Inn.

The Quayside at Alderney had two pubs – the Sea View and the Diver's. By 7.30pm both were packed solid with fishermen. By 9.30pm, you can imagine the scene. Handstands in the corner trying to drink pints upside down, the odd scuffle and drinks all round: the best party you'd ever been to. By 10.30pm, the game was up. Eileen had taken a fortune. Everyone had had

FISHING TRIP TO CHERBOURG

a ball. By 11.30pm most crew members had staggered back to the right boat. A few had fallen by the wayside and a few heavy drinkers could be seen still drinking in the odd wheelhouse. I finally crawled into my bunk at midnight, having had a final drink with Scruffy and Jappo, a skipper from Guernsey.

I was in a good deep sleep when I was woken up by the sound of *Kastel Paol*'s engine. It was just after 3.00am. We had been in our bunks three hours. The noise soon faded and Scruffs was on his way – first one out. Stewpot's engine came to life almost simultaneously with ours. Rich had crawled into the engine room and managed to pull the appropriate levers. We were an air start engine, as were all of us, making it easy to start after a night ashore.

It was the tradition that skippers would leave the crew in their bunks and chuck the ropes off themselves. I staggered out on deck. Stewpot had already chucked off our ass end stern. I pulled in both ropes and jumped back into the wheelhouse. I put her in gear and *Burutu* gently headed out, past what we called the 'sunken end' and then on past the main breakwater. I turned on the radar and Decca. I could just see Scuffy's stern light, so I followed that until we got clear of Bray Harbour. I'm sure Stewpot was following my stern light and Jappo, his. I lit up a fag and squeezed back into the galley to put on the kettle. Too late! Rich had not gone back to his bunk, but had made two mugs of strong coffee spliced with rum. Good old Rich.

'Christ! That was some night,' he commented.

I just looked at him and smiled.

'Yeah,' I said.

*

St Peter Port Radio was still giving out gales. I don't think the wind had dropped much below Force 7 since the start of the trip. By midday they were forecasting 8-9 south west, going west to north west Storm Force 11. At 4 o'clock that afternoon, Jappo came over the Radio to say it was too much for him. His boat was smaller than the rest, just under 50ft. *Burutu* was 70ft. He was heading back to Alderney. There was too much south in it to get home to Guernsey. The *George William C* and the *Northern Clipper* both stopped fishing at around 5pm. The *Crusader*, a boat from Dartmouth which was fishing about 20 miles to the north of us, also threw in the towel and headed for shelter. This left four of us still on the ground; *Kastel Paol, St Sylvair, Primel* and us. After consultation on the Radio between the four of us, it was decided that it would be prudent to take shelter. The 6pm Shipping Forecast increased the wind strength to Hurricane Force 12, with heavy snow showers. The decision was made – run into Alderney.

I had just started hauling in a string. It would take another hour and a half to haul and shoot. We pressed on into the stormy darkness. The string was fishing well. By 7.30pm we turned to the south east to shoot away. A big sea was running but the wind had eased to about Force 4.

'Huh! … the lull before the storm, Scratch,' Rich yelled up from the deck.

He was dead right. Within twenty minutes of us getting the gear back over the side, it was screaming from the north west. The Radio screeched into life.

'*Burutu, Burutu* – *Kastel Paol, Kastel Paol.* You getting me, Scratch?'

'Aye aye, Scruff. Got you fine. Yeah.'

'Don't bother trying to come into Alderney. It's well north west now. You would never get in through the breakwater end. The outer end of the breakwater is buried. We are in Bray Harbour, dodging. We can't get alongside. Wing Nut and Battle of Britain have just come away from the Quay. They can't get alongside.'

Wing Nut was skipper of the *Gurkha Brigade* and Battle of Britain was his first mate. Wing Nut had a bigger pair of ears than Prince Charles.

The *Christmas* lay alongside the Quay, raging up and down. Scruffy finished his transmission by saying her skipper, Kenny Corbett, was most likely 'anchored under the lee of Bum Island'; a seagoing saying for a sailor who had gone ashore and fallen into good fortune in a lady's bedroom. Kenny was good at that. *Christmas* would have to take her chance alongside. Sadly, the *Christmas* was lost a few years later on Beer Beach while under the command of Skipper Dick Baylay of Salcombe. There was no loss of life.

After receiving the news from Scruffy, I had to reappraise the situation. Cherbourg lay about eighteen miles south east. I turned the *Burutu* another 20 degrees and lay a course for the western entrance of Cherbourg. This put the storm directly behind us. *Burutu* liked that a lot more and settled into a surfing motion down the giant waves. Rich and Long Hair entered the wheelhouse from the galley end.

'What's the crack then, Billy Whizz?' asked Long Hair. I never knew why Long Hair always called me Billy Whizz, never Scratch.

I told them that Alderney was a no goer so we were going to run to Cherbourg, now about fifteen miles away to the south east. Richard's first comment was, 'Bugger, I haven't got any French money.' Long Hair said no problem, we could sell a few lobsters. Rich then disappeared and came back with a bottle of rum, de-corked it and threw the cork out of the wheelhouse window into the raging wind and snow. All three of us had a good belt of rum and Long Hair produced three Villager cigars. The wheelhouse was soon filled with the rich smell of rum and cigar smoke: eight miles to run.

The radar screen was dotted with dense snow showers, but

they seemed to be passing mainly to the west of us. Every so often a huge sea would come crashing over our quarter and run up the deck, at least clearing the snow. I had a last look at the chart. It was simple enough to run into the western end. The purple A.74 lane on the Decca ran straight into the entrance. Two miles to run and the bottle of rum was well down. Long Hair produced three more cigars and we lit up.

'Half a mile to go, boys,' I said . At the same time I noticed, taking up the bottom half of the radar screen, a huge snow shower, dead astern. I could see that it would be upon us as we hit the entrance.

Snow had completely blocked the radar and the screen was blank.

I had to make a quick decision: turn into this roaring tempest or run on for the entrance blind.

I think she would have turned in that sea, but I remembered at that moment that the Decca A.74 lane goes straight through the entrance.

Caught up in this sudden blizzard, visibility was down to nil, the forward mast disappearing into the night and the driving snow.

So I steered her in on the Decca needle.

I estimated that we were roughly 500 yards from the entrance when the radar had gone blind. Five minutes later, with the gale still raging and the snow horizontal, the sea began to calm.

We all looked at each other. 'I think we're in,' I whispered.

It had been a bit unconventional steering in on the Decca needle, but it worked. We were definitely in.

Now that the sea had calmed, I rounded the *Burutu* up and shut the throttle down. The snow slowly cleared and blow me down, we rounded up by the Ocean Terminal from which I had sailed in the *Queen Mary* fourteen years before.

As usual in a strange port, I looked around to see where

the fishing trawlers were tied up. We cruised up past the Ocean Terminal and I saw ten big Caen and Cherbourg registered trawlers alongside what must have been the fish quay.

'We'll drop alongside these trawlers.' I said to the boys.

We rounded up and soon secured ourselves alongside the outside trawler. Rich went down to the engine room and shut down the faithful old Baudouin. Thank God it had not let us down when we needed it most. Just as I came out of the wheelhouse, for the first time in nearly twenty four hours, a little face appeared out of the accommodation hatch. John had crashed out in his bunk when we stopped fishing and had slept like a baby all the way in. He didn't know what he had missed – the rum, the cigars and all the excitement of coming in blind to Cherbourg Harbour.

*

The wind was already starting to ease and I could see the stars. The depression that had caused the storm had taken a more southerly track than most that come flying across the North Atlantic at that time of the year. Most pass over the top of Scotland, but this baby had crossed southern Ireland, Wales and the Midlands before racing out into the North Sea. My observation was that winds around the back of a depression always seem fiercer than the ones leading it. Hence the 70 – 80 mph winds from the north north west that we had encountered for six to eight hours.

It was too late to go ashore. France usually shuts down by 10.30pm and it was almost midnight, so Rich knocked up a bit of a snack meal that we washed down with beer and red wine. Then we all crashed out until morning.

Next day was fine. There was no point in sailing again until the following evening and so we pulled half a dozen lobsters out of the vivier and with these as currency, set off ashore to enjoy a long lazy lunch. The first restaurant we picked welcomed us with open arms. Our currency was good and we staggered back in the late afternoon feeling pretty happy, ready for a good kip and then, on with the rest of the trip.

We left Cherbourg the following morning at 2.30am. This got us to the gear at first light. The storm had done the fishing good and four days later we had a fair old trip aboard. We landed down in Primel in Brittany and made a good grossing, after the usual battle with Square Neck about price.

Rich and I spent the rest of the day in Primel at the Café Du Port and then went on to Louis Ozard's house for supper and more wine. Louis was half French and half Channel Islander, a good fisherman and a good drinker. He was skipper of the 70ft trawler *Le Gaulois*. Louis and his wife Michelle always made us very welcome at their house in Primel and I have never forgotten their hospitality. Sadly, two years later, Louis and all hands were lost in a storm in the Irish Sea aboard the 70ft trawler *Dawn Waters*. Nothing was ever recovered.

We left Primel around 6.00pm, as soon as the *Burutu* floated. After a twelve hour steam I brought her back into home port, Salcombe, moored up and was back in time to see the children off to school.

Five

RETURN TO ROCKALL

By late February '79, I decided on a good refit and set sail again for Scottish grounds. Having organised the refit, Jane and I decided on having a really good holiday as I was away from home a lot, fishing again. Sarah was now six and Rob coming up to five. We decided to go to Key West, Florida. We had three weeks away and it was fabulous, although it did take me about a week to unwind. We finally had three days in Disneyworld – that was good, and then we finished up on Daytona beach for a week. That holiday always sticks in my mind as the best ever. It was many years until we went on holiday again. I think we just forgot to go and other things were appearing with the kids, horses and sailing.

By late March we were ready to sail. Richard was at a bit of a loose end. He had sold the *Silver Spray* earlier that year and signed on with me again. It was really good to be sailing with Rich again, he took an awful lot of the responsibility of being skipper away and, of course, was well capable of skippering himself.

The next new crew member to join was Nigel Davis. I always thought his nickname should have been Kirk – he was the spitting image of Kirk Douglas, dimple and all. He was a good, reliable hand and went on to skipper the *Burutu* after my ownership was transferred to Jersey owners. He became a good skipper, but the sea finally claimed Nigel in the Atlantic about five years later In heavy weather, the trawler he was working on capsized due to flooding in the engine room. He was never found and so, like Louis Ossard and his crew in the *Dawn Waters*, Nigel joined the legions of other sailors and fishermen across the world whose only gravestones are the relentless grey topped waves that continually cross our oceans. Spud Cudd and Willy Brown, two other Salcombe boys, were also on the same trawler but miraculously survived the capsize. When your number is up, off you go. Fourth crew member was a fella called John Pullman. He wasn't too experienced but was keen and showed good promise.

With the *Burutu's* refit now complete, we sailed from Salcombe bound for Rockall in about late March 1979, loaded with five hundred and fifty pots, 2000 gallons of fuel and enough bait provisions and booze to last about twenty one days. It was my first visit back to these northern waters since we last fished up there in the *Kenavo,* back in '75, so I was quite excited with the prospect of around two weeks fishing before we would have to land.

An eighty five hour steam saw us about 800 miles north of Salcombe, just south west of the Flannan Isles. I decided to start fishing here and move south as we fished. This was far enough north at this time of year. Fishing was good but patchy. There were more crayfish as we moved south down the Benbecula shore towards the Wellington Reef, west of Barra. I always remember that trip. We were completely on our own. I don't think we saw another ship or trawler the whole trip. It is a very desolate piece of coastline, especially at that time of year. The weather wasn't too bad though, but it wasn't calm.

We landed our first catch in Oban to a fella called John Arrow. He was a pretty prominent shellfish buyer of the day. It was rumoured that he had done a bit of boxing in the past and was a bit of a hard case. But I always got on well with John and sold to him often.

We gave ourselves a couple of days off in Oban to prepare the boat for the next voyage. We sailed from Oban, back out across the Minch, through the Sound of Barra and back to the gear which was all shot away west of Barra Head. The first two days were not too promising, so it was back down to the golden ground west of Islay.

I shot half the gear, about 250 pots, on the Blackstones Bank, roughly 20 miles south of the Skerryvore lighthouse marking the southern tip of Tiree. This was a shot in the dark. I just happened to stumble on it as we sailed across it and the reef appeared on the echo sounder. We started hauling at first light the following day and 'Jackpot!' as Wills had said back in '74. There they were, three or four lobsters every pot plus crayfish. The Blackstones Reef was not big enough to accommodate all the pots we had, so we steamed about 20 miles south to another reef – the Stanton Bank – and shot the remainder of the gear there. Then we were full speed back to the Blackstones.

*

Weather was calm, fishing was excellent, spirits were high on the *Burutu*. These sort of days were the bonus days for all the bad weather and poor fishing days every fisherman has to go through, but when it does come good, the feeling is indescribable. After seven days we had an excellent catch aboard. This trip was a record for my fishing career on the *Burutu* – I would never see fishing like this again.

*

We landed back in Oban having only been away for eight days, with 2 tons of lobster, mostly select size that brings a better price, three quarters of a ton of good large crayfish and a good ton of large cock crabs. We didn't keep the female crab, they would have taken up too much room in the vivier. It is always better to keep only the high value fish. The gross figure that we landed was well in excess of what I had paid for the *Burutu* only six months before – better born lucky than rich. I always remember something that John Arrow said to me that night when we landed that catch. 'Congratulations, Scratch,' he said, 'but what about the quality of life?' It made me think a bit, but he was right. I was spending more and more time away from Jane and the children. I would have to rectify this over the next few years or I may as well have stayed in Africa or South America. 'Quality of life' rang in my ears as we sailed away from Oban for another trip.

Sailing down the Firth of Lorn on that beautiful, starry, moonlit night, bound for the golden grounds south of Skerryvore, little did I know that immediately after the best trip of my life, I was about to experience what was probably to be the worst.

Six

HEBRIDES, STORM FORCE 10, IMMINENT

We started hauling gear again at first light. Weather was still fair but the forecasts were talking of an exceptionally deep depression departing the eastern seaboard of America and due to pass north of Scotland within forty eight hours. Not good news with gear – all pots in less than 20 fathoms of water – or 120ft to the landlubber. From past experience, back in '74 with the old *Kenavo*, you needed to have everything in thirty fathoms plus if this intense type of storm was approaching (one fathom is equal to 6ft).

The first haul was good, but the lobsters and crayfish had also heard a storm was approaching – it's strange how. at that depth, shellfish can tell what's happening up on the surface, but they can. The second haul was down by more than half – the signal to move the gear and quick! By midnight, forty eight hours after leaving Oban, we had all the gear in 30 fathoms plus. The intense depression was rapidly closing in on the west coast of Scotland, gale warnings were now coming in at regular intervals and it was no longer 'six to eight gale', but 'eight to storm force ten'. By 2am I told Rich and the boys we were going to run into Scalasaig, a small and very sheltered port on the Island of Colonsay. I knew there was good shelter there and a good pub. We rounded the north end of Colonsay. The wind was a full gale and right behind us, but as we rounded up into the lee of Colonsay and headed south to Scalasaig, all was calm, in spite of the screaming wind and driving rain. We pulled into Scalasaig just before first light. I expected the pier to be empty with this weather. Most other fishing boats I had talked to over the radio had headed back to Oban.

Through the wind and rain I made out two 120ft sidewinders, Icelandic trawlers on their way home from Icelandic waters to Milford Haven to land – The *London Town* and the *Andrew Wilson*. They were both old ships, built in the fifties, but trawlers of that class that worked Iceland and as far as Greenland, represented possibly the most seaworthy vessels ever designed. The only thing they could not cope with was the icing up of the superstructure and rigging in those cold northern latitudes, causing them to become top-heavy and capsize. Apart from that, they could cope with anything. 'Huh,' said Richard, 'Must be a bit scatty out there if those two have taken shelter. You made the right move, Scratch.' We tied up alongside the *London Town* and all turned in.

It took five days for the storm to blow itself out, the depression stopped and anchored itself about one hundred miles east of Peterhead causing storm force winds to blow from the northwest all down along the west coast of Scotland. We were all trapped in Scalasaig. The pub made a fortune. We thought we could drink but these two trawler crews put us to shame. I remember the cook on the *Andrew Wilson* drank himself unconscious. I don't think he came to for about forty eight hours but his crew mates weren't going to abandon him, they carried him up to the pub every lunchtime and every evening and sat him in a corner, just in case he came to. They said he would be very sad if he came to on board and there was no-one around; that's what you call good shipmates.

Finally, the storm abated. The two trawlers gently slipped away astern out of Scalasaig and headed down through the Sound of Islay to finish their homeward journey to Milford Haven. We never saw them again – ships that pass in the night. We sailed from Scalasaig at about the same time, but our course took us north around the northern tip of Colonsay, then due west to Skerryvore and Tiree. There was still a fair old sea running but the *Burutu* handled it well and we arrived back on the fishing grounds in around six hours. There were a few dhan buoys missing, but the gear was well safe in 30 fathoms – not much in it though, a few crabs and plenty of dogfish. The following day, most of the gear was fishing well but, with the depression still out in the North Sea, there was still a continual six to eight gale blowing from the north, down through the Hebrides.We had been away from Oban now for nine days and we barely had half a ton of lobster aboard. It shows you how one trip can be so different from the last. But a bigger and almost fatal drama was about to unfold.

Seven

'... FOR THOSE IN PERIL ON THE SEA'.

Because of the strong northerly wind, I was creeping closer up to the island of Tiree to try to fish, hopefully, in more sheltered water, but Tiree is very low lying and not much of a lee can be found. We were shooting away a string of around 75 pots on the west side of Tiree, about half a mile west of the Outer Hurricane Rocks. We were working with a following sea to try to make it a bit more manageable on deck. Nigel was passing the pots to John, who was on the starboard gunwale, dropping them overboard. Suddenly a hell of a big sea broke just astern of us and pushed the *Burutu* ahead at about twice the speed I wanted for shooting away. In a flash, there was a scream from the deck. The rope had suddenly snaked out across the starboard gunwale, taking John with it like a rag doll. I can clearly remember the view I had from the wheelhouse window – the rope came tight on his ankle. He must have travelled 60ft through the air before he disappeared below the cold, grey sea. I immediately put the *Burutu* full astern, but 70 tons of boat is not going to stop quickly, especially in that sea. Two more pots went over the side after John disappeared – that is about another 180ft of rope. That's how far John was away from the *Burutu*, but underwater. Finally I got the ship back, head to sea and Richard managed to get the rope to the winch, we could now start hauling John back in. I told Nigel to get into the wheelhouse and keep her head to sea for fear of breaking the thin line to which I hoped John was still attached.

Nigel slowly came ahead, I took over the winch control and Richard was on the gunwale. It seemed like an age before the first pot came back in, another age and then the second, still no John. Then, at last, Richard yelled to me over the driving wind and spray, 'Ease her down, Scratch, he's coming up.' I eased the speed of the winch down and John appeared over the gunwale at the hanging block, upside down and with what seemed like gallons of water pouring from his open mouth. I was sure he was dead. If the 60ft flight through the air hadn't killed him, then surely, he had drowned. I never timed it, but we all reckoned he had been underwater for at least seven to ten minutes.

Richard and I immediately cut him free of the rope, or the backline as we call it, and lowered him down to the deck. I yelled up to Nigel to get us into some sheltered water south of the Hurricane Rocks. He turned *Burutu* east to find some sheltered water. I dropped down to my knees alongside John, he was motionless and looked very white and pale. Suddenly, one of his eyes flickered, 'Christ almighty, Rich, he is still with us.' I grasped his chin and hair to give mouth to mouth resuscitation. Having never done it before, I wasn't sure whether to blow or suck, so I did both. Not a pleasant task as John hadn't shaved for about a week. A sudden cough, then he shook quite violently. He then became conscious. I shall never forget the first thing he said. 'Christ, Scratch, I saw the pearly gates.' Rich and I looked at each other with great relief and a smile. Nigel got us into calmer water and we got John down to his bunk. I remember he was very cold and shivering uncontrollably.

I called Oban Coastguard to ask for a doctor's advice on the next move with John. They decide to take him off by helicopter and get him to the Inverness Chest Infirmary, in case he still had water on his chest. So, within three quarters of an hour, he was lifted off by a big Sea King helicopter and taken to Inverness. After ten days he was back on the starboard gunwale as though nothing had happened.

Once again I had witnessed the unbelievable power of the sea and how, at a moment's notice, it can snatch life away and give it back.

If John had not stayed connected to the backline, we would never have seen him again. Shooting away gear off fishing vessels in bad weather, is definitely when the crew on deck are at their most vulnerable and when most fatal accidents are likely to occur. Little wonder that fishing is rated as possibly the most dangerous occupation worldwide. All through my fishing career, people would invariably ask me the same old question. 'What were the biggest seas you ever saw, Scratch, and when were you the most frightened?' An impossible question to answer. I suppose the biggest and most dangerous waves were to be found in shallower, coastal waters with strong tidal flow and very rough, rocky seabed. The deeper the water, the smoother the seabed combined with less tidal flow gave an easier type of sea. One very bad place for dangerous seas, was two or three miles west of the Rhinns of Islay, on the southwest coast of Scotland, just before you come down into the north channel between the Mull of Kintyre and Malin Head, the northern tip of Ireland or the Innistrall Light. We used to call it 'the wall'. Passing over it with the echo sounder you can see why. The seabed looked like the French Alps with one very sharp, steep wall. The sea was always bad there even in moderate weather. Many ships and trawlers have come to grief in this small stretch of water. In daylight you can see it boiling but in the dark, it would be a killer. As for being frightened, well you don't get frightened – you wouldn't be there if you got frightened, a little anxious perhaps sometimes. Maybe you just think you are invincible, it could never happen to you. I suppose, if it does, you don't know much about it anyway.

Eight

RECUPERATION

After the almost fatal accident with John, I decided this trip had gone on long enough, so I arranged a landing with John Arrow in Oban. After we had landed our well earned catch, we had a couple of days off. There were several jobs and repairs to do to the *Burutu*; she had pushed through some pretty rough weather since sailing from Salcombe seven weeks earlier. We did one more quick trip before John rejoined us, but the fishing had gone very poor and combined with dropping prices, I decided a couple of weeks at home was overdue. So, after one more landing at Oban, I steamed the boat to Crinan at the western entrance of the Crinan Canal, where she could sit in fresh water for two weeks while we went home.

I always reckoned if there was any gribble worm in the *Burutu*'s hull, then the fresh water would sort them out. We hired a brand new Ford Grenada from Glasgow airport and drove home in record time – six hours from Glasgow to Kingsbridge in South Devon, most of the journey at around one hundred and twenty miles per hour. Never saw a copper. The final years of freedom.

The best catch I ever made! Jane on *Buturu* - summer 1979.

Norian lies forlorn - scrapyard, Plymouth, 1983.

It was late May '79 when we got back. The weather at home had been very good, Jane had just spent most days on the beach at East Portlemouth with the kids. She was tanned all over and seemed to look even better as time went by. My guardian angel was surely looking after me when I drove up Totnes hill and picked her up that summer's day in '72.

I stayed at home almost three weeks and it was glorious. The weather was good, Jane and I raced our Salcombe Yawl in the regattas and open meetings. We had managed to buy Y35, the Salcombe Yawl I had raced in the late '60s and early '70s – we had ten good years with her.

One fine day, we all went to Cornwall for a long day out and a picnic. The kids were just getting mobile now and were good fun, well, most of the time. On the way home, we stopped in Plymouth for a couple of hours in the Barbican area. Robert was in a pushchair and Sarah spent most of the time standing on the front of it. We bumped into a street artist called Robert Lenkiewicz who was doing sketches for a couple of quid each. He did one of Sarah and one of Robert. They were very good, we have them today, still hanging in one of our bedrooms. Robert Lenkiewicz, in time, became a very well known and respected artist doing many famous paintings and murals around Plymouth's Barbican area.

A little while later, we were looking around a second hand type antique shop and I just happened to notice a beautiful ship's wheel for sale. Looking at it more closely. it seemed to stir some distant memory within me. With horror and shock, I read the small note attached to it, 'Ship's wheel from the Steam Yacht *Norian*,1910, £300.' I couldn't believe it. Of course, I just had to buy it but £300 was a big sum in those days. Jane agreed that we should buy it and so we did. It represented a big part of my history. I asked if they knew the whereabouts of the *Norian*. They told me she was being broken up at the scrapyard on the

Plym River. We immediately went down to the yard and there she was looking very forlorn. My mind raced back to Cowes Regatta 1963, Simon Sitwell, 'Can you peel spuds and shovel coal?', learning to splice wire and rope, paying off in London. A tear came to my eye and we headed home.

Nine

GOOD LANDINGS, COURTESY ADMIRAL DONITZ

The three weeks I was at home flew by but it was a very welcome break from the recent dramas in Scotland. It was now time to get the boys together and return to earning some money. A wise old fisherman said to me once, 'The sea is like a huge piggy bank, it's just difficult making a withdrawal sometimes.' What a true saying that was. Try as I could, the fishing never came good again until the autumn of that year and, heaven knows, we steamed hundreds of miles in search of the ever elusive lobster and crayfish.

I kept in touch by radio with my old mate Scruffy who was still in Rockall sea area on his usual stamping ground between St. Kilda and the Flannan Isles. He was also finding it hard going and had managed to sit the *Kastlel Paol* on the rocks through the Sound of Vatersay, the western approach to Castle Bay and Barra. I knew the rock well, it certainly was not on any chart.

The west coast of Scotland holds many surprises lurking just below the surface. Scruffy came off on the next tide with not too much damage. The *Kastel Paol* was another Camaret-built boat built for the purpose, not to the rule.

By late June of that year, I had found some better fishing about ten miles north of the Inishtrahull light which marks the northernmost tip of northern Ireland. There were about fifteen wrecks on the seabed, all pretty close together and all about the same size. There was quite a good bit of lobster all around and amongst these wrecks. We lost a few pots that got caught up in the wreckage, but the fishing outweighed the loss of gear, so I persisted. Years later, I read about the German U-boats that surrendered at the end of the second world war. They were all taken into Londonderry, Northern Ireland, but at a later date, they were towed out north of Inishtrahull Light and scuttled. Lobsters do like to live in and around wrecks. If it was the U-boats on which we were fishing, then thank you, Admiral Donitz. I clearly remember the wrecks were all about the same size which would definitely point towards the scuttled U-boats. We got a couple of good landings there, that was the main thing.

Ten

THE THIRTY-SIX
HOUR TOW

Late one afternoon, we had just finished fishing for that day when a squeaky little voice came over the radio. All I could really hear was, '…are you picking me up, Scratch?' I answered the call a couple of times, then suddenly it came across much clearer. *Burutu, Burutu, Cawsand Bay, Cawsand Bay*, are you getting me now, Scratch?' I think the *Cawsand Bay* had been transmitting on low power earlier, that's why I could not receive him too well. I immediately went back to them as she was a boat from Plymouth and I knew the owners well. The *Cawsand Bay* was about thirty miles due west of us with a fouled propeller. The wind was force five to six, north east, blowing her further and further out into the Atlantic, if I didn't go and rescue her, the next land she would see would be America. To just run thirty miles out into the north Atlantic, knowing you had to tow another sixty foot vessel back against the weather, was a pretty depressing thought. It was to be a long old tow, but had to be done.

Within four hours, I was alongside the *Cawsand Bay*. I held off to windward and floated a towline across. Once secured, we started what turned out to be a thirty six hour tow. The *Burutu* only had 180 hp and the Cawsand Bay had around thirty pots around her propeller, so the progress was pretty slow, especially against half a north east gale. Finally we made it around the north end of Islay, down the Sound of Islay to Port Askaig, where we got her alongside. A diver went down to clear her propeller and it took him most of the next day. An unwritten law of the sea says you always help another boat in trouble; it was certainly the longest rescue I ever made. The owners of the *Cawsand Bay* were very good and made it worth my while from their insurance company, compensating for fuel and loss of fishing time. It's funny how things work out. Two years later, I skippered the *Cawsand Bay* on two voyages to the west coast of Scotland.

Eleven

BRUSH WITH WELSH FISHERIES

After that incident with the *Cawsand Bay*, I decided it was time to head for home, we had been away for nearly fourteen weeks. On the way back down through the Irish Sea, we needed to refuel. The *Burutu* carried just over two thousand gallons of diesel and had a hell of a range, but we had steamed thousands of miles in those fourteen weeks and were pretty low on fuel. We would stop at Milford Haven on the way home, fuel was always pretty cheap there, but rounding the Smalls, the south west tip of Pembrokeshire, I could not resist a quick try for some crayfish. The Hats and Barrels where Jeff, Marilyn and I had that bit of drama on the *Linnet* and *Panorama*, a few years before, was always known to be good for crayfish, so, in the dark, over the side the gear went. Fishing was good but, within forty eight hours, we were boarded by the Welsh Fishery protection vessel. Simple mistake – I thought the limit for 60ft and over vessels was three miles. It was six.

To cut a long story short, the next morning I appeared at Haverford West Magistrates Court and was fined three hundred pounds for being inside the six mile limit. The fine was no problem, I was afraid they were going to confiscate the catch. I had a lot of lobster and crayfish down the hold from Scotland; to lose that lot would have been a disaster. They let me go with just the fine, thank God. We refuelled and sailed from Milford Haven with all haste, loaded our gear at the Smalls and set course for Land's End. We took more than three hundred pounds worth of good size crayfish from the Smalls though.

By late July we landed our catch in Newlyn after shooting all the pots away just to the south of the Wolf Rock, about twenty miles south of the Lizard and Land's End. We did a ten day trip for crab around the Wolf Rock but a major tragedy was about to unfold just to the north of us.

Twelve

THE 1979 FASTNET

The 1979 Fastnet Yacht Race passed around sixty miles to the north and what a disaster it was. Quite a few yachtsmen were drowned. The main problem was in the Celtic Sea, north of Land's End. I think many of them abandoned their yachts before it was really necessary, but, as I have said before, the sea is a powerful lady, if she wants you, she takes you.

The worst wind passed through in the night and we had stopped fishing but some of these summer storms can be as bad as any winter storm. Two days after the race had been abandoned, we were hauling away at first light. I was on deck working the winch, Richard was in the wheelhouse, suddenly I had the fright of my life, a huge porbeagle shark came flying over the gunwale. A porbeagle shark is a very fat, chunky member of the shark family but this was a big old boy. He must have been 8ft long and as fat as a pig. These sharks live on the seabed. He must have become caught up in our gear as we shot it away. If a shark can't swim, he drowns. This old chap was as dead as a hammer but what scared me was, for a moment I imagined it was one of the yachtsmen from the Fastnet Race. Because it was the last day of our trip and we were to land in Roscoff the following day, the shark kept well enough without ice and I remember it made a very good price in France. We spent the remainder of the year just crab fishing, forty miles south of Salcombe – very monotonous but a steady income. For most of the period we were day tripping and in every night, so life was a little normal for two or three months.

Thirty six hours after the ill fated '79 Fastnet race, a big old porbeagle shark jumped aboard. Myself, Richard and Mark Grundy.

Thirteen

'I WILL RETURN AND SEE YOU AGAIN'

In November of that year, I asked Mike Atfield, another old school mate of mine from way back in the East Portlemouth days, to build me a brand new Salcombe Yawl. Mike was a year older than me and, on leaving school, did a six year boat building apprenticeship at the local boatyard of Edgar Cove and Sons. Mike went on to become a master boatbuilder. It was Richard Cove, one of the sons, who was wild-as-the-wind skipper of the *Newbrook*. That winter Mike built the yawl for me and she was a beauty; mahogany planking on elm frames with teak ply decks. Her sail number was Y 123 which roughly means she was the 123rd yawl to be built. Jane and I launched her in the spring of the following year. We called her *Kenavo* after the first fishing boat I bought, back in the early seventies with Richard. *Kenavo* is a gaelic word meaning 'I will return and see you again'; a good name. Jane and I had many successes in *Kenavo* during the 1980s, the best win was the prestigious hundred guineas race held in

Dartmouth. We sold old Y35 to a Dr. Doorward of Edinburgh who sailed her extensively on the Forth until returning her to Salcombe in the late nineties.

Fourteen

SALVAGE OFF THE FRENCH COAST

At Christmas I brought all the gear ashore. The pots were in a pretty poor state of repair and all needed to be gone through before the next fishing season. At least this meant time at home with Jane and the kids. Towards the end of January, 1980, I had a call from Square Neck; quite a surprise really as I had not landed to Primel for a couple of years. He wanted to know if I could run a few loads of crab across the channel, from Newlyn-Penzance to him in France. Because we were not fishing, just repairing the gear, I agreed to do two trips for him. We didn't need a full crew for this sort of job, so Colin signed on to come across. It was Colin who had come to Scotland with me, back in '75 on the *Kenavo*.

First trip, no problem, we landed ten ton of female crab from a company called Harvey in Newlyn. Second trip – a little more interesting. We left Newlyn bound for Roscoff, a run of about twenty hours. The wind was from the south, force five to six so the old *Burutu* was plunging into the sea, just chucking a bit of spray back, nothing out of the ordinary. It was dark as we approached the French coast and I was looking forward to getting under the lee of the land. I think it was around four in the morning and we were due in at six, when Colin spied a tiny little light flashing away off our starboard quarter. After watching it for a while, it became pretty obvious it was someone with a small torch flashing SOS. I turned to starboard and approached the solitary little light which, as we got near, stopped flashing. I then turned on our powerful searchlight and what we saw, we couldn't believe!

In the beam of the searchlight was a 'Marie Celeste'. A big, very expensive French schooner, about 90ft foot long, wallowing around with sails torn and flapping in the wind and rain. Sitting on the bow, hanging on to the forestay was the little Frenchman who had been flashing SOS. He was soaking wet and looked pretty well all in. He could stand up but just remained where he was, thankful he was soon to be rescued.

Colin and I soon assessed the situation. If we were to take her in tow, one of us would have to leap aboard to secure the tow line. There was no way the little Frenchman was going to be any use at all. After several attempts to come alongside without damaging the yacht too much, Colin managed to leap aboard. Pretty soon we had a tow rope attached and I headed for the Ile de Batz light and Roscoff. About twenty minutes passed and Colin got the VHF radio working on the schooner, he then revealed the mystery that surrounded the vessel. The little Frenchman was the last one standing out of a crew of nine, the rest were all down below in their bunks having been overcome with seasickness and fatigue. They had literally thrown in the towel. I think seasickness can do that to people, they just want to lie down and die. They would all probably have died, had we not picked them up as they were drifting north into the busy, west going shipping lanes of the English Channel. A ship could have run them down and not even felt the impact.

Finally, I rounded up off the Roscoff ferry terminal. I got the schooner alongside the *Burutu* and then at last, alongside the quay. By this time the crew were slowly starting to emerge from below. They looked a sorry sight but couldn't thank us enough for saving them. Pound note signs began to appear in my mind, this was a very expensive yacht we had just salvaged. It turned out she had been chartered from St. Malo to sail to the Azores but whoever let this tribe loose on the ocean, should have had their brains tested, I could see there wasn't a seaman amongst them. Claiming salvage is not an easy process, especially when you are told the case will be heard in Paris in a few months time and you will need to be represented by a French barrister at God only knows how many francs per hour. Colin and I were advised by Square Neck to forget our salvage claim and put it down to experience; we took his advice.

Looking back on that night, I should have towed it back to Salcombe, I could then have made a good salvage claim with the yacht under my control. You live and learn but at least we did some good that cold January night off the Brittany coast.

Fifteen

OVERCOMING A
PERSONAL OBSTACLE

As I mentioned in the early part of this autobiography, school for me had not gone well at all. Mathematical skills were nil, I could write a little but reading was a terrible problem. The main difficulty with reading was that I could not remember what I had just read, so could never put anything together. Reading small signs I could manage, but to attempt a book was impossible. Many years after I left school, they put a name to this unhappy state of affairs – dyslexia. It is fairly obvious now that this is what I suffered from and if you were not careful in those days, you were just called thick. The way I coped was to steer a completely different course through life and overcame my learning disabilities. It had been a huge skeleton in the cupboard for me throughout my life but I mastered the art of disguising it with great success. Even Jane didn't know I was dyslexic until I told her after more than thirty years of marriage. That's how good you can get at it, if you try hard. Dyslexia can surely be overcome if you look for a different route through life, have a positive attidude and above all, a passion. The sea and ships were my passion and that is what saved me. Even now, in later life, I often see numbers back to front – sixty four becomes forty six and so on. The best approach is delegation – don't fight it, go with it.

I may well have taken on the French marine barristers in Paris with the salvage claim on the French schooner, but I knew immediately I would be out of my depth. For me, it was a no go area. The invention of the calculator in the 1970s was a huge relief for me. It opened up a whole new world of which, beforehand, I had only been able to scratch the surface.

Looking back, I give great credit to those men on the *Norian* all those years ago, who instilled in me the self confidence to go off and conquer the world and take on all it had to throw at me. It was a good day the day I rowed over to the *Norian* and met Simon Sitwell.

Sixteen

IRISH WATERS

Late February 1980 and the *Burutu* was ready for sea again. Several trips up Channel to north of Alderney and Cherbourg got us through to the spring of that year. Scruffy had done well with the *Kastel Paol* and had a new boat built for him in Camaret. He sold the *Kastel Paol* to his first mate called Tony Sangan, another Jersey man who fished her well but I seem to remember he had a few problems with the Irish limits, not dissimilar to my encounter with the Welsh authorities. Scruffy called his new boat the *Paulanda* after his two daughters, Paula and Amanda. She was a fine ship, but very low in the stern. He did well with the *Paulanda* but mainly stayed in the English Channel for the next five years.

*

By June 1980, I had the wanderlust again. I had heard the *Kastel Paol* was doing well west of Ireland but could not fish inside the twelve mile limit because of her Jersey registration. Most of the rougher, good lobster ground was within that limit. A brainwave hit me regarding registering the *Burutu* in Dublin so that I could fish inside the limits. Having hatched the idea, I couldn't wait to set sail.

I chartered a small aircraft and flew from Exeter to Jersey, picked up my registration documents for the *Burutu*, flew from there straight to Dublin, walked into the registration of shipping office in Dublin and asked to register *Burutu* as an Irish fishing vessel. Try that today, it would be an impossible minefield of bullshit and bureaucracy. The registrar of shipping in Dublin could not have been more cooperative. He asked me what my Jersey registration number had been. I told him it was J 633. 'Oh, b'Jeysus!' he said, 'Just change the J to D and you will be D 633 for Dublin'. I just could not believe it. It was that simple. I'm sure any fisherman reading this today will find it hard to believe that it could be so easy, but it was. I flew back to Exeter with my new registration, changed the J to a D and, within forty eight hours, set sail for the west coast of Ireland.

Once again, good old steady Rich was with me. Dino also signed on for the voyage and the third hand was a fella called Dave Curly. There was an ulterior motive for signing on Dave Curly. He was an Irish man with the strongest Irish accent I think I have ever heard, a stocky fella with a huge shock of black hair and a long, black beard – not a lot of fishing experience, but a good willing hand. His big contribution to the voyage was his accent. I reckoned it would go down much better with the Irish Fisheries patrols and Irish fishermen if a strong Irish accent came back over the radio in any radio communications. I put this into practice several times over the coming weeks with great success, often unable to understand a word of what either of them was saying, but I think it was a politically good move. We were not boarded by any patrols the whole voyage.

First landfall in south west Ireland was the Fastnet Rock, the rounding mark for the infamous Fastnet Race, but I didn't shoot away the gear until we were well west of the Old Head of Kinsale where the famous White Star Cunarder, the *Lusitania*, was torpedoed during the First World War. We slowly fished our way from there past Mizzen Head, Valencia Island, on past the mouth of the Shannon River and up into Galway Bay and Connemara. By this time, it dawned on me I would have been better off just sailing straight up to Scotland where I knew the ground well. We caught more crayfish than lobster. The ground looked very good but the lobsters were just not there in any great numbers. One haul, at a place called Brandon Bay, all the gear had filled up with spur dogs. Spur dog is a member of the shark family, about a metre long. We had a hell of a job to clear them out of all the pots; how the last one got in each pot, I shall never know. All I can really say about that trip is that it was a beautiful experience, the weather was good and the west coast of Ireland is stunning.

On we pressed, ever northward across Donegal Bay and Bloody Foreland, finally arriving off Malin Head about twenty four days after shooting away west of the Fastnet. Fishing is always a gamble, I had gambled but came out even. We had a good catch aboard but had fished for three weeks to get it – about ten days longer than a trip like that should have taken.

Now, not being able to fish in British territorial waters, I was faced with a strange dilemma. Should I simply lean over the bow and paint a J back in place of the D, or just fish on around the top end of northern Ireland? I don't think anyone would have taken a blind bit of notice what registration was painted on the bow but, remembering my run in with the Welsh authorities at Milford Haven, I played the white man and we loaded all the gear aboard as we approached the British limits. We had a good old catch down below, it would have been a disaster to have that confiscated, which is often the end result in these cases. We landed a good catch of Irish lobster and crayfish to John Arrow in Oban. A six hundred mile steam home, a few telephone calls and we were once again J 633; our Jersey registration was restored.

Seventeen

FIREMAN HITS THE DECK

By August and September 1980, I was back and well established in the hen crab grounds, forty miles south of Start Point and that's where I fished for the next four months; good, steady fishing all through the autumn of that year. That autumn the hen crab price in the UK was good, almost the same as the continental price, so I just day tripped out of Salcombe. This meant, for the first time almost since I married Jane, our life together resembled some sort of normality. I was spending most nights back in Salcombe and in my own bed, seeing the children off to school some mornings, taking my wife out to lunch, sailing the yawl at weekends. This was the first period of normal married life we had experienced in eight years and, guess what, I thought it was quite good. Jane and I decided that perhaps one more year with the *Burutu* would be enough. We should sell her and get a small dayboat out of Salcombe that would force me into leading a much more civilised life. Those eight years with the *Kenavo* and *Burutu* had set us up well – we owned a lovely home, there was money in the bank and things looked good. So

1981 was to be my last year deep sea and after that I would be an inshore fisherman for the rest of my fishing career – or so I thought.

It was always hard going in the eastern English Channel, always a lot of tide running and invariably nasty weather. Fishing off Ireland, the south west approaches and Rockall and Malin were always easier going somehow, mostly because of the lack of tidal flow. The English Channel is wide at the western end and then suddenly compresses down to twenty miles in the Straits of Dover. All this water has to go somewhere every six hours, so the tide just goes faster. Combine this with a rougher seabed as you go east and you can easily see the problem.

*

Around Easter that year we had an interesting run. It was to be just the usual ten day trip and we were about six days into it with the usual nasty old weather, not full gales but a good force six most of the time. Richard, for some reason, was down below and just happened to poke his nose into the engine room. It was flooded, the water level only inches from the main air intakes. Without hesitation, he jumped into the water and shut down the engine. If water is drawn into the engine through the air intakes, it will 'hydraulic'. This will cause huge damage to the engine and require an engine rebuild. Thank goodness he shut down just in time, but, of course, when the engine stops, she becomes a dead ship.

*

I ran down to the engine room to find Richard up to his waist in water. 'We've got a problem, Scratch,' and he wasn't kidding. Although we were rolling around quite heavily, the water level did not seem to be increasing, thank God. The whole ship was flooded from the forepeak back to the cabin at the stern. Rich continued trying to find where the water was coming in, but to no avail. I quickly went back up to the wheelhouse and got on the radio to Scruffy on the *Paulander* who was about three miles north of us. It was reassuring to know he was close by and could be with us in about twenty minutes, should we need him. I then called Brixham Coastguard to inform them of our situation. Our pumps were no good without power from the main engine. We did have another pump on an auxiliary engine but, like a lot of things when you want them most, they don't work; lack of use, I think.

*

After another hour or so, with the situation not getting any worse or any better, Brixham Coastguard decided to send a Sea King helicopter out from RNAS Culdrose in Cornwall with a powerful pump. It was incredible. Within the hour, the Sea King was hovering above us with a massive pump dangling on a line. The pump was supplied from Camborne Fire Brigade. The *Burutu* was rolling quite badly and it was difficult to land the pump on our deck with our masts and radio antennae, but after a few attempts, we landed and unclipped it safely. Rich soon understood how the pump worked and, within a few minutes, had it running. I looked aloft again to give the thumbs up to the Sea King but, to my horror, dangling just above the mast top, was a very frightened looking fireman who they were sending down to operate the pump, quite surplus to requirements, but down he came. He hit the deck and that almost knocked him out and he immediately turned green and was violently sick. He must have thought he had landed on some hideous ride at Disneyworld. He clung to the rail like a limpet. The poor chap was well out of his comfort zone. Finally, they sent the wire back down and, to his great relief, we hooked him on and back up he went to the sanctuary of the Sea King. Within an hour, we had the engine room pumped out dry. But the mystery was that water was no longer entering the ship – a little similar to the situation in the Irish sea a few years before, just south of the Isle of Man on the *Kenavo*.

Richard tried all his magic but could not get the main engine restarted. We reckoned it may have taken in some sea water. Perhaps it was a good thing it would not start because we could well have caused damage if it had started. So, Scruffy to the rescue and he towed us into Alderney. Once he started to tow us, she began to take on water again and an inspection of the forepeak revealed we had lost a load of caulking between the stem and the planking right on the bow. A temporary repair with a couple of sleeping bags and we were watertight again.

That night in Alderney I managed to repair the bow with some rope used as caulking and covered it with thick bitumen paint. She had somehow taken water into the fuel system but by midnight Richard had the engine running as sweet as a clock. All was good and we were back on the fishing grounds by first light the following day. We finished our trip and made a good landing in Roscoff five days later where the bow was properly repaired by French shipwrights.

Eighteen

COVEY

For the rest of 1981, I continued to fish the English Channel in the F sector, approximately thirty miles due south of Salcombe. The only other boat to be fishing in the same sector at that time was Richard Cove's *Newbrook*. Covey himself had given up going to sea. I think he was just too knackered to carry on. He was around fifty five years old then and was lucky to have made that age. Excessive consumption of gin each day, combined with a very hard seagoing life had taken its toll. I know he suffered badly during the last few years of his life. I remember having a drink with him one day in his house, he was well pissed and writhing around in pain. 'It's not bloody fair, this life, Scratch,' he said. 'If I was a dog, they would shoot me.' I always remember him saying those words and felt compassion for him. He only made a couple more years after that, but a legend he was.

The *Newbrook* was now skippered by Owen Burner, nick name Scour. He had been with Covey since the early sixties and I'm sure was the longest serving crew aboard the *Newbrook*. He was a good skipper and an excellent fisherman and was definitely what can only be described as Covey-trained in more ways than one. The *Newbrook* was an excellent sea boat with seven ton of lead attached to her keel. As long as you could hold on, she could go through anything and she did. Weather hardly ever stopped her with alcohol playing a huge part. The other two crew members aboard *Newbrook,* at that time, were my old mate Wills and a fella called Bert Moss. Bert, Wills and Scour could all drink for England but I can honestly say alcohol never stopped the *Newbrook* from going to sea. Bert Moss went on to be a very successful skipper making his mark in the industry with a similar boat to the *Burutu* called *Pen Glas* – a Camaret built boat. Wills, Willoughby, as he was often known, bought a forty-footer called the *Independent,* another Camaret boat, and did very well with her off the west coast of Scotland. Scour finished off his seagoing days with a small netter aptly named the *Summer Wine*. The *Newbrook* is still fishing today, as good as the day she was built, but I reckon soon some senseless Government rule will spell the end of her career and she will be scrapped, but what history.

PART THREE

PROSPECTOR

One

_____

THE *CAWSANDS BAY,* DISASTER BOAT

And so in the late autumn of that year, I put the *Burutu* up for sale. She had served me very well. We had had hard times and good times, she had taken me thousands of sea miles and I always had great confidence in her but now it was time to part. The *Burutu* was bought by a fella from Jersey called Bob Viney. Sadly, she was lost on the borders of Rockall and Malin eight years later, but there was no loss of life and the crew were all taken off by helicopter.

Bob was a successful fisherman in his own right and owned two or three trawlers and shellfish boats. He was also a good mate of Mo Deboucier whom I had got to know quite well since it was he who first inspired Rich and me to go to Scotland back in '74. Mo, by this time, had sold the *Finarbed* and was running a big beam trawler called the *Peter.*

*

So now I was at a bit of a crossroads again – to stay deep sea, or did the future lie inshore? I had two or three good months ashore then a situation arose I could not afford to turn down. The *Cawsand Bay* was for sale – the same *Cawsand Bay* I did the mammoth tow in from the Atlantic with a couple of years previously. The *Cawsand Bay* had been built in Camaret, Brittany, which was, I am sure, probably the most renowned port in France for the building of the vast majority of their huge shellfish fleet. *Kenavo, Burutu, Kastel Paol* and the *Paulander* were all Camaret built boats to list just a few of the many hundreds of vessels built there by highly skilled shipwrights and engineers who passed down generations of knowledge to each other. All this was about to change however with the construction of the *Cawsand Bay.*

I shall probably ruffle a few more feathers but I am sure there is not a fisherman at sea who would not agree with me, once again, on this.

The *Cawsand Bay* was a disaster boat. She was built with a White Fish Authority grant to aid her cost. The White Fish and the Department of Trade and Industry became involved in her construction. Out of the window went the hundreds of years of experience between boatbuilder and fisherman, in came the experience of the bureaucrats who thought they knew better. Ships before this time were being built for purpose, now they were being built to the rule but the bureaucrats held the upper hand, so things were about to change for the worse. Compared to Scruffy's *Paulander,* she was a mess. This reflected on her short and infamous career. Scruffy had spent the final few months of the construction of the *Paulander* almost living aboard to make sure she was right and because she was Jersey registered, he didn't fall foul of the crazy rules being enforced by the DTI and White Fish. Sadly, the net of bureaucracy was soon to close around the Jersey fleet as well.

I had sold the *Burutu* just in time; the final years of freedom were drawing to a close. I agreed with the owners of the *Cawsand Bay* on a trial period of six weeks before I bought her but I did not know she was such a death trap. I was under the illusion she was another thoroughbred Camaret boat.

During the trial period, I did two trips up to the west coast of Scotland in her. What a nightmare they were! Fishing was almost out of the question, just to keep her afloat and her engines running was a full time job. Everything about her was far too complicated – alarms, wires, so-called safety hatches in the wrong place, badly thought out fuel systems, bad positioning of the auxiliary engine. The two trips were a disaster. Don't allow the government to get involved in your business. It will cost you money and time. I finally managed to steam her back to the English Channel where her main engine blew up – a piston going right through one of the fuel tanks. That was the end of deep sea fishing for me. We got towed into Brixham by a beam trawler called the *Kornbloom*. I handed her back to her owners and walked away a little the poorer but a little wiser. The *Cawsand Bay* was repaired and did go back to sea but sadly, a couple of years later, was lost in the Celtic Sea taking one crew member with her. I'm sure Jane was pleased to see me home safe and sound. She knew I was not happy about even being on the *Cawsand Bay*, let alone trying to make a living.

Two

SETTLING DOWN INSHORE

So in the late summer of '82, it was time to go back to sea but, this time, as an inshore fisherman. In basic terms that means not venturing further than perhaps six to eight miles from your home port. I did comply with this restriction, apart from a quick venture to the Isles of Scilly a couple of years later thinking I still had a 60ft boat beneath me; old habits die hard. In about August to September of 1982, I bought a 33ft Lochin. My knowledge of boats of this size was quite limited but I had picked a winner.

She was called *Prospector*.

Little did I know at the time of purchase that twice I would come within reach of the pearly gates not half a mile from home. I bought *Prospector* second hand from a Weymouth fisherman called Phil Corbin. Once again, unbeknown to me then, the Lochin 33 was renowned as a very seaworthy hull design, at that time used extensively by the RNLI for their Brede class lifeboat. I can only say that, for all the years I owned and fished her, I

Prospector, speed and power could get you out of a lot of trouble.

never doubted her sea keeping capabilities. I felt as safe in her
as I ever did in the *Burutu* or the *Kenavo.* However, it was a
completely different way of going to sea. She had good speed,
around seventeen knots. That alone would get you out of a lot
of trouble, but she would lift to any sea that came at you, never
took water on deck, rather like a clever boxer, she just seemed to
dodge everything – unlike a conventional displacement hull in
bad weather, spending most of the time with decks awash. You
never get anything for nothing though. Her carrying capabilities
were not good so I always had to be sure not to overload her with
the weight of fish caught. Believe me, it's very difficult to stop
fishing if you are doing well. To call it a day and start steaming
home, knowing full well you could catch another half ton of fish,
is difficult and this situation has caused the loss of many fishing
vessels trying to return home overloaded in a bit of weather; not
a good situation.

When I sold the *Burutu* to Bob Viney, I included all the
fishing gear in the deal, so, when I bought the *Prospector,* I had

no pots or gear of any description. The fact that the *Cawsand Bay* was lying in port with a blown engine, worked to my advantage. All six hundred of her pots were still at sea, shot away in the G sector about forty miles due south of Salcombe. I agreed with the owners of the *Cawsand Bay* that I would work and look after their gear until such time that the vessel was ready to sail again. This was a good deal for both of us. It meant I could start fishing immediately with the *Prospector* and their gear would be looked after. The only slight drawback being the distance of the gear, forty miles offshore and as I only had a 33ft boat, not the best combination but it was late summer and the weather was still good.

The *Prospector* had the speed to cover forty miles twice a day but, as I said before, not the carrying capacity required for the homeward forty miles with three quarters of a ton of crab on deck. With this load, she was down to about 7 knots. But the good Lord smiled on me. The weather held fair for about three weeks and I made hay while the sun was shining. I was backwards and forwards out to the *Cawsand Bay*'s gear almost continuously for three weeks, bringing in around three quarters of a ton every day. The *Prospector* was paid for in those three weeks and there was money in the bank – better born lucky than rich.

During these three weeks, I had four hundred pots made up by a couple of fishermen I knew who were ashore for a while. They did a good job for me so, by the time the *Cawsand Bay*'s engine was repaired, I was ready to put my own gear back to sea. I shot my own gear away in the D sector around fourteen miles south of Salcombe, not such good fishing but a far safer distance to be offshore in a 33ft boat with the onset of autumn and winter.

Three

A MAN CALLED ANIMAL

And so, in that autumn of '82, I settled into life as an inshore fisherman, a way of life that I would adopt for the final twenty odd years of my seagoing career. It was a fairly difficult adjustment in more ways than one. Firstly, we were only two-handed so I was back to full time work on deck. I was skipper and deckhand rolled into one. I had to buy a set of oilskins and some sea boots. I had had a pretty cushy ten years as skipper on the big boats, spending most of the time in the wheelhouse, now I was back on deck amongst the blood and the guts and the sea. Could I cope?

Another adjustment was watching the weather more carefully. I would often find myself at sea knowing I should have been more vigilant considering the weather that came in. However, the *Prospector* was an amazing bit of seagoing kit. She just lifted to all the waves and you never really noticed just how much sea was running until a bigger vessel was close by really making heavy weather of it. Her power and speed were also great assets. You could put the hammer down and get out of a nasty looking wave situation, whereas with a conventional

Animal, a top hand, moving gear on *Prospector* 1985.

fishing boat, you had to sit there and take what was thrown at you. Her only weak link was going head on into weather; she didn't like that at all.

First crew member to join me on the *Prospector* was young Gasook – Steve Cooper. Gasook was a good hand and had been with me on the two disastrous trips to Scotland on the *Cawsand Bay*. For some reason he had to finish fairly soon after I bought the *Prospector*, so immediately into the breach jumped Animal – Jeremy Bricknell.

All fishermen seem to have nicknames, it seemed to be just the way of things, very few were ever known by their first names and in fact I could probably count them on one hand. Animal was brilliant in all respects and was definitely skipper material. He had sailed with me a few years previously on the *Burutu* and showed good promise then from a really young age. He must have stayed with me on the *Prospector* for six to eight years, skippering her several times during that period. Sadly in the early '90s, he started to get serious disc trouble in his lower back which curtailed his seagoing career. I'm sure he would have become a successful skipper owner had his seagoing career not been brought to a sudden end. Animal was quite tall, a slim build but very strong. Often these slim, wiry types were stronger and had more staying power than chunky, more muscular guys. A huge shock of dark, curly hair and several tattoos on his arms were his other distinguishing marks. He was a keen biker when ashore and was known as the 'nicest hell's angel in town'. He even called his daughter Bonnie after his motorbike – a Triumph Bonaville.

Life had really changed now. I was home every night, seven days a week. Robert and Sarah were both enrolled at Malborough Primary School, not a stone's throw away from our back door so, needless to say, they were invariably late for school. The 80s were very good years to me, life was sweet, but I felt I had deserved it. I had been away at sea for many years, from the age of fourteen, but now at last I was home for good, or so I thought.

Animal and I fished the *Prospector* well for the next eighteen months and in the spring of '84, I had to re-engine her. She was fitted with a 180hp Ford Mermaid – basically a Fordson Major tractor engine marinized by Mermaid Marine in Dorset and raised from 120hp to 180hp by a turbo charger. Mermaid engines were very good marine engines at that time. I could never fault them in any way. They were both powerful and economical.

Because I continued to fish around fourteen miles offshore in the D sector, I decided to up the horsepower by another one hundred and ordered their latest engine – a 275hp Mermaid turbo plus. I think this was about as powerful as they could make the old six cylinder Ford engine without blowing it up. It made the *Prospector* almost fly. I didn't often use the full power, but ran a lot at half to three quarter throttle. Believe me, never under-engine a boat, better to over-engine her. It will always be more economical and reliable and you have that extra power up your sleeve if you need it.

With the new engine fitted and all run in, I got itchy feet again. It's actually quite difficult to lose the wanderlust once you have it. I met up with another fisherman I had known from the deep sea days, a fella called Mike Rouse from Penzance. He had fished around the Isles of Scilly quite a bit but his boat was too big to go within the limits. I seem to remember it was nothing within three miles for 40ft boats and above. With the *Prospector* I could fish right up to the beach if I wanted.

Four

THE SCILLY ISLES

I met Mike on his boat one stormy night in Plymouth. He was sheltering from the weather so I drove down to see him to collect any information he could pass on to me about inshore at the Scillys. Fishermen don't usually give away much information but Mike was very helpful, mainly telling me where not to go, rather than where to go. Inshore fishing at the Scillys in January, February and March is not a walk in the park by any means. Ninety percent of it was in under fifteen fathoms of water, so great caution was needed and there were many unmarked rocks just below the surface. After explaining to Jane I was just going to give it a quick try, I got permission to sail but I don't think she was that thrilled with the plan.

Animal and I had to do three trips to the Scillys and back to get all the pots down there. That was a bit of a marathon. The *Prospector* could only carry about one hundred pots, hence the three trips to get all the gear there. To put it in a nutshell, I was trying to do a man's job with a boy's boat – as one wise old salt told me about a year later. Still, it wasn't a complete disaster,

Myself on *Prospector*, 1985.

thank goodness. The weather was kind to us and we found some good fishing. We fished around all the western extremities of the islands, going as deep as seventy fathoms just west of the Bishop Rock lighthouse but the crayfish were still there even at that depth. The Bishop Rock lighthouse was still manned in those days. The lighthouse keeper must have thought we were nuts to be there in a 33ft boat at that time of year. Looking back, perhaps it was a bit stupid, but we got away with it, crayfish and lobster being our main quarry. Most of the time we managed to sleep on the *Prospector,* there was only one bunk in the wheelhouse so we took it in turns. If we were caught in St. Marys for weather, we would book into a B&B for the night.

We fished the Seven Stones reef, where the huge oil tanker Torrey Canyon had come to grief in the 1960s but, by May, we had slowly moved back around the south west Cornish coast to the Lizard Light and from there made the final move back to Salcombe.

Jane had a good talk with me and that truly was the last time I left home. My travels were definitely over, I was home to stay. Once again, I fished only in the D sector for crab until the Christmas of '84, moving inshore for the rest of the winter until the spring of '85.

Summer of '85 was pretty good as far as the weather was concerned. As a fisherman, when you say the weather is good, your only real concern is the wind strength which determines whether you will be able to go to sea or not; sun and rain are not at all important. So, if a fisherman tells you it will be a fine day tomorrow, that means there will be no or very light wind. One old fisherman friend of mine, who is now deceased, came home from sea one day quite late and asked his wife if she had seen the television forecast for the following day. 'Oh,' she said, 'sunny periods with a few showers perhaps later.' 'No,' he said. 'Which way were the arrows pointing?' 'Towards the settee,' was her reply. He never again asked her for the forecast.

Shooting away pots on *Prospector*, 1990. Back to the blood and guts

Five

TRAWLER RACING

Hope Cove, as I mentioned earlier, in the spider crab days, was a small port a few miles west of Salcombe. Every August Bank Holiday they have a big festival which they call Hope Cove Weekend. It must have been the summer of '85 when the organising committee decided to have a trawler race. All the fishing boats from Salcombe, Hope Cove and a few from Plymouth would assemble for a race. The race would be run around a triangular course directly off Hope Cove – the start line and finish were to be in the harbour entrance. This would give the spectators a bird's eye view of the race.

The day of the first Hope Cove Trawler Race dawned with great excitement amongst all local fishing boats and crews. What a spectacle it would make, in more ways than one. Alcohol always played a big part and the partying began early on the morning of the race. By 2.30pm, the official start time, most crews were in no fit state to walk, never mind race fishing boats. All boats assembled and the gun was fired to the cheering of crews and the roar of twenty or so powerful diesel engines. Black

Prospector. I only won one trawler race. Winning was too expensive!

smoke, spray, water bombs, hose pipe fights, eggs, tomatoes, any ammunition to hand was used between crews to gain the upper hand. The actual race lasted possibly for about an hour. Finally boats were strung out depending on size of engine and speed but, on assembling again after the finish, the water battles between the boats continued until everyone was wet through and all ammunition had been used. I won that first trawler race, not through skill but simply because I had the fastest boat. I learned a good lesson that day – never win a trawler race.

After the race all hands assembled for prize giving and told the landlord of the Hope and Anchor Inn to put all drinks on Scratch's account as he had won. The final bill came to over two hundred pounds, a considerable sum in 1985. I've been in around thirty trawler races since then but was never ever first again. The Hope Cove Trawler Race of that year was the first of many such trawler races to be held annually in Hope Cove. Within five years, local fishermen and fish salesman, Peter Watt,

Salcombe Trawler Race c 1994

nicknamed FD, started the Salcombe Trawler Race which is held every year during the first week of August to this present day. Rules are just the same … the most horse power wins, but taking part, that is the real fun.

Six

A NATURAL SAILOR

Having always been involved with sailing, which is quite unusual amongst the fishing community, it was only natural for my son, Rob to come sailing with me. From a very young age, he would crew for me so, by the age of around eight, he was quite a competent helmsman and, at that tender age, could helm and sail a Salcombe Yawl single handed. In teaching him to sail, I applied the same strategy that old Jeff Scott used on me many years before. I never really went about trying to teach him to sail or told him very much, he just watched what I did, copied me and it worked like a dream. By the age of ten, he was South West England Junior Champion, the top end age limit being sixteen. By twelve years old, he was a National Champion, winning the prestigious Eric Twiname National Youth Championships and at thirteen retired from sailing, much to my horror. I always wished I had had his racing ability. During those few years that Rob was racing, the house was stuffed with trophies from all over the country. We would drive hundreds of miles to race meetings and always come home with some trophy or other. I've won a few races in my time but never with the ease and natural talent that Rob had: he would just made it look so easy. I honestly really don't think Rob knew how he did it. It was just a natural thing you did, I'm sure people are born with these talents. You can teach some people to race but you can't teach them to win – that's the difference. Rob went on to become a boatbuilder and was awarded Young Boatbuilder of the Year from the British Boatbuilding Federation.

Seven

TRAGIC NEWS

September of '85 saw Animal and me fishing once again in the D sector about fourteen miles due south of Salcombe – all pretty repetitive stuff. They call crabbing out in the English Channel, where we were working, factory fishing. The gear is all shot in straight lines within a square box around eight miles square. I really did miss the excitement of fishing on the big boats, away from home where you were free to roam wherever you wanted, but no, those days were over, I had to get used to inshore fishing and like it. The winters were a bit better. We would try a bit of netting to get away from the monotony of just crabbing, also I would go lobstering along the coast to the west of Salcombe, but always had to be very careful not to site the gear in shallow water with any bad weather around. Fifteen fathoms was the cut off point, shallower than that in bad weather and your gear was definitely at risk. I can remember, many times going back out to sea on a winter's evening to get the pots into deeper water because of an impending gale.

October 24th, 1985 was a sad day for Salcombe. I remember the day well.

At about 2pm, we had just finished fishing in the D sector when shocking news came over our VHF radio on Channel six which was the channel used by all fishermen off Start Point: "Griff is missing".

Nigel Davis and Gasook were working a boat called the *Midbrook*. They had noticed Griff's boat, the *Sunseeker* fishing quite close to them, going round and round in a circle. Nigel tried to call Griff on the radio but with no response and so steamed over to the *Sunseeker* to investigate. What he found was not good. The *Sunseeker* was still attached to her gear, causing her to circle round, but Griff was not there. He had been pulled overboard by the gear in exactly the same way that I had lost John Pullman over the side a few years earlier off Tiree.

Griff was working single handed so once he had gone overboard, it was curtains. There was no one aboard to help. It was, and always will be, the most frightening thing about working single handed – you are completely on your own and if the sea wants you, it will take you.

Nigel and Steve managed to get Griff's winch going then hauled his lifeless body aboard – not a pleasant or easy task. A drowned body is very heavy but manage they did and then they slowly started to steam back into Salcombe, surrounded by most of the Salcombe inshore fleet. I think what shocked us all so much about losing Griff was that he had seemed to represent the strong, central character of our small fishing community. He was the sort of unelected leader and it was as though nothing could ever happen to Griff. But it did and he left behind a gaping hole in our small tight-knit community.

Griff's funeral was well attended. Salcombe church was packed for the Service and in the afternoon we took his ashes to sea and scattered them on Salcombe Bar about which Tennyson had written his poem, Crossing the Bar. Fishing communities all around our coast, from Scotland to Land's End, deal with grief in their own quiet, private way. It always amazes me, however, that the loss of fishermen is rarely reported on national news. Often it is only by word of mouth that I have heard of the loss of a boat and its crew.

Griff's death also left behind a bit of a situation for the RNLI. He had been coxswain of the Salcombe Lifeboat for several years but now the job of cox fell to second coxswain, 'Horse' Cater. Horse was at retirement age so Salcombe Lifeboat was soon in need of another new coxswain. In the spring of 1986, I was approached by the RNLI to become coxswain but it was never really going to work. I lived three miles away from Salcombe and it was before the days of pagers to alert for a shout, so Frank Smith, or Smee as he was always known, took over the new post of coxswain mechanic. Smee was an old school mate of mine from way back at Salcombe boys' school. He too would have felt the wrath of Chimp Child's cane. He went on to become a brilliant cox for the RNLI for maybe the next twenty years or so.

Griff. His loss was a sad blow to Salcombe.

Eight

GONE WITH A FLOURISH

And so the 1980s slipped by, life really became quite routine. In about '89 or '90, Animal hurt his back quite badly so had to go ashore; his fishing days were over. A sad loss he was a good hand in more ways than one. A fella called Alan McGill took his place, or Gilly as he was always known. Gilly was a good hand, slim and wiry but strong with good stamina. He had survived a sinking on a boat called the *Flourish* and had spent time in a life raft in the middle of the English Channel before being picked up by another fishing vessel. That sort of experience always breeds a strong animal. The *Flourish* had sailed from Dartmouth in South Devon at around midnight under the command of local skipper Nobby Clarke. She was bound for the F Sector but never made it. She was run down by a tanker or freighter at around 3am about twenty miles south of Start Point. The ship that ran them down probably never knew he had done it. Gilly, Nobby and Kenny Corbett (later to skipper the *Christmas*) and a fourth hand just managed to scramble into the life raft. Nobby told me later she went down in minutes as they scraped along the side

Gilly and me on *Prospector*, 1989. Gilly gave up on the sea after two close scrapes.

Racing Salcombe Yawl Y61 with a client

Three generations of Scratch, Grandson Will, myself, son Rob 2008.

Large cock crab from north of Cherbourg 1982.

Prospector, with Gilly on the rail, 1989.

of the huge ship. Nobby tried to get her name but it was too dark. Fortunately for Nobby and his crew, within about an hour Squeaker Squires, skipper of the *Concord*, came across them. He picked them up in his powerful searchlight before another ship ran them down. Squeaker's first question to Nobby was, 'Where's the *Flourish*?'. 'Bottom of the English Channel, 'was the reply. The *Concord* then steamed back to Dartmouth much to the relief of the four shipwrecked mariners.

The F and G Sectors, in the middle of the English Channel, are the best and most prolific crab grounds in the Western Approaches, but, to a fisherman working these grounds, there is not only the ever present dangers from fishing, but also the terrifying prospect of being run down by a cargo ship or tanker doing perhaps 15-20 knots. The Fs and Gs are in the middle of all the westbound shipping that leaves Europe for the rest of the world. A ship will pass within half a mile of you every five minutes, twenty four hours a day, or 'twenty four seven', as they say. A sharp lookout is required at all times by the skipper

SALCOMBE HARBOUR

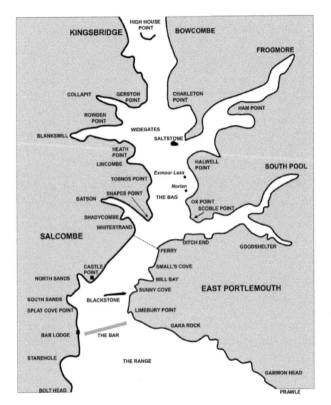

Salcombe Harbour

because he is the only one in the wheelhouse. Combine this with working on what we call fixed gear, that is gear attached to the seabed and you can imagine the number of close scrapes occurring daily. No, Sir, you don't get anything for nothing.

Nine

YET MORE TRAGIC NEWS

Early January 1991 I received tragic news from Jersey. My old chum Scruffy Ingram had been pulled overboard by his own gear and drowned in what was a carbon copy of the accident that had claimed Griff's life, back in 1985. Scruffy, like me had sold his boat, the *Paulander* and bought a small inshore boat, a bit smaller than my *Prospector*. But poor old Scruff was working single handed and, just the same as Griff, was pulled overboard and that was curtains for Scruff as well. I flew to Jersey to attend Scruff's funeral. It was a pretty big event on the island. Many fishermen were there from all corners of the English Channel. A strange situation arose for me at Scruffy's funeral. It was difficult to recognise other fishermen, seeing them always in maybe a smock, jeans and sea boots but now with them all dressed formally with collar and tie, suits and jackets. We spent most of the time introducing ourselves to each other. Many I had never even met in person but had had long conversations with them over the radio during long nights at sea, steaming to Scotland and back or dodging ships in the mid-channel grounds. It did seem like rough justice for Scruff, having sailed tens of thousands of sea miles to go just a couple of miles from home. But, if the sea wants you, she will have you. Perhaps it's more dangerous closer to home. A lot of fishing tragedies seem to happen close to home in small inshore boats and during the next two years I would come closer to the pearly gates than I had ever been before.

In August 1991, more bad news got back to Salcombe. Nigel Davis, who had sailed with me on the *Burutu* back in the early '80s, when we almost lost John Pullman off Tiree, had been lost in the Atlantic when the trawler he was skippering had capsized in poor weather. Another face was missing from the quayside in Salcombe, never to return. His body was never found – his grave was at the bottom of the Atlantic.

Ten

WHITE FISH AUTHORITY AND A NEAR FATAL SITUATION

In 1991 I re-engined the *Prospector* again but this time, made the almost fatal mistake of letting the Government become involved in my business. At that time, the then 'White Fish Authority', as they were known, were giving fishermen grants for new engines. It wasn't much, about ten or fifteen percent of the total installation. Like a fool, I applied for a grant, heaven only knows why as it had always been my policy to stay well clear of anything to do with Government and Council business and I had always done well adopting that policy. During the final fitting of the new engine, a chinless wonder turned up from the White Fish Authority, to inspect the boat and the engine installation. It can only be described as an insult. This fella was obviously just out of university and was clueless. Every time I asked him a question, he had to look in the folder he was carrying to give me an answer. I stayed cool and tried not to lose my temper with him but the bottom line was, unless I did what he wanted, the engine would have to be removed and the grant would be withdrawn. I was keen to get back to sea and although wishing I had not involved the WFA, I agreed to do the two stupid things he wanted done.

The first thing was to increase the scupper size. The scuppers are the drain holes that let excess water drain off the deck in heavy weather. They also let water on to the deck if they are the wrong size. He didn't seem to appreciate that. He made some calculations with pen, paper and a calculator, but he was doing them for a displacement hull, not a semi-displacement as was the *Prospector*. I don't think he knew the difference. I had been at sea since the age of fourteen and I knew exactly what size scuppers the *Prospector* needed.

The second thing he asked me to do was the silliest and the most dangerous and it almost cost me my life a year later and that of my crew. The *Prospector's* fuel pipe was a strong gauged, clear plastic pipe. The reason for me using this pipe was simple. When a diesel engine runs out of fuel, the whole system has to be, what they call, bled through to get all the air out of the system before it will start again. I won't get too technical, but with a clear pipe, you can see if the diesel fuel is coming through. He wanted all this pipe renewed with some black rubber pipe with a steel wrapping around. I was not at all happy with this but finally agreed and changed the fuel line. He finally signed me off, saying the grant could be paid but also curtly informed me not to change anything back, as he would return to check it all again in a few months.

When I set sail again with my new engine, I added something in the engine room the ministry would never have thought of in a thousand years – a five gallon outboard fuel can with a rubber pipe and a squeeze bulb on it with five gallons of diesel. In an emergency, I could quickly connect that to the engine and be going again in seconds. Carrying that, without a doubt, saved Gilly's life and my own.

Sure enough, only weeks after Scruffy's funeral, we had finished fishing about three miles west of Salcombe, a nasty south east gale was setting in our course home and brought us within one hundred yards of the very rocky coast around the entrance to Salcombe called Off Cove. It was around six in the evening, late January, cold and dark with the wind and rain. 'Ten minutes and we will be in,' I said to Gilly. Simultaneously the engine died. Christ almighty, what now! I flew out of the wheelhouse to the engine compartment and sure enough, there was the split fuel line that the White Fish Authority had told me to install, spewing diesel into the bilge. I told Gilly to chuck the anchor out immediately which he did but the it had gone into rock and the rope parted like a carrot when we came upon a big sea. This was serious. In the darkness we could see the giant waves breaking white on to the jagged rocks. I knew that one of those waves alone would smash the *Prospector* to a thousand pieces. We couldn't call for help on the radio as we were the last boat out. The only chance we had was the five gallon outboard fuel tank. I honestly thought I would never get it rigged up in time, but somehow I did. I connected it directly to the fuel pump, a bit unconventionally, but it worked. I yelled through the wind, rain and spray to Gilly, now in the wheelhouse, to turn the key and try to restart the engine while I squeezed the bulb in the fuel line for all I was worth. The engine spluttered and started but then stopped again. 'Keep turning, Gilly,' I yelled. She started again but ran a bit rough, then the good Lord smiled. Mother sea changed her mind and didn't want us after all. The engine burst into full life; it was the best sound I had ever heard. 'Chuck her in gear, Gilly,' I yelled, 'and get the hell out.' We slowly clawed our way off the deadly rocks to deeper water. When the engine restarted, I could feel the backwash of the rocks, two more waves and it would have been the end for us. We crept around Bolt Head and limped into the sanctuary of Salcombe Harbour. That five gallon fuel tank had saved our lives, without a shadow of a doubt. I thought about the chinless wonder from the Ministry and what I would do to him if I could get my hands on him. The real irony of it was, if we had been lost that night, the *Prospector* would have been shattered to a thousand pieces and no one would ever have known what caused the accident. They did when I got ashore!

Looking back now on my sea-going life, spanning over more than fifty six years, I did manage to dodge and steer clear of many of the senseless rules and regulations made up in the name of safety by the people who have no practical experience of the situations about which they are attempting to make safe. I feel that the youngsters of today are at far greater risk than we were. Only last year I heard of two trawlers who had their wheelhouses flooded in heavy weather. In both cases their engines stopped and could not be restarted because of clever electronic cut-out systems and safety devices. It is a bit like looking under the bonnet of your car, these days. You don't need a spanner, you need a computer geek.

Eleven

CROSSING THE BAR

In 1993, Gilly signed off the *Prospector*. He gave up fishing and went to find a new life in Spain. I only saw him a couple of times after that but I think he made a good life for himself over there. He never made old bones though, and we lost him around 2008. Perhaps, after a couple of close scrapes like the one with Nobby on the *Flourish* and me on the *Prospector*, you think maybe, it's time to come ashore. Not for me though, I was destined to knock on those pearly gates one more time before coming ashore.

Spud Cudd signed on when Gilly left. Spud was a very experienced and seasoned old hand by now; it was Spud who had miraculously survived the capsize of the trawler that had claimed the life of Nigel Davis in 1991. We had sailed together on the *Burutu* in the late seventies. I seem to remember he came to Scotland with me on the ill-fated *Cawsand Bay*. Having been at sea since he left school, he certainly was a top hand.

It must have been about the winter of 1995, we had all been trapped in harbour for about two weeks; just one gale after another, all the boats were itching to get to sea again. I can

clearly remember, it was around 9pm when the wind finally gave up. All was calm and the stars were out. The wind was forecast to decrease and become variable from the north; that should certainly calm the sea off. At 2am the next morning, I phoned Spud to say it's all calm, let's give it a go. 'Ok, Billy, I'll be ready in half an hour.' Spud was the same as Longhair and Griff, they always called me Billy, never Scratch. By 3am, Spud and I were aboard and slowly proceeding down Salcombe Harbour towards the notorious Salcombe Bar at the entrance. I have read and heard about freak waves but was very soon to encounter one. Spud was just behind the wheelhouse, cutting bait and generally getting things ready for the day's fishing. I was in the wheelhouse as we approached Salcombe Bar. I had put her on automatic pilot and was setting up the Decca and tuning in the radar, getting the kettle on; everything was all very normal and routine. I had just pulled on my oilskins when, about one hundred metres in front of us, on the radar, was a large definite white line closing in on us very quickly. I had seen lines similar to this come up on the radar in Scottish waters, but they had turned out to be flocks of geese. This was no flock of geese closing in on us now. As I said, the sea was dead calm but what hit us was unbelievable. It was just a solid wall of water, thirty to forty foot high; a 'freak'. I am sure we were lucky in so much that the wave had broken just as we hit it, so we went straight into the tunnel of the wave; had we hit it seconds earlier, it would have pitch-poled us backwards and that would have been the end for both of us. It all happened then in a flash, we emerged through the trailing edge of the wave, but minus the wheelhouse; it had been smashed to pieces. The *Prospector* was absolutely full of water, how she was still afloat, I shall never know. The front of my oilskins were red with blood, but I could feel no pain.

Looking over my shoulder, I saw the back of the freak wave – it was like the side of a large house but now, thank God, running away from us on into Salcombe Harbour. Our electrics were all knocked out, so it was pitch black, I could just see Spud clinging to the rails around the stern of the *Prospector*. I turned back to face forward amongst the broken glass and wood and gave her full throttle. The 275hp Mermaid engine came into its own as she almost leapt out of the water, draining her deck of water and debris. It was an odd feeling, lying there wrecked in flat calm water once again. In that calm, I can remember the thunderous roar as the freak wave broke over Blackstone Rock that sits in the middle of the entrance to Salcombe. After that, everything was quiet again apart from the gentle throb of the Mermaid. Spud came forward and entered what remained of the wheelhouse. I shall never, ever forget his opening few words, 'I think we had better go back in, Billy,' accompanied by another few choice words describing what had just happened. Then he noticed all the blood down the front of my oilskins; my mouth also felt full of blood. Some sharp object, I think maybe glass or a wood splinter, had gone right through my upper lip to my upper jaw. I felt nothing when it happened but now, it was starting to throb a bit. 'Better get you up to the quack when we get in, Billy.' The steering was not working too well, I think the hydraulic pipes had fractured with the impact of the water, so I basically steered her back up Salcombe Harbour, by the odd kick astern to bring the bow round.

It took another two weeks to get the boat ready for sea again, all new electronics and a major repair to the wheelhouse. I had to have a new wheelhouse fitted the following year to make her A1 again. Perhaps I should seriously consider a new occupation; was someone up there trying to tell me something, but it would be another seven years before I finally came ashore.

Twelve

YACHT DELIVERY

The summer of '97 brought an interesting job along for me, a good old friend of mine called Jeremy Thompson, bought a fifty foot Dutch built steel motor yacht in Greece, called *Agir*. One evening, in the local pub, he asked me if I would be interested in bringing it back to the UK with him. Spud had finished by then on the *Prospector* and my old chum, from back in the *Kenovo* days in Scotland, Bimbo was now crew, he teamed up with Barney Powlesland who was skipper of the *Frances* all those years ago when he and Richard had met Mo Debuchia at the Hurd Deep and told them of the big lobster catches in Scotland. Bimbo and Barney agreed to run the *Prospector* while I went on this yacht delivery job back from Greece. Well, this was first time back on a yacht for almost thirty five years and I was quite looking forward to it.

She was lying in the Port of Lefkas and had to come back to the UK. Easy, as old Jeff Scott would have said. Cross the Adriatic, round the toe of Italy, through Messina, up the Italian coast, cross to Marseilles, up the Rhone, out at Le Havre and home. Well, that's exactly what happened. Well, it would have been that simple but for two facts. She had the dirtiest fuel tanks in the Med and her starboard propeller stern gland was worn out. It would have been much easier had she been a sailing boat; sails never let you down. She had two big diesels. Almost as soon as I got one going, the other one packed up. For the first three hundred miles I was hardly out of the engine room, but it did get better after we rounded the toe of Italy. We called into Messina to try and get some help with the stern gland but Messina didn't seem to be a very friendly place, so on we plodded up the Italian coast. Somehow we got close to a prison island around Monte Cristo and were chased off by armoured police waving AK47 guns. Finally, we rounded the top end of Corsica and picked up a load of plastic cable on the starboard prop. Jeremy, being a good swimmer, dived overboard and cleared it. We were lucky with the weather, though, it was flat calm the whole trip but we just got into Marseilles before a Mistral gale set in, however, we had entered the mighty Rhone river by then.

As we entered the Rhone, there was a cutting leading off to port, it had a large sign with a huge arrow saying Etang – the huge inland lake that runs parallel to the coast west of Marseilles. Seeing this immediately stirred memories of almost forty years ago, sailing with John and Jeff in the *Corunna of Burnham* to Port Andrax when we saw the beautiful white horses of the Camargue. I had certainly sailed a few nautical sea miles since then. Another thing that occurred to me towards the end of that delivery of the *Agir*, Jeremy's motor yacht, was that, for the first time in thirty five years, I had completed a voyage without having to catch anything. This did seem a bit odd, if you came in with nothing when you were fishing, simple – you didn't get paid anything. But this was easy. Perhaps I should go back into the delivery business.

Thirteen

A GENTLE SPIN ROUND

On arrival back in Salcombe, I seriously considered that this yacht delivery type business could be a good finale to my seagoing career. Fishing is a very hard way of going to sea, to say the least, yacht delivery seemed like a walk in the park. Bimbo and Barney were quite happy running the *Prospector*, so I soon lined up another yachting type job with a fella called Peter Hartley. Peter had an American yacht, I think it was a J-40, a very nimble and fast racing yacht but Peter's seagoing credentials weren't too good, so he asked me to take him on about a week's cruise around the English Channel. This was no problem to me, but Peter specially asked if we could do a night crossing. Something he had never experienced before.

We duly left Salcombe for the French coast at around 9pm with a run of around a hundred miles to the port of Primel where I had landed hundreds of times with the old *Kenavo* and the *Burutu*. Well, I couldn't believe the performance of this yacht. The wind was easterly fifteen to twenty knots, a broad reach right across the channel. A broad reach being the fastest point of sailing, we planed all the way across, through all the westbound and eastbound shipping lanes at around twelve knots; much faster than I had envisaged, arriving off the French coast at dawn. I think Peter and his wife, Maggie enjoyed their first night crossing but couldn't believe the number of ships going east and west. We pulled into the tiny port of Primel just after first light.

After breakfast, I took Peter up to the Cafe du Port where Richard and I were regular customers back in the 1970s with old Louis Ossard. Bearing in mind it was almost twenty five years since I had last been in there, Michelle, the landlady appeared looking as gorgeous as she had twenty five years ago – leather trousers and a tight fitting white tee shirt, it was as though time had stood still. After about an hour, the Michelle I knew from the old days appeared, the years had taken their toll – it was her daughter I was chatting up at the bar! Peter found this all very amusing, but anyone can make a mistake.

We left Primel and I sailed them up through the Meloine Channel to the east of Roscoff – a rocky, narrow channel, but they loved it. Past the Roche Douvres Light and up the Russell Channel to St. Peter Port, the capital of Guernsey. To my great surprise, tied up in Guernsey was my old mate Richard so that gave cause for a hearty night ashore. It was about twenty years ago we had stopped there to buy cheap diesel when we started to transport the spider crab to France. How time flies when you are enjoying yourself. Richard had bought himself a fine yacht – a Halberg Rassy 42 called *Miriad* and spent most summers cruising the French coast and down into the Bay of Biscay.

We arrived back in Salcombe after being away about a week. Peter came ashore a little wiser about the sea, he had learned things they don't teach you in a book. He was most intrigued when I could tell him exactly where he was mid-channel by reading the names on the fishing dhans but, as I explained to him, you had to know which boat was fishing where, but they were just like signposts if you knew that.

I did seriously look into full-time yacht delivery in the late 1990s but bureaucracy and bullshit wouldn't allow it. Although I had done those two yachting jobs on a commercial basis, to go any further with it was no good. For insurance purposes, I had to have an Ocean Yachtmaster's Ticket. The chances of getting that were nil with my education so it was back to fishing for the final few years of my seagoing career. The net was surely closing around 'the final years of freedom'. I wasn't to have the easy life for my last few years at sea, so I put on my sea boots and oilskins and returned to fishing and the blood and guts.

In the late summer of 1999, my two children were both married within eight weeks of each other. They were both simple, home-grown ceremonies, in both cases the families from both sides shared all the catering. Aunts, great aunts and cousins made scrumptious cakes, buns and puddings and, needless to say, all the tables were groaning with the weight of lobster, crab and crayfish. Robert and I nipped across to France in a van and purchased all the wine, champagne and beer for both weddings. Robert married his childhood sweetheart from school. Kate Andrews became Kate Hitchen and Sarah Hitchen became Sarah Bromwich by marrying Ed – also a childhood sweetheart. I explained to all four of them that the first thirty years would be a bit sticky but after that, it really starts to get good. Within four years, Jane and I had four grandchildren, William, James and Harry and a beautiful little girl called Frankie. God bless 'em.

My old mate, Bimbo with whom I had sailed thousands of miles, retired and came ashore in around 2000 and, as the new millennium dawned and the turbulent and bloody twentieth century was left behind, it occurred to me I had been at sea for over forty years. It was definitely time to think about 'swallowing the anchor' and coming ashore. My son Robert signed on with me for the last three years of my life at sea. It was the perfect ending to have him come to sea with me, we had always got on well and since leaving childhood behind, he became more like a brother to me than a son.

PART FOUR

FRANCES

One
_____

SLOWLY SLOWING DOWN

In 2004, I sold the *Prospector* to the Harvey family from Newlyn, Cornwall; the same company with which I had taken the two loads of crab across the channel when Colin and I rescued the big French schooner. I delivered her down to Newlyn and she never missed a beat all the years I owned her apart from when I let the Ministry get involved and we almost lost her on the rocks off Bolt Head. She had been a faithful old horse and I was sad to let her go along with a way of life the sea had given me. Harvey gave her a big refit after they bought her and she is still fishing today, out of Newlyn.

The autumn of 2004 left me scratching my head – what to do next? I was like a jockey without a horse, but I had no boat – a strange feeling to say the least. Since the two yacht deliveries with Jeremy and Peter back in the nineties, I had got a little more back into sailing and racing. In the summer of 2005, I started a boatyard business looking after as many as twenty Salcombe Yawls. I was also teaching sailing full-time, from the basics right up to the very competitive. Racing people always said they felt very relaxed sailing with me, I must say I did find it so easy after a lifetime at sea, but you had to have the patience of a saint, I think that was something I was blessed with. By winter of 2005, I was at a loose end again as sailing finished during winter months. I couldn't just retire, I had to do something. It was Richard's elder brother Bob Murray, who hatched the idea – why not supply restaurants in the middle of England with prime lobster and crab and any sort of fish they want. This sounded right up my street with knowledge of the fishing industry at my fingertips. Within two years, I had almost thirty restaurants on my books, all up through the Cotswolds, across south of Birmingham and back down through Wales. The real secret of my success in this business was a knowledge of where to buy top quality fish, certainly not off a trawler that has been at sea for a week, but from day boats that land their catch every evening. I used to buy most of the wet fish from Looe in Cornwall, all from day boats. You wouldn't buy any shellfish from Cornwall though, that had to come from the Strawberry Patch off Start Point – quite a small area but it produces the best shellfish around the UK. Crab processors drive all the way to Salcombe from Newlyn to buy this crab because the yield and taste is so good. I imagine the reason for this top quality shellfish is caused by the tidal flow off Start Point stirring up some very nutritious food every six hours when the tide turns.

Two

A DECOMMISSIONED BEAUTY

In 2005 I went down to Mevagissey in Cornwall and bought the *MFV Frances*. It was the *Frances* that Barney had skippered when he and Richard on the *Ibis* had ventured to the Hurd Deep and met Mo Debuchier, back in 1972. She was now being decommissioned, by the Chesterfield family, after thirty five years of trawling out of Mevagissey. I had always remembered the *Frances* from way back in 1960 when I was a kid living on the *Exmoor Lass*, Mum and Dad's houseboat. She has the most beautiful lines I think I have ever seen, from every angle she is kind to the eye. She did look a bit rough around the edges when I bought her. I think it was the closest I ever came to divorce in forty years when I steamed her back into Salcombe and Jane saw her. 'Huh!' she said, 'What an idiot, spends a lifetime at sea, finally retires and what does he do? Go out and buy an old decommissioned trawler!'

Within about two years, I had her looking like a million

Richard, left, myself and Barney, depart Mevagissy to bring *Frances* home, 2009.

Richard, myself, Winkle and Barney bringing *Frances* home, 2009.

dollars and we have had endless fun and parties on her. She is now fitted out like a yacht. I re-engined her, turned the fish room and forecastle into a large cabin with en suite loo and constructed a new wheelhouse. On her stern deck, under an awning, you can sit twelve people for dinner. Jane and I just go on short coastal hops in her but only if the sea is like a mirror, if

The *Frances* arrives back in Salcombe, the closest I came to divorce in 45 years.

Frances off Bolt Tail, 2015. No more white water on deck, only calm waters from now on.

it's at all choppy, Jane comes home on the bus – and so doI! The days of white water on deck are well behind me.

By around 2009, the restaurant supply business was starting to fade a bit, caused by stronger competition from larger fish suppliers. My last real foray into the business world was exporting live female crab to the far east. I had a good five years

Me and my First Mate, Jane on *Frances*, 2015.

doing this, flying, on average, one ton a week from Heathrow to Shanghai. Other companies sent more, but I was only a one man band – a ton was good business for me. Once again sadly, the bureaucracy and senseless paper work got the better of me. I was too old now to put up with too much nonsense from the paper pushers, so, in 2014, I sent my last consignment to China and called it a day. The sailing and boatyard business are still going quite well, but just at a pace I want them to. I am not really right out of the fishing industry though, I supply many top restaurants in London and the Home Counties with large cock crabs. These top chefs seem to go mad for them, long may it last.

Richard

9th June 1943 – 9th September 2017

Richard, 'Huh! the lull before the storm, Scratch!'

EPILOGUE

'Home is the sailor, home from the sea
And the hunter home from the hills ...'

Arriving home after a long voyage, my mother would often quote these lines from Robert Louis Stevenson and this is where I find myself today. As my story draws to a close, I sit on the afterdeck of *Frances* with Jane, a drink in one hand and an occasional cigar in the other and look back on a life filled with close scrapes, adventure, good luck and love. Now in the sunset years, my thoughts go back many times to my old shipmates who have passed through the pearly gates and how I have come to knock on that door so often but have been turned away. One thing is for certain, the day will come and I hope they will all be there, sitting in a pub with free beer. God bless 'em!

Simon Sitwell, '... can you peel spuds and shovel coal?'

Covey, '... hold tight boys, another one coming.'

Mr Profit, '... no catering department for you, then.'

Canberra Star 4ABs, 2 Greasers, 1 Donkey Man 1 Deck Boy South Africa Australia New Zealand Round the World

Tony Wiltshire, '... come on Shag, we're off to Danny's bar.'

Scotty, '... always look up in fog.'

Joe McCoy, ' ... pull up a chair son.'

Lil, ' ... you want to marry 'er, boy.'